# Special Needs and Early Years

## A Practitioner's Guide

### Kate Wall

P·C·P

Paul Chapman
Publishing

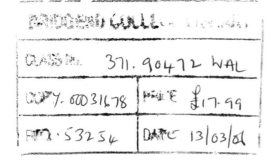
ISBN 0-7619-4075-8 (hbk)
ISBN 0-7619-4076-6 (pbk)
© Kate Wall, 2003
First published 2003
Reprinted 2004

Paul Chapman Publishing
A SAGE Publications Company
1 Oliver's Yard, 55 City Road
London EC1Y 1SP

SAGE Publications Inc
2455 Teller Road
Thousand Oaks, California 91320

SAGE Publications India Pvt Ltd
B–42 Panchsheel Enclave
PO Box 4109
New Delhi 110 017

**British Library Cataloguing in Publication data**
A catalogue record for this book is available from the British Library

**Library of Congress Control Number: 2002115861**

Typeset by Dorwyn Ltd., Rowlands Castle, Hampshire
Printed and bound in Great Britain by
Cromwell Press Limited, Trowbridge, Wiltshire

# Contents

*Foreword by Tricia David*                                                          *viii*
*Glossary of acronyms*                                                               *ix*
*Acknowledgements*                                                                    *x*

**1 Definitions of special needs and relevant legislation**                          1
   Introduction                                                                       1
   Current provision in the UK                                                        1
   Development of nursery provision in the UK                                         2
   Discussion of development of provision                                             8
   Range of early years provision                                                    10
   Historical development of special needs provision and legislation
      in the UK                                                                       11
   Summary                                                                            19
   Definitions                                                                        20

**2 Families of children with special needs**                                        23
   Introduction                                                                       23
   Children and their families                                                        23
   Children with special needs and their families                                     27
   Parental acceptance of special needs at or soon after birth                        28
   Parental acceptance of special needs at a later stage                              30
   Grandparents                                                                       33
   Siblings                                                                           34
   Implications for practice                                                          39
   Increase in numbers of children with special needs                                 39
   Summary                                                                            40

**3 Partnerships with parents**                                                      43
   Introduction                                                                       43
   Parental involvement                                                               44
   Parental issues affecting partnership                                              45

Quality of partnership                                                45
Home–school liaison teachers and family centres                      47
Positive change or enforced change?                                  48
SureStart                                                            48
Characteristics of positive partnerships                             49
Positive outcomes for practitioners                                  51
Positive outcomes for parents                                        51
Positive outcomes for children                                       52
Levels of partnership                                                52
Legislation and guidance                                             53
Inspection requirements                                              56
Foundation Stage requirements                                        56
Parental involvement in observation, assessment and reviewing
     progress                                                        56
Factors supporting positive partnerships                             57
Issues compromising partnerships                                     60
In working practice                                                  60
Summary                                                              61

4 **Interagency working**                                            **64**
Introduction                                                         64
Definitions and models                                               64
Historical developments                                              66
Progression to date                                                  67
The need for interagency working                                     68
Understanding the roles of other professionals                       70
Skills and qualities needed                                          71
Professionals involved                                               71
Working together                                                     76
The role of the SENCO                                                77
Planning and coordination in early years settings                    78
Factors affecting collaboration                                      80
Issues supporting future progression                                 80
Summary                                                              84

5 **Observation and assessment**                                     **86**
Introduction                                                         86
Children's rights, legislation and guidance                          87
Purposes and values of observation and assessment                    90
Principles of observation                                            93
Methods of assessment 1 – observations                               95
Methods of assessment 2 – checklists and questionnaires              102
Methods of assessment 3 – observing through play                     104
Methods of assessment 4 – involving the children                     106

Methods of assessment 5 – children's behaviour                    107
Profiling                                                          108
Summary                                                            109

**6 Programmes of intervention**                                  **111**
Introduction                                                       111
Definitions                                                        111
Effective interventions                                            112
Differentiating the curriculum                                     114
Individual Education Plans                                         116
Specific intervention programmes 1 – speech and language difficulties  118
Specific intervention programmes 2 – autistic spectrum disorders   122
Summary                                                            131

**7. Responding to the affective needs of young children**        **134**
Introduction                                                       134
Definitions and terminology                                        135
Legislation and guidance                                           136
Personal, social and emotional development                         137
Causal factors                                                     144
Self-concept                                                       146
Behaviour                                                          151
Summary                                                            156

**8 Inclusive education for young children**                      **159**
Introduction                                                       159
Historical development and legislation                             160
Definitions and models                                             163
Reasons for inclusion                                              166
Enabling inclusion in early years settings                         167
Issues and barriers                                                169
Including disadvantaged children                                   173
Summary                                                            178

**9. Issues for consideration**                                   **180**

*Bibliography*                                                     190
*Index*                                                            196

# Foreword

Some 30 years ago a little boy called John came into my life, as his grandparents, with whom he lived, brought him on visits to the nursery where I worked, over a period of several weeks, prior to his admission. After a few of these sessions, my Nursery Nurse colleague and I shared our feelings – we were both anxious that we would fail John, and most importantly, the area in which we feared we would fail him most was that relating to affection and loving interaction. For John came to us with multiple physical difficulties. He did not seem the kind of child who would inspire spontaneous, mutually joyful exchanges. How wrong we were – and how much we both learnt about the human spirit, about being and belonging and loving, from that one little boy. We were privileged to be the adults who worked with him and shared his achievements.

Once again I feel I am privileged. This time, to write the foreword to Kate's impressive book. Her ability to combine practical experience and expertise with personal observations, evidence from research, theoretical perspectives and philosophical reflections is rarely matched. Kate provides us with an exemplary model to which we can aspire, with her thoughtful and humane interweaving of all these aspects of life with very young children, especially those for whom life has set extraordinary challenges. Kate's exhortations to encompass a multi-professional and multidisciplinary approach, to recognise the needs of all our children, their families and communities by advocating changes in societal attitudes, are timely. Being a parent – mother and father – is probably more difficult now than it has ever been and I am filled with admiration at the ways in which young families cope with all the demands made on them and the stresses they encounter. Kate's work will help practitioners towards a better understanding of how to reflect on these demands, how to question policies and practices, and how to provide vital support so that all our children may achieve their optimal potential and feel valued by the society to which they belong.

*Tricia David*
*Emeritus Professor of Education*
*Canterbury Christ Church University College*
*September 2002*

# Glossary of Acronyms

| | |
|---|---|
| ACE | Advisory Centre for Education |
| ADD | attention deficit disorder |
| ADHD | attention deficit hyperactivity disorder |
| AIT | Auditory Integration Training |
| ASD | autistic spectrum disorder |
| CLIC | Cancer and Leukaemia in Children |
| CMO | clinical medical officer |
| CSIE | Centre for Studies on Inclusive Education |
| COP | Code of Practice for Special Educational Needs |
| DfEE | Department for Education and Employment |
| DfES | Department for Education and Skills |
| DoH | Department of Health |
| EEC | Early Excellence Centres |
| ELG | Early Learning Goals |
| ESN | educationally subnormal |
| EP | Educational Psychologist |
| EYDCP | Early Years Development and Childcare Partnership |
| GEST | Grants for Education, Support and Training |
| GP | general practitioner |
| HI | hearing impairment |
| HV | health visitor |
| IBP | Individual Behaviour Plan |
| IEP | Individual Education Plan |
| IQ | intelligence quotient |
| IT | information technology |
| LEA | local education authority |
| LSA | learning support assistant |
| MLD | moderate learning difficulties |
| NAS | National Autistic Society |
| NASEN | National Association of Special Educational Needs |
| NNEB | nursery nurse |

| | |
|---|---|
| OECD | Organisation for Economic Cooperation and Development |
| OFSTED | Office for standards in education |
| OT | occupational therapist |
| PBCL | Pre-school Behaviour Checklist |
| PE | physical education |
| PECS | Picture Exchange Communication System |
| QCA | Qualifications and Curriculum Authority |
| SEN | special educational needs |
| SENCO | special educational needs coordinator |
| SENDA | Special Educational Needs and Disability Discrimination Act |
| SLD | severe learning difficulties |
| SLT | speech and language therapist |
| SN | special needs |
| SPELL | Structure; Positive approaches and expectations; Empathy; Low arousal environments, and Links with parents |
| SSD | severely subnormal difficulties |
| SSD | social services department |
| TEACCH | Treatment and Education of Autistic and Related Communication Handicapped Children |
| UNESCO | United Nations Educational, Scientific and Cultural Organization |
| UNICEF | United Nations Children's Fund |
| VI | visual impairment |

# Acknowledgements

As this is my first book there are many people who have supported and encouraged me throughout the process, to whom I owe my sincere gratitude. I am indebted to Estelle, Guy, Angela, Tricia, Jo and Carly for the time they have given reading and commenting on each chapter as well as ongoing support and consideration. Tricia, in particular has been a key motivator for me.

Mark and Ian have always believed in me, even when I doubted myself, and I thank them for that, even Mark's constant nagging (or was it encouragement?).

Michael has shared each high and low point with me and encouraged me throughout, without which I am not sure I would have completed the work.

Sam and Tracy have always had faith in my abilities and have supported and encouraged me all their young lives. They continue to be my inspiration.

I dedicate this book to mum, and everyone who knows me will understand why.

# 1

# Definitions of Special Needs and Relevant Legislation

## Introduction

The term 'special needs' is frequently used in a generic manner and has become indicative of a separate and discrete area of education and wider society. Yet we are currently undergoing societal changes that promote inclusion in all aspects of our lives. It could be suggested that all people have needs and that these needs will vary as their lives develop and change. Events may have severely traumatising effects demanding very specific short- and/or long-term support, but at other times occur more gradually, causing less impact. At times we all require very specific, individual support and provision but this does not necessarily imply that we are different, or have special needs, more that we are human. We should therefore strive to provide effectively for the individual needs of *all* children at *all* times, enabling each child to achieve his/her full potential. Provision should ensure that each child is offered a range of appropriate, challenging experiences, support development at his/her own pace and ensure success. High-quality early years provision would then be responding to the needs of all children, whether or not they have identified special needs.

This chapter discusses definitions of special needs and special educational needs, clarifying commonalities and differences. The changes within early years and special needs are also chronicled to clarify understanding and to place later discussions in perspective. The knowledge of progress to date should help to make sense of how best we can provide for children's individual needs and where we may be heading in the future.

## Current provision in the UK

Within the UK there is a well-documented diverse range of early years provision that has undergone periods of growth and expansion, mostly on a needs-led basis (e.g. Oberhuemer and Ulich, 1997; Pugh, 2001). This chapter identifies significant developments over the twentieth century reflecting on research, government initiatives and legislation. Combined with an examination of the range of provision available to today's youngest children and their families, this leads to the clarification of definitions for the purposes of this book.

# Development of nursery provision in the UK

### *Late 1800s–early 1900s*

At the beginning of the twentieth century there was no statutory pre-school provision in the UK, although in Europe the importance and value of pre-school provision had been identified and early years settings were encouraged. As far back as 1869, the French government, recognising a specific need, supported the development of crèches and continued to support further expansion and development. Van der Eyken commented on early European developments, concluding that:

> What we see throughout the nineteenth century in Europe therefore, is a ferment of ideas, of quick development and of official recognition for the world of the young child, and by 1908 it was possible to say that half the children between two and five in Belgium, a quarter of those in France and between 2 and 10 per cent in Germany were regularly attending institutions of some kind. (Van der Eyken, 1967: 60)

In the UK at this time there was no such perceived need for early years provision. Few women worked, with most remaining at home to fulfil their duties as wives and mothers. However, some 3- and 4-year-old children were placed in elementary classes alongside their older peers, remaining seated for the majority of the school day and following inappropriate curricula set for older children. Learning, sometimes in classes of 60 children, was by rote and severe punishments were administered for misdemeanours. Today, at the beginning of the twenty-first century, we would express grave concern at this scenario and the resulting effects of inappropriate curricula and early formalisation on very young children, yet these very issues are still debated. Discussions regarding the age of school entry in the UK compared with other European countries are frequently highlighted in the media, as are discussions about the formalisation of early learning.

In 1908 the Education Act gave local education authorities (LEAs) the power to offer free nursery education in nursery classes housed within elementary schools. This followed the 1905 Board of Education's report highlighting the inappropriateness of these elementary classes for under 5s. However, without legislation to enforce such provision this was not a move securing nursery education for all 3 to 5-year-olds, simply those living near to schools which offered the service. By allowing, rather than compelling, LEAs to provide nursery education, the government of the day missed an opportunity to create a coherent and comprehensive nursery education service for all children. Subsequent governments have followed a similar pattern, although the current government, at the beginning of the twenty-first century, is working towards a free nursery place for every 3- and 4-year-old who desires it.

## *Some early pioneers*

In the early 1900s, and even in previous centuries, despite the lack of government support there were early years pioneers who recognised, very clearly, the value of early years education. There was an increasing need to provide for the growing population of children requiring daycare, due to a continuing increase of the female workforce, but also for children with special needs. These special needs could be the resultant effects of poverty and war, major factors of the time, resulting in 'over-crowding, malnutrition, poor hygiene, disease and the ravages of poverty' (Van der Eyken, 1967: 65).

Robert Owen (1771–1858) was one of the earliest and most influential early years pioneers. A cotton-mill manager in New Lanark, Scotland, Owen reduced the working hours of young children in his mill and set up a school for the children of mill workers. Owen, according to David (1990: 18), 'believed that environmental factors, particularly during the earliest years of life, shaped the future citizen, and what he worked for was the education of an engaged future citizenry, not a subjugated and underachieving one'. Although we may question Owen's motives, his school encouraged children to explore play activities within a philosophy similar to Froebel.

Friedrich Froebel was a German educator responsible for opening Germany's first kindergarten in the mid-1800s. He acknowledged the importance of play for young children and advocated kindergartens that encouraged exploratory play using appropriate resources to stimulate and extend children's knowledge. This philosophy still exists today but is, in the eyes of some, compromised by the introduction of the Foundation Stage that they view as too formal and structured for 3- and 4-year-old children in the UK. The issue surrounding the importance of play in the early years remains as contentious today as ever.

Sisters Rachel and Margaret McMillan devoted their lives to the plight of young, poor children. Margaret's main interests lay in children's education while Rachel's energies were related to children's health, perhaps an early example of health and education working together. In 1906 the sisters were instrumental in the introduction of the school meals system and in 1913 opened their first nursery school in Deptford with its own outdoor play space, which prospered rapidly. Due to the poor general state of the nation's children at the time the McMillan sisters were providing for many children with special needs and at the same time campaigned for nursery education for all, as Bradburn summarised:

> She (Margaret) realized that poverty, ignorance and disease were not only harming an adult population but mortgaging the growth of the next generation also.
>     She yearned to change the system which created the conditions she abhorred. At the same time she realized that sick children could not wait for political reform. She fought to cure the dirt and disease that she saw everyday in the mothers and children around her, and kept up the fight for political reform as well. (Bradburn, 1976: 45–6)

The McMillan sisters continued throughout their lives to work for a nationwide nursery education system for all children.

Maria Montessori, founder of the Montessori Education system, first published her work 'the Montessori Method' in 1912, based on observations of her own young children and placing the child at the heart of their own learning process. Within a Montessori classroom the adult is a guide to the child, supporting the child's exploration and discovery but not intervening nor imposing. A range of Montessori materials (didactic teaching materials) enables the child to explore, develop skills and self-check. These central materials are part of a broader range of stimulating experiences offered to the child. Beaver et al. (2000) summarise the method:

> The child is at the centre of the Montessori method. She (Montessori) believed that children learn best through their own spontaneous activity and that they have a natural inquisitiveness and eagerness to learn. The role of the adult is to provide a planned environment that will allow the child the opportunity to develop skills and concepts. (Beaver et al., 2000, p. 81)

## Early–mid-1900s

In 1907, and again in 1916, a case for separate and discrete early years provision was raised, as was the suggestion that children should not be compelled to commence formal education at the age of 5, but without positive results. It was, however, the beginning of an understanding that a different form of education was required for our youngest children.

In 1918 the Maternal and Child Welfare Act separated daycare and education, placing responsibility for daycare provision within the remit of the Department of Health (DoH) with education remaining under the Board of Education. This division is still evident today, despite continued efforts to blur the divisions and ensure a coherent service for young children and their families. The recent advent of Early Years Development and Childcare Partnerships, bringing together all early years agencies, is a move towards creating a coherent early years network.

At the same time, the 1918 Education Act gave local authorities the power to support nursery education for children aged 2 to 5 years, but specifically to promote healthy physical and mental development.

By the late 1920s the UK government appeared to view nursery education from a more positive perspective with an education enquiry committee report in 1929 recognising the different needs of under 5s and identifying a need for separate nursery education.

Grace Owen (1928: 15), the honorary secretary to the Nursery Schools Association, concluded at the time that: 'It cannot be long before nursery schools for children between two and five years of age are the accepted instrument for securing adequate nurture for very young children'. This is an ideal yet to be achieved in the twenty-first century.

## 1940s

Until the start of the Second World War there was little change in the range of provision available. Benefits to children, short and long term, were still not well researched and children's developmental needs and the importance of appropriate early years provision not recognised by all. Robson (1989: 4) highlighted: 'The developmental needs of the child seemed secondary to political, economic and social factors and the pamphlet (Nursery Schools and Nursery Classes 1936) described the under-fives "problem" as being due to modern housing conditions, the growth of traffic and all kinds of pressing social, industrial and financial considerations'.

In 1943, the Board of Education White Paper preceding the 1944 Education Act again highlighted a need for nursery provision, concluding that nursery schools were needed nationwide to offer appropriate educational experiences to the very young. The 1944 Education Act that followed continued to support the notion of nursery education, stating that: '(the 1944 Education Act) placed the duty to provide nursery education in the hands of LEAs' (David, 1990: 21). Sadly the country then experienced economic difficulties and the hoped for expansion of nursery provision was severely compromised before it had started.

During the Second World War the government supported pre-school provision by way of grants, predominantly to release women to war-related workplaces as the majority of the male workforce was fighting for their country. In addition, the women needed to supplement the poor wages sent home by their husbands. Once the grants were removed after the war, many of the nurseries closed, thus returning the nation to an array of pre-school provision and most parents to a lack of useful provision, dependent on where they lived and their financial status.

## 1950s–1970s

Since the end of the Second World War growth in pre-school provision has continued in an ad hoc manner, and availability varies geographically. Throughout the 1950s and 1960s, when the population was fast overtaking available housing, the sheer lack of available space for housing development resulted in the building of high-rise flats. This produced additional concerns for young children and families as the basic design of such accommodation limited socialisation for adults and children alike, and left many families isolated from friends, family and their local community. Over the years many of these tower blocks became run-down and high-rise estates were often known for their problems of vandalism, crime, drug and alcohol abuse and social deprivation. Young children housed in such tower blocks were often 'prisoners' in their own homes as parents experienced tremendous difficulties in simple tasks such as taking small children down to ground level to meet with friends and playmates. As many parents chose to have their children within two or three years of each other, even the most basic trip to the supermarket was problematic, with two or three under 5s to cater for. At a time when nursery provision was still not available to all, the quality of opportunities and experiences offered to these children could be described as minimal and lacking challenge. This is a view supported by Willis:

> One aspect of designing flats which has not hitherto been given sufficient attention is that of providing adequately and imaginatively for children's play. Very many comments have been made as to the undesirability of bringing up children in flats and general regrets are expressed that this should occur at all; nevertheless, with the present density standards for inner and middle rings of London, large numbers of children will inevitably be spending their formative years on flatted estates. It is therefore of urgent importance that a suitable environment should be planned for them. (Willis, 1953: 19–20)

The Plowden Report (CACE, 1967) highlighted the value of early years provision that led to some expansion of nursery provision, but these developments were predominantly in inner-city areas deemed to have exceptional needs (educational priority areas). Additional expansion at this time came mainly from the private sector and voluntary agencies, with an increase in campaigning for more provision for the under 5s.

## The playgroup movement

Throughout the 1960s the playgroup movement expanded nationally, responding directly to local need and the lack of state provision. As Van der Eyken concluded:

> The efforts of these groups have done a great deal to stimulate concern about the under-fives. No one, however, would suggest that these self-help solutions are in any way an alternative to the provision of proper facilities and trained supervision for young children. They have arisen out of a growing recognition by parents of the needs of their children. At considerable personal sacrifice these parents are doing what they can to fill a void that they recognise exists. Inevitably their efforts can only alleviate the need. To satisfy that need is the responsibility of society as a whole. (Van der Eyken, 1967: 83)

Often being held, and still being held, in church halls, playgroups were predominantly run by mothers who maintained a rota to attend and supervise 3 to 4-year-olds at play, charging a nominal fee to cover expenses. Few of these mothers had formal training, qualifications or experience of such work. Since the first playgroups were introduced the Pre-School Playgroups Association (now the Pre-School Learning Alliance) has been instrumental in providing guidance, training and support to all playgroups. It has campaigned continuously for improved terms and conditions for workers as well as raising awareness and recognition for early years work and workers.

## 1970s–1990s

In 1972, the Conservative government boldly pledged to provide free nursery education for every 3- and 4-year-old within ten years, another government commitment to early years education that remains unfulfilled today. However, when statistical evidence is presented regarding UK provision for 3- and 4-year-olds, the fact that few 3-year-olds are provided for is masked by the high percentage of 4-year-olds now attending school. In addition, the majority of 3-year-olds are provided for by childminders, not in playgroups or nurseries. By the mid-1980s, little progress had been made, as highlighted within the Policy Analysis Unit report which concluded that:

> In Britain there is hardly any provision at all for two year olds and part-time care only for 20 per cent of three year olds. Low priority has been given by successive Governments to child-care for under-fives, and there is no longer any statutory responsibility on local authorities to provide facilities for pre-school children, except those 'at risk'. (Policy Analysis Unit, 1986: 2)

## The Children Act, 1989

The Children Act (1989) brought together preceding public and private law relating to children and identified a core value of the welfare of the child being 'paramount'. The Act also reinforced the importance of the family and of those who have 'parental responsibility' for children, trying to redress the balance between 'the needs and rights of children and the responsibilities and rights of parents' (Beaver et al., 2000: 196).

The Children Act defined 'children in need' and made clear how local authorities should provide for them, enabling them to remain at home with their families whenever practicable. In addition, regulations were set for daycare providers covering such issues as space available, staffing ratios and qualifications of staff, all of which are monitored via the annual inspection process.

The terminology within the Children Act (children in need) should not be confused with educational terminology (special needs or educational needs). Refer to the 'definitions' section at end of this chapter for clarification.

## 1990s to date

From this point in time there was little change in early years provision offered to 3- to 4-year-old children until the 1990s when the Conservative government introduced nursery vouchers as part of a renewed drive to expand nursery provision.

The Nursery Education and Grant Maintained Schools Act of 1996 formalised the Nursery Voucher Scheme and offered parents of children in their pre-school year vouchers, worth £1,100 each to exchange for sessions with local providers. Instead of the anticipated expansion of available provision offering greater choice to parents, many playgroups were forced to close. The incentive of monetary gain encouraged schools to open empty classrooms as nursery classes and some parents, perhaps misguidedly, perceived pre-school provision in schools as more educational and thus preferable to playgroups. Some schools added to parents' dilemmas by guaranteeing reception class places to nursery class attenders only. Playgroups were also subject to inspection by the social services department (SSD), whereas nursery classes on school premises were not.

For voluntary sector providers, registering with the scheme meant increased income, without which they were no longer financially viable, but also brought about the introduction of Office for Standards in Education (OFSTED) inspections demanding changes in methods of assessment, monitoring, recording and policy production. Groups registered on the scheme were expected to follow the Desirable Learning Outcomes of Learning (SCAA, 1996), outlining six areas of learning to be addressed with the children.

At this changeable time, training for playgroups and other voluntary providers was instigated around the country, as was support for groups to cope with the extra administrative tasks. As from 2000, the Desirable Learning Outcomes were replaced by the Early Learning Goals (QCA, 1999) as part of the Foundation Stage of learning designed to prepare children for the National Curriculum following school entry. The Foundation Stage applied to children from the age of 3 years until the end of the reception year in primary school, so more changes and expectations were placed on early years providers.

## Discussion of development of provision

Over the last 20 or 30 years the effects of legislation and the development of early years provision have been considerable. Day nurseries have always provided care for children but have not always set out to provide education, whereas nursery schools and classes have emphasised the educational elements. Within this context the term 'education' applies to a more directed academic process which should not be confused with learning, which all children take part in, in all contexts, at all times. Playgroups, conversely, have provided both care and education, the latter becoming more formalised since the mid-1990s. The end result is a diverse range of provision with some commonalities but many differences. Some providers offer overlapping services and the move is now towards combined early years centres offering daycare and education (sometimes called 'educare') to young children. However, while the concept of providing for all needs under one roof may seem logical, it raises many issues. To enable effective provision we are becoming dependent on combined centres and, therefore, on professionals from different backgrounds and with different training and qualifications working together. This is a positive move forwards but, in reality, issues of pay, terms and conditions of employment, professional boundaries, local authority bureaucracy and administration can pose very real difficulties.

A change of emphasis in policies and practices should therefore be encouraged before effective multidisciplinary working systems can provide for all the needs of all the children all the time. Pugh suggests:

> The starting point of a policy must therefore ensure that the underpinning principles, the aims and objectives, and the mechanisms for planning, delivering and managing services are developed in a coordinated way, drawing on the skills and expertise of parents and of all those who come to work with children from different professional backgrounds. (Pugh, 1996: 11)

## National Childcare Strategy and Early Years Development and Childcare Partnerships

Following the 1996 Act was a requirement that LEAs should establish Early Years Development and Childcare Partnerships (EYDCPs) and produce Early Years Development and Childcare Plans, from April 1998. McKenna (1999: n.p.) outlines the role of EYDCPs as having: 'an initial remit for ensuring that all four-year olds have access to a free, good quality nursery education place if their parents wish it. This partnership had to include representatives from the statutory, voluntary and private sectors, the health authority and others.'

Following this development the government issued its National Childcare Strategy aiming to 'ensure that all families have access to the childcare which meets their needs' and continuing: 'We want to ensure that good quality, affordable childcare is available to meet the needs of all neighbourhoods' (Internet 3 [see Bibliography]). At this stage membership of the partnerships was extended to include all agencies working with early years children, such as childminders, special needs providers and parents. The remit now includes a responsibility for children from 0 to 14 years of age. These considerable extensions to existing partnerships created some initial complications as, first, so many representatives now attended meetings and, secondly, the range of provision for 0–14 is hugely complex and diverse.

Early Years Development and Childcare Plans were devised by each local authority and submitted to the Department for Education and Employment (DfEE) for approval. If successful, grant funding was allocated. Guidance was issued to authorities outlining such requirements as:

- plans for the extension of current service levels
- staff development, including training
- links with employers
- developments of information services to ensure all parents are able to make informed choices.

## Early Excellence Centres

As our knowledge and understanding of providing for young children and their families have expanded, so has awareness of the need for multidisciplinary settings offering a wide range of services from health, social services and education departments as well as those from the voluntary sector. Early Excellence Centres (EECs) have developed offering high-quality education and childcare within a multidisciplinary framework, responding directly to government initiatives and family needs. Pugh (2001: 18) summarises the range of provision in such centres:

- Excellence in integrated education and care services.
- Access to extended day and holiday childcare for children from birth.
- Support for parents, including parenting education.
- Links to other key services, such as community health services.
- Accessible and affordable adult training opportunities.
- Outreach through local EYDC [Early Years Development and Childcare] partnerships to improve the quality of other early years services through training and practical example.

## Range of early years provision

Providers can be divided into three broad categories and are well documented (e.g. Pugh, 2001). The range of provision includes:

1 Statutory services:
(a)  primary schools – providing for children from 4 to 11 years
(b)  nursery schools and classes
(c)  day nurseries and family centres
(d)  home based support.

2 Private services:
(a)  childminders
(b)  private nursery schools
(c)  private day nurseries
(d)  workplace nurseries
(e)  nannies/au pairs
(f)  out-of school clubs.

3 Voluntary services:
(a)  playgroups (pre-schools)
(b)  groups affiliated to charitable organisations.

This wide range of provision may appear to offer considerable diversity to respond to the needs of individual families, but, in reality, the options available to any one family are limited by finance, inappropriate opening hours and geography, as Pugh (1996: 11) summarises: 'Whilst there is value in diversity which can be sensitive to local needs, the current divisions between one form of service and another owe more to history and the professional jealousies of providers than to the needs of children and their families.'

Questions arising might include:

- Is this 'diversity' of provision available to all children and families?
- How can we ensure parents make informed decisions when such a wide range is available?

In conclusion early years provision has developed according to need and at varying rates due to a lack of consistent government funding. The current range of provision is only now becoming more unified following very recent legislation and guidance.

## Historical development of special needs provision and legislation in the UK

An exploration of the development of special needs provision will highlight key chronological events, indicating a progression from eighteenth-century perspectives to the present day.

An early example of special needs practice occurred in Paris at the turn of the nineteenth century when Itard began working with a 'wild child' discovered in Aveyron, France, who had reputedly been brought up by animals in the wild. Itard's work identified the boy's apparent deafness. Sèguin, a pupil of Itard's, who later worked in the USA, identified that people with significant difficulties could have communication difficulties that impaired their development and ability levels, and therefore they were not necessarily imbeciles or ineducable.

During the eighteenth century the first public schools for the deaf and the blind respectively were opened, followed in the early nineteenth century by the development of asylums for 'idiots'. Throughout this historical period children with special educational needs were, for the most part, unacceptable to society. For religious and/or cultural reasons parents often experienced great shame and tremendous guilt, and in some cases either abandoned their children or kept them hidden from society.

In 1870, Forster's Education Act provided education for all children – a significant move forwards – including those who had previously been considered young adults as opposed to children, and whose needs, special or otherwise, were clearly misunderstood.

In the 1890s, LEAs were required to make special provision for all blind and deaf children and were given the option to provide for 'mentally defective' children.

Following the Boer War it became apparent in the UK that the standards of health and fitness of the armed forces were of an unacceptably low standard, creating a national concern. School meals and medical inspections were introduced under the 1909 Education Act in an attempt to alleviate future problems. During this period Binet's intelligence tests were introduced to assess the intelligence of the young.

Throughout the 1920s and 1930s Freud's work was becoming established, offering explanations for adult behaviours and feelings and linking them back to early childhood experiences. This highlighted implications for the importance of those early experiences. At this time the first child guidance clinic was founded to respond to the prevalent problems of poverty and lack of work, and their impact on the young children of the time.

The Education Act 1944 instigated the appointment of a Minister for Education and the formation of the Ministry of Education, and stated that LEAs 'should have regard to the need for securing that provision is made for pupils who suffer from any disability of mind or body by providing special educational treatment' (ibid.: 5). The Handicapped Pupils and School Health Regulations of 1945 identified 11 categories of disability: blind, partially blind, deaf, partially deaf, delicate, diabetic, educationally subnormal, epileptic, maladjusted, physically handicapped and with speech defects. At this stage medical practitioners undertook diagnoses and children were placed in the most appropriate facilities, resulting in many children being sent away from their homes to boarding schools. Within the 1950s many parents rebelled against this 'medical model' of diagnosis as their children, often very vulnerable, were transported considerable distances from their families and local communities resulting in the children becoming even more vulnerable.

The 1970 Education (Handicapped Children) Act (DES, 1970) placed the responsibility of special needs provision within the remit of LEAs and, as a result, special schools were created for children with:

- moderate learning difficulties (MLD)
- severe learning difficulties (SLD)
- severely subnormal difficulties (SSD).

Perhaps one of the earliest references specifically regarding special needs within the early years was the Court Report of 1976 which highlighted the need for focus on the screening of health and development in the early years to identify difficulties early within a developmental framework.

In 1978, the Warnock Report (DES, 1978) was published having examined in great detail the provision available at the time for all 'handicapped children and young people'. This report, innovative at the time, was to inform subsequent legislation and significantly change the face of special needs provision. One of the key issues raised was that all children have the right to an education and, as society was now more accepting of 'difference', that for children experiencing difficulties we should be committed to 'educating them, as a matter of right and to developing their full potential' (ibid.: 1.11). The fact that this basic principle needed stating reflects somewhat negatively on the education system and societal perspectives prior to 1978. The report continued to suggest a continuum of special needs as opposed to children fitting into one or more categories. The report clarified that children can experience short- and/or longer-term needs and that provision must be flexible to accommodate change.

Within the report were clear recommendations for LEAs (not health authorities) to assume responsibility for assessing and identifying young children with possible special needs. Furthermore, methods of assessment were detailed to move forwards from the sole use of intelligence quotient (IQ) tests. The report made clear that a variety of methods should be employed to ensure the most effective provision according to need and that within child factors should be considered in conjunction with additional possible causal factors, including those within the school/provision.

Within the report parental partnerships were seen as crucial for effective provision if all children with special needs were to achieve their full potential. The child should be assessed as an individual with a differentiated curriculum reflecting this, if appropriate.

The Warnock Report also debated the notion of integration through a reflection of existing practice in special schools, concluding that there were, at that time, three main forms of integration:

1 Locational – where special provision is available as a separate entity on the same site, but the children are not a part of the mainstream classroom.
2 Social – where children remain in their special unit/class for core subject teaching but attend mainstream classes for some subjects such as art, music, physical education (PE).
3 Functional – where children with special needs are full members of the mainstream classes and class teachers take full responsibility for their education.

The ensuing Education Act of 1981 echoed the key principles of the Warnock Report and placed special educational needs provision firmly on the legislative agenda. Key points included:

• LEAs were given the responsibility of identification and assessment of special educational needs.
• Multidisciplinary assessments could lead to a formal assessment of special educational needs, culminating in a statement of special educational needs, which would be reviewed annually.
• Focus to be placed on individual needs rather than categories of need.
• Provision for children with special educational needs to become the responsibility of the LEA.
• All categories of handicap were removed.
• Effective parental partnerships should be established.
• Integration should occur wherever practicable.

In addition, definitions of special educational needs were consolidated (DES, 1981, s. 1.1):

Children have a learning difficulty if:
    They have significantly greater difficulty in learning than the majority of children of their age, or
    They have a disability which prevents or hinders them from making use of the educational facilities generally provided in schools, for children of their age.

It continued, that a child has a learning difficulty if he/she:

> Has a learning disability which requires educational provision that is additional to, or otherwise different from, the educational provision made generally available within the school, or:
> If he/she has a physical disability.

The Children Act (1989), as mentioned previously, consolidated previous public and private laws regarding the welfare of children. Additional definitions and revised terminology were clarified:

> A child shall be taken as 'in need' if:
> He is unlikely to achieve or maintain, or to have the opportunity of achieving or maintaining, a reasonable standard of health or development without the provision for him by services by a local authority under this Part;
> His health or development is likely to be significantly impaired, or further impaired, without the provision for him of such services;
> Or,
> He is disabled. (DoH, 1991: s. 2.3)

Further definitions include:

> a child is disabled if he is blind, deaf or dumb or suffers from mental disorders of any kind or is substantially and permanently handicapped by illness, injury or congenital deformity or such other disability as may be described ... (Ibid.)

> 'development' means physical, intellectual, emotional, social or behavioural development; and 'health' means physical or mental health. (Ibid.)

> and family, in relation to such a child, includes any person who has parental responsibility for the child and any other person with whom he has been living. (Ibid.)

The Children Act also clearly identified a need for effective multidisciplinary working systems, as summarised by Anderson-Ford (1994: 20): 'The Children Act, like the 1981 Act, clearly defines the need for communication between teachers, the school health service and social services departments (SSDs) as well as between the LEA and SSDs at a senior management level.'

The Education Reform Act 1988 (DfEE, 1988) introduced the National Curriculum, outlining core and foundation subjects, with flexibility for modification to accommodate the learning needs of children with special educational needs. A key focus of the Act was to ensure that all children had equal access to a broad and balanced curriculum.

The Disability Discrimination Act, in 1990, demanded that all schools should have admission statements for children with special educational needs, but specifically for those with physical disabilities. Schools needed to ensure that all pupils had equal access to facilities, resources and curriculum and that an anti-discriminatory philosophy existed. One may have argued, however, that the limitations, general conditions and planning of some school and pre-school buildings rendered this Act difficult to adhere to, despite the best of intentions of staff and governors alike.

In 1993, part three of the Education Act (DfEE, 1993) addressed problems and issues that had arisen since the implementation of the 1981 Act. Major reviews of the 1981 Act highlighted two key areas for change, as outlined by Lindsay (1997: 20): 'The Act was inconsistent, inefficient and clearly did not meet the objective of ensuring each child with SEN received a quality assessment, and provision to meet the needs identified.'

As a result, the 1993 Act offered guidance on both identification and assessment and created special educational needs (SEN) tribunals to offer parents opportunities to debate decisions with LEAs. Interestingly, several voluntary agencies (e.g. Network 81) had been established over the previous decade to address the issues of children with special educational needs and their families, in many instances working with parents on individual cases, offering advice and support, but at the same time campaigning for the rights of children with special educational needs. Further examples of supporting agencies can be found at the end of this chapter.

In summary, the 1993 Education Act revised the 1981 Act and introduced the following amendments/additions:

- School SEN policies must reflect the new approach.
- Greater responsibility should be given to parents within positive, effective working partnerships.
- Independent tribunal system should be established.

The Code of Practice (DfEE, 1994) guidance document (as opposed to a legislative document) was introduced in 1994, detailing the responsibilities previously laid down within the 1993 Act. It offered LEAs and practitioners very clear and specific guidelines on all aspects of special educational needs provision, including:

- identification of SEN
- assessment of SEN
- a new five-staged assessment process, culminating in a statement of SEN
- regular reviews of progress, provision and statements
- the introduction of the special educational needs coordinator (SENCO).

One of the key issues for all early years practitioners was that provision for children below the age of 5 years was included within section 5 of the Code of Practice giving support to the philosophy of early identification and intervention within a multidisciplinary framework. All maintained schools and registered early years providers were expected to adhere to the guidance given within the Code of Practice, which was intended to be a working document, within which changes could be accommodated, depending on the child's responses to the intervention given.

Early years providers were to establish policy documentation for special educational needs and ensure:

- all parents were familiar with such documents
- all members of staff were knowledgeable in special educational needs provision
- familiarity with a range of agencies who work with children with special educational needs and their families.

At that particular time, with playgroups dominating pre-school provision, these requirements were considerable as, although very skilled and knowledgeable adults staffed such groups, they often lacked formal qualifications and, more specifically, special needs training. Training programmes were introduced nationwide, mainly through either LEAs or the Pre-School Playgroup Association to ensure that all children's needs could be addressed.

The newly created role of SENCO (DfEE, 1994: para. 2.14) brought with it considerable requirements and responsibilities, as summarised by Smith (1996: 9):

Taking responsibility for the day-to-day operation of the school's SEN policy;
- Liaising with and advising fellow teachers;
- Coordinating provision for pupils with SEN;
- Maintaining the school's SEN register and overseeing the records of all pupils with SEN;
- Liaising with parents;
- Contributing to staff in-service training;
- Liaising with external agencies.

In reality, many SENCOs were already full-time practitioners and these responsibilities were therefore additional, although in some instances new appointments were created. However, pre-school providers also had to maintain a SENCO and with many playgroup employees remaining in post for relatively short terms this created ongoing difficulties for many groups.

The five stages of assessment detailed within the Code applied to children from birth, although the Code did not expect special educational needs to arise during the first two years of a child's life, unless the child had a specific condition from birth and/or major health and development difficulties. The Code stated that for children under 5 years of age and not yet attending school, the five-stage approach should still be applied but it was not anticipated that many formal statements of need would result. In summary the stages of assessment are:

Stage 1: Class or subject teachers identify or register a child's special educational needs and, consulting the school's SEN coordinator, take initial action.
Stage 2: School's SEN coordinator takes lead responsibility for gathering information and for coordinating the child's special educational provision, working with the child's teachers.
Stage 3: Teachers and the SEN coordinator are supported by specialists from outside the school.
Stage 4: The LEA consider the need for a statutory assessment and, if appropriate, make a multi-disciplinary assessment.
Stage 5: LEA consider the need for a statement of special educational needs and, if appropriate, make a statement and arrange, monitor and review provision.
(DfEE, 1994: s. 1.4)

The final statement of need was to be the result of a multidisciplinary assessment, gathering information from all practitioners involved with the child, plus the parents.

The Code outlined the requirements for effective planning of provision for individual children on the special needs register (Individual Education Plans – IEPs) which could include such information as: summary of the difficulties; steps taken to accommodate those needs; details of parental views; resources (materials and human) required; detailed targets for future working and information on assessments, monitoring and reviewing the provision.

Within the Code was a clear direction that if parents were to request an assessment of their child's needs then the LEA *must* carry this out but, conversely, if social services or health professionals identify a child's needs then the LEA *may* carry out an assessment if they feel it appropriate, and then only with parental consent. If schools requested an assessment then, at stage 4 or 5 of the assessment process, the LEA will decide whether a statement of need is appropriate or not.

The Code of Practice was a positive step forwards for children with special educational needs but created considerable additional responsibilities and tasks to be undertaken by existing staff. Rarely was the situation such that a SENCO would be appointed to ensure the introduction of and monitoring of the requirements of the Code. The Code of Practice has now been revised, with the National Association for Special Educational Needs (NASEN) being instrumental throughout. A consultative document was sent to all members with resulting recommendations and comments passed to the Department for Education and Skills (DfES).

One important change within the Revised Code of Practice (DfES, 2001d) is a whole chapter relating to identification, assessment and provision in the early years. Consecutive governments have begun to acknowledge the value and place of early years provision and are working towards a place for all 3- and 4-year-old children that require it. In addition the importance of early intervention for special educational provision is now well documented, as referred to by the DfEE (1997: 13) within their Green Paper, outlining government intentions and future pathways for meeting special educational needs: 'early diagnosis and appropriate intervention improve the prospects for children with special educational needs, and reduce the need for expensive intervention later on. For some children, giving more attention to early signs of difficulty can prevent the development of SEN.'

The Nursery Education and Grant Maintained Schools Act (DfEE, 1996) was a major advancement and acknowledgement of early years provision which introduced the Nursery Voucher Scheme with concise requirements for providers who wished to become a part of the scheme and receive vouchers redeemable for funding. Although previously discussed within this chapter, a reminder at this juncture is appropriate when reflecting on special educational needs provision within a historical perspective. All providers needed to have 'due regard' to the Code of Practice, again requiring additional training and resources for many pre-school providers which were jointly addressed by national organisations and LEAs, often in a collaborative manner.

The Special Educational Needs and Disability Discrimination Act 2001 incorporates further changes for education and as a result the Special Educational Needs Code of Practice 2001 has now been published and the Disability Discrimination Code of Practice is also available.

The Special Educational Needs Code of Practice (DfES, 2001d), as previously mentioned, includes a section on identification, assessment and provision of special educational needs in early education settings. The five-staged approach from the 1994 Code is now replaced by a 'graduated response' incorporating Early Years Action and Early Years Action Plus:

> Once practitioners have identified that a child has special educational needs, the setting should intervene through *Early Years Action*. If the intervention does not enable the child to make satisfactory progress the SENCO may need to seek advice and support from external agencies. These forms of intervention are referred to (below) as *Early Years Action Plus*. (DfES, 2001d: s. 4.11)

The new Code of Practice (DfES, 2001d) identifies key changes from the original Code of Practice (DfEE, 1994) as:

- A stronger right for children with SEN to be educated at a mainstream school
- New duties on LEAs to arrange for parents of children with SEN to be provided with services offering advice and information and a means of resolving disputes
- A new duty on schools and relevant nursery education providers to tell parents when they are making special educational provision for their child
- A new right for schools and relevant nursery education providers to request a statutory assessment of a child. (DfES, 2001d: iv)

Another area emphasised within the new Code of Practice is the value and need for effective multidisciplinary working systems, providing for the needs of children within a 'seamless' service that addresses the needs of children as well as their parents. However, practitioners and organisations such as NASEN have identified possible shortcomings within the guidance, including the lack of provision for non-teaching time for SENCOs to allow for planning, preparation and record-keeping (although the guidance suggests that this should be reviewed within settings), plus the recurring issue of training and funding. Considerable importance is placed on parental partnerships and multidisciplinary working, but these place additional demands on SENCOs' time to create, monitor, review and maintain systems and processes. It could be that without the allocation of specified time to undertake such activities the outcomes may be limited, although working practices inform us that SENCOs achieve this despite the time implications.

In a similar vein practitioners working with early years children need additional training to ensure they have the up-to-date knowledge and understanding of the new guidance documents and the necessary skills to implement them. There is a need for specific and extensive special educational needs training for early years practitioners, and new guidelines and legislation will intensify this need. A comprehensive nationwide training system would accommodate this, but funding would be needed.

The Disability Discrimination Act Draft Code of Practice (Schools) (2001: 7) offers guidance to educational establishments on 'preventing discrimination against disabled people in their access to education'. A person with a disability is defined as one 'who has a physical or mental disability which has an effect on his or her ability to carry out normal day-to-day activities' (ibid.: 14) and the Code continues to identify two key duties relating to educational settings to ensure that pupils with disabilities are not discriminated against:

- Not to treat disabled pupils less favourably; and
- To make reasonable adjustments to avoid putting disabled pupils at a substantial disadvantage. (ibid.: 15)

With the array of human rights legislation that now exists (United Nations Convention on the Rights of the Child, 1989; Human Rights Act, 1998; Special Educational Needs and Disability Discrimination Act, 2001) early years practitioners must ensure that the special needs provision we offer reflects the rights of the children and their families. Whilst we may, as a society, be moving towards inclusive education for all children we must not ignore those children and/or parents who request a separate form of specialised education for their children.

## Summary

Early years provision has expanded over the last century to offer a diverse range of opportunities to young children and their families and all registered early years providers must now have due regard to the Special Educational Needs and Disability Discrimination Act, 2001 (DfES, 2001c), hopefully ensuring appropriate special educational provision for all children within a multidisciplinary framework. However, issues such as funding, training, resources and accommodation can impact on the levels of provision available and the range offered in different areas of the country and in different settings, so we are still a long way from a system that is truly equitable to all children at all times. Huge strides have been made, but further progress is still needed to ensure optimum achievement for all very young children.

As the field of early years has been incorporated within special needs legislation and guidance comparatively recently, monitoring and reviewing provision must continue to address any current and future issues. Continued evaluation and research in the field will support this process.

Special educational provision, both generally and in the early years, has received more national attention over the last 20 years than ever before and, while we can acknowledge that the central aim is to strive continuously to improve systems and provision, the current situation (and relevant legislation and guidance) is not necessarily the answer to ensure equal and appropriate provision for all. As Farrell concludes, we are currently in a situation balancing both positive and negative aspects:

> On the positive side parents now have a much louder voice, there are more mechanisms to support them and they have far greater rights of appeal ...
>
> Perhaps more important are the continued problems associated with the bureaucratic and cumbersome statutory assessment procedures which, despite the proposed changes in the new Draft Code, still seem to be a millstone round the necks of all those involved in striving to provide the best quality education to pupils with SEN and their families. (Farrell, 2001: 8)

## Definitions

The following terminology is used throughout this book:

*Early years/young children* are those aged 0–8 years, but this book will focus predominantly on the under 5s or pre-school children as there is a plethora of information available on children of statutory school age.

*Early years provider/provision/setting* refers to any practitioner or establishment providing opportunities and/or support to 0–5-year-old children. This will include pre-school groups, nurseries, nursery classes, childminders, daycare, special needs units/classes/schools and educare groups.

*Parents* refers to any person, parent or otherwise, assuming 'parental responsibility' for the child.

*Professionals/practitioners* refers to any person working with children in any setting, whether or not they hold professional qualifications.

*Special educational needs* (SEN) are any difficulties experienced by a child requiring additional or different educational provision to be made.

*Special needs* (SN) are those difficulties experienced by a child that do not necessarily result in a special educational need.

---

### *Special needs or individual needs?*

Despite legalistic, educational and societal definitions I would suggest from personal experiences that all children, like all adults, have individual needs that will change in type, severity or nature during different phases of their lives. It should be our aim as early years practitioners to enable all children to achieve their optimum potential whether they are identified as having 'special needs', 'special educational needs', or not.

## Key issues

❖ Early years special needs provision is now placed on the legislative agenda placing considerable expectations on early years practitioners.

❖ Legislation and guidance now incorporates special educational provision, disability discrimination and human rights.

❖ While we can continue to work towards inclusion, with the individual needs of all young children and their families being met, there are still key issues to address.

❖ Monitoring and research should be encouraged to ensure progression.

## Some suggestions for discussion

### Item 1

Assess the training needs of all practitioners in your setting with regard to special educational needs. Examine in particular:

• Knowledge of recent legislation and guidance.
• Knowledge and skills to provide for the special needs of all attending children.

### Item 2

In the light of your responses to item 1, identify any training needs and how you might address them.

### Item 3

Examine the special needs policy for your setting.

• Does it need updating in the light of recent guidance and legislation?
• Does it offer clarity of understanding for practitioners and parents?

### Item 4

Assess the special needs recording systems you have in place.

• Are they up to date, reflecting recent legislation and guidance?
• Is the documentation system practical to manage?
• Is documentation accessible to parents and, if so, is it written in an appropriate language and presented in an appropriate format?

## 📖 Suggested further reading

Department of Education and Science (1978) *The Report of the Committee of Enquiry into the Education of Handicapped Children and Young People* (Warnock Report). London: HMSO. (Chapter 2, 'The historical background'.)

Farrell, P. (2001) 'Special education in the last twenty years: have things really got better?', *British Journal of Special Education*, 28 (1): 3–9.

Pugh, G. (ed.) (2001) *Contemporary Issues in the Early Years, 3rd edn.* London: Paul Chapman. (Chapter 8, 'Meeting special needs in the early years' by S. Wolfendale.)

## Useful contacts: some examples of supporting agencies

Advisory Centre for Education (ACE)
Unit 1c Aberdeen Studios, 22–24 Highbury Grove, London N5 2DQ
☎ 0207 354 8318      💻 www.ace-ed.org.uk

British Association for Early Childhood Education (BAECE)
136 Cavell Street, London E1 2JA
☎ 0207 539 5400      💻 www.early-education.org.uk

Disability Rights Commission (DRC)
Freepost MID 02164, Stratford-upon-Avon, CV37 9BR
☎ 08457 622 633      💻 www.drc.org.uk

Independent Panel for Special Educational Advice (IPSEA)
6 Carlow Mews, Woodbridge, Suffolk IP12 1DH
☎ 01394 382814      💻 www.ipsea.org.uk

National Association for Special Educational Needs (NASEN)
4–5 Amber Business Village, Amber Close, Amington, Tamworth B77 4RP
☎ 01827 311500      💻 www.nasen.org.uk

National Children's Bureau, Early Childhood Unit
8 Wakley Street, London EC1V 7QE
☎ 0207 843 6000      💻 www.ncb.org.uk

National Early Years Network
77 Holloway Road, London N7 8JZ
☎ 0207 607 9573      💻 www.neyn.org.uk

Network 81 (for parents of children with special educational needs)
1–7 Woodfield Terrace, Stanstead, Essex CM24 8AJ
☎ 0800 770 3263      💻 www.network81.co.uk

# 2

# Families of Children with Special Needs

## Introduction

In this chapter we consider the child within the context of his/her family to ensure that the needs of every family member are addressed. Having a baby or a young child with special needs can be traumatic in many ways such as:

- at the time of initial diagnosis with the possible feelings of grief and loss
- when confronted with a diverse range of 'expert' professionals, each having their own perspective on the child
- when dealing with the possible feelings of lost control over decision-making
- when feeling confused within an unfamiliar and complex system.

Different family members may deal with the issues in opposing or concurring ways, so it is important that early years practitioners understand and respect each of the individuals involved. If we support the needs of each family member then, in turn, we support the child. Effective multidisciplinary working systems will support this process but it is imperative that we do not make assumptions about parents' needs and views. In addition we should always listen to, and attempt to understand and respect, their perspectives and feelings.

## Children and their families

Today's family is often far from the stereotypical image of two parents with two children. In the mid-twentieth century there were fewer broken marriages and more extended family members who usually lived nearby and supported their families, particularly the young and elderly.

In my early childhood perhaps I was fortunate to live with both parents, behind the family shop. Both parents were, for the most part, on hand at all times, but when they were ill or away from the house, my grandmother, who lived locally, was available to help out. Similarly when I had my own children my mother was able to support me when I returned to full-time work, so neither my own children nor myself needed to use daycare provision. In contrast my own daughters, who do not live nearby and who have a mother who is still working full time, will need early childhood services for their children.

## Family structures

Besides these fundamental changes the structure of families has also changed dramatically and we should reflect briefly on the range of family structures that currently exist and in which the children we work with are growing up. Barnes (1995) suggests five family structures:

- *Conjugal nuclear*: two married people of the opposite sex living together with their children.
- *Non-conjugal nuclear*: two people living as man and wife but not being legally married (co-habiting or common law).
- *Lone parent*: generally as the result of death, separation (for a range of reasons) or divorce where a parent lives apart from his/her partner.
- *Reconstituted or 'blended'* (Hayman, 1999): when one lone parent establishes a relationship with either another lone parent or a single person.
- *Extended*: when more than one generation from one family lives together.

In addition there are also relatively new family structures such as:

- same-sex families, e.g. a mother and an aunt taking parental responsibility
- gay/lesbian families
- adoption
- foster families
- care homes
- grandparents, aunts or other relatives taking care of their young relatives.

Family structures vary considerably and, if we accept that family members have significant influence upon the children growing up, there are implications for early years practitioners.

## What support does a family provide?

There are four key features of family support:

1 To provide a safe and secure environment in which children can develop their full potential.
2 To pass on culture, e.g. how we behave, aspects of history, languages.
3 To pass on norms and values. (Religious organisations and schools also do this.)
4 To pass on family biology.

Naturally, different families have differing standards, so norms and values passed on to children vary. Acceptable behaviour within one family may be considered unacceptable in another. The effects of different standards of behaviour are evident in early years settings, and practitioners need to respond appropriately. Children are not born behaving inappropriately but adapt to and learn from behaviours modelled around them. We would like all young children to demonstrate positive behaviours at all times, but must acknowledge the behavioural learning that has taken place within the home and community and consider working with parents as well as the child, to alleviate difficulties and support the child. Practitioners should also acknowledge that inappropriate behaviours are often a child's attempts at achieving independence.

Practitioners should also reflect on their own practices as they may inadvertently compound a child's behavioural difficulties. Tasks that are too hard or too easy may bore a child, as they see no valid reason for trying to complete them. In this position children may resort to unacceptable behaviours as a way of avoiding the task but this may result in the child being reprimanded for 'not getting on with their work'. The outcome is that the child is being blamed for the practitioner's inappropriate planning.

## How does a family impact on a child?

What is a family? Barnes suggests:

> 'Those who have loved us' may be parents, siblings, grandparents, other relatives, teachers or peers. Although other groups and social factors affect socialisation, the family is typically seen as the most influential agency in the socialisation of the child. It is the context within which the most direct and intimate relationships are forged. Our concept of family is greatly influenced by our personal experiences and our culture. (Barnes, 1995: 84)

While accepting this perspective society should also acknowledge that, sadly, not all children are loved in this way. However, if, as Barnes suggests, 'family' comprises those people who love us and each member is a great influence on our development, then we need to begin to explore all those individuals and groups that impact on the lives of children which will extend far beyond the primary notion of the immediate family. Bronfenbrenner (1979) offered an ecology of human development extending beyond the immediate family to national and societal levels through four distinct levels:

1 Microsystem – comprising all family members, the home environment and early years providers, all of whom spend considerable amounts of time with the child. Thus each of their behaviours informs the child's development.
2 Mesosytem – extending beyond the home and provider, we develop links and interaction between them.
3 Exosystem – this includes the social networks of the family, the local neighbourhood and the employment of family members, each of which can directly or indirectly affect the child.
4 Macrosystem – relevant national policies, education and welfare systems, economic systems and cultural systems.

While we may initially consider that only the immediate family affects the child, it is clear to see that, directly or indirectly, there are many influences on a child's life, such as the television. A child's parents may not have direct control over the programme content, but this content can affect a child's development in many ways, cognitively, socially, developmentally and behaviourally.

Goldenberg and Goldenberg (1985: 136) highlight key family features: 'Families are systems influenced by many factors; the ethnic and cultural backgrounds; the stage of the family life cycle; environmental events; external factors; individual relationships and the personal and collective experiences of family members.' Therefore, when considering a child's development we should consider all positive and negative influencing factors, including the family, or, at least, as many as are practically possible. The changing faces of any one family must also be considered, as the family itself is an evolving entity that will change, develop and grow through interaction with significant others and wider society.

## Government initiatives for family support – SureStart

A recent government initiative, SureStart, is an investment in young families specifically aimed at fighting deprivation. Millions of pounds have been set aside to finance and develop SureStart programmes across the country in an attempt to break the existing cycle of deprivation. The key philosophy is one of empowerment. Through giving initial direction and professional support, staff work to enable families to develop and deliver their own provision. The government summarises its intentions as:

> SureStart aims to improve the health and well-being of families and children before and after birth so children are ready to flourish when they go to school. It does this by:
> Setting up local SureStart programmes to improve services for families with children under four
> Spreading good practice learned from local programmes to everyone involved in providing services for young children. (Internet 1)

### Reflecting on the whole child

If we are to consider the individual, and sometimes special needs of each of the children with whom we work, we should understand their differing backgrounds and the resulting effects in order to assess the 'whole child'. We must acknowledge and respect family differences. In some instances specific familial effects may compound a child's difficulties and be beyond our control. If we are aware of and acknowledge these difficulties we can still support the needs of the child effectively.

# Children with special needs and their families

## Perspectives of families of children with special needs

While the preceding discussion of the family equates to all families, those bringing up children with special needs undergo a range of experiences that can have additional positive and/or negative effects on individuals. Parents of children with special needs may have different perspectives on development, learning, opportunities and the future for their children, themselves and the family as a whole. Attwood and Thomson (1997: 130) identifies five key features that distinguish parents of children with special needs:

1 They are long-term players.
2 They tend to become isolated.
3 They are more concerned for their own children than others.
4 Their emotional involvement is heightened.
5 They know that the welfare of their children is much more dependent on the continued effectiveness of the family.

Research is readily accessible to identify specific, individual family needs, e.g. Carpenter (2000), Dale (1996) and Hornby (1995), identifying a need for professionals to acknowledge and understand the perspective of each family member.

## The father's perspective

Current national processes and systems for the identification, assessment and intervention of special needs occur most frequently during the working day, immediately prohibiting attendance and participation for many working fathers. Their understanding of discussions is therefore often second-hand and may lack clarity and/or depth. As one of the main carers for children it is imperative that fathers are included fully in all decision-making and information giving meetings. Carpenter (2000: 137) concludes that: 'They (fathers) need to be offered increased access to information and support, to be provided with opportunities to network with other fathers and to have their need for information and support within the family addressed. In order to achieve these aims, greater training and awareness among professionals is necessary.'

While we may not be able to accommodate paternal involvement at all meetings and discussions, or to change paternal working conditions, we should at least address the issues by ensuring that local systems are in place to inform and support fathers.

## The professional perspective

Mallett (1997) highlights that as professionals we enter a chosen career and those who work with children with special needs often progress to this work after an initial period of working within mainstream settings. We therefore choose to work with children and families experiencing difficulties and are paid an arguably respectable salary. Ongoing training and support are available and, theoretically, we can leave work behind at the end of the day (although in reality few achieve this).

Parents, on the other hand, have little or no advance warning of having to bring up a child with special needs and, in many cases, were expecting a healthy child for whom they had plans and aspirations. Suddenly their dreams and expectations are eradicated and they are faced with a barrage of professionals, confusing systems, some lack of control of events, possible rejection by their friends, community and family, and an overwhelming feeling of failure and disappointment. The way parents are supported is crucial to their future, their child's future and the future of other family members.

## Parental acceptance of special needs at or soon after birth

Children experiencing complex disabilities are often diagnosed at or soon after birth, as are children with specific conditions such as Down syndrome. Sometimes parents may have known during the pre-natal period, but to many the news will be totally unexpected and will arrive at a time when parents are already experiencing tremendous emotional turmoil.

During the first days and weeks following childbirth parents experience major adjustments to a totally new way of life. There is extreme joy and celebration of the joyous event plus excitement and anticipation for the future, but this sometimes conflicts with the overburdening sense of responsibility for this brand new, totally dependent life. When one parent is feeling that the responsibility is overwhelming then, hopefully, their partner will be able to support them and vice versa. Extended family and friends will be visiting, so time for the new family can often be interrupted and compromised by welcome and well-meaning visitors. So what happens when this turbulent period is interrupted by the news that the much loved, newborn child has special needs? Dale (1996: 49) suggests: 'Parents rarely expect their child's disabling condition or life-threatening illness. The confirmation or diagnosis, whether at birth or later, often creates an immense crisis of changes, expectations and hopes, and parents may experience intense reactions during the early days.'

### The impact of the initial diagnosis

Undoubtedly parents need to know if their child is experiencing difficulties and to be informed as soon as practically possible by a professional who is aware of the implications of the specific difficulties and is able to respond to any questions or issues raised, but at this emotional time the handling of this initial discussion is crucial. Coming to terms with an early diagnosis can be made easier or more difficult by professionals and there are many reports highlighting parents' negative experiences, resulting in increased difficulties over and above the natural turbulence of emotions at the time. Birrell offers such a report highlighting one family's passage from delivering an apparently healthy little girl to discovering she has considerable difficulties:

> Then he (the paediatrician) requested that we got Iona dressed before telling us, in a gentle voice: 'I am afraid it appears that Iona is profoundly brain-damaged.'
> They (the words) seemed to reek of despair, of hopelessness, of her condition being incurable, her life unbearably bleak. Our hopes for her, and for us, seemed to plunge further into the abyss with each echo. (Birrell, 1995: 1)

Such examples only begin to give professionals an inkling of the feelings parents' experience. Unless we have actually been through a similar experience, and naturally there are practitioners who have, we cannot fully appreciate the implications and effects on each and every member of the family. Carpenter (2000: 135) suggests that too often at this very difficult time: 'The professional approaches were insensitive and ill-timed as they did nothing to enhance their quality of life or parenting confidence.'

## Including the father

In this difficult period professionals often spend most time with the mother who is seen as the primary carer. Fathers can too easily be overlooked as they are expected 'to be the strong one'. Herbert and Carpenter's study of seven fathers highlighted this 'marginalisation' of fathers after mother and baby had returned home:

> All help was focused on the mother and baby. The father's needs were not addressed or, perhaps, even noticed. They were seen as the 'supporters' and as such adopted the role society expects – that of being competent in a crisis (Tolston 1977). All seven fathers talked of returning to work and trying to search for normality and keep a sense of reality in their lives. (Herbert and Carpenter, 1994: 27)

If we acknowledge that mothers and fathers affect their children then it follows that we should support them individually to account for their specific needs. The more involved the father from the day of conception onwards, the more informed and empowered he can become.

## Maternal issues

Quite often new mothers of babies with special needs are moved to a side ward for 'privacy', theoretically to support sensitivity, but these parents are immediately being segregated from other new mothers who may well be incredibly supportive. While I understand the reasons behind this policy and respect that some mothers would wish to be segregated, each case should be considered individually. A generalised assumption for all is not necessarily helpful.

Professionals may avoid conversations with new mothers of children with special needs as they feel uncomfortable and simply do not know what to say, but this can isolate mothers even further.

If professionals can begin to at least acknowledge some of the difficulties experienced, then perhaps we can support parents positively at this time. Any professional dealing with this emotive situation must demonstrate empathy, understanding, respect, tact and diplomacy. They must be informed and well trained to deal with questions, whether they relate to the condition, the future, the baby or the parents and their handling of the news. Sensitivity is an essential personal characteristic needed, but is sensitivity a quality that can be taught?

# Parental acceptance of special needs at a later stage

As previously mentioned, many specific conditions and/or complex disabilities will probably have been identified prior to, at or soon after birth. Other special needs may emerge at a later stage or develop gradually over a period of time raising concerns by parents, family members, friends and/or professionals.

## When initial concerns are raised

Parents may observe a gap between the development of their young child and older siblings or friends' children and raise the issue with the general practitioner (GP) or health visitor (HV). However, in many cases it will be the GP or HV who notices delayed development or specific problems such as hearing impairment. Alternatively it may be the early years practitioner who identifies difficulties and undertakes a period of observation and assessment to confirm or dispel the concerns before raising the issue with parents.

## Child observation

Observation can clarify and focus thinking, and thus inform the practitioner, parents and future intervention. In some instances observation will show that a child is not experiencing difficulties, as Roffey (1999: 53) acknowledges: 'Although early intervention is desirable there is no point in intervening, perhaps inappropriately, before there is some clarity about what is needed. Observing the child in different situations over a few weeks and presenting different activities to see how he approaches them will give a lot of information.'

A more detailed examination of observational methodology occurs in Chapter 5.

## Discussing concerns with parents

At this point we are again faced with discussing concerns with parents in a sensitive and caring manner, and the professional issues raised previously apply equally here. General practitioners and health visitors may be trained to deal with such situations but this may not necessarily be the case for early years practitioners. Under the Schools Standards and Frameworks Act 1998 (DfEE, 1998) which introduced Early Years Development Plans, all registered early years providers have a qualified early years teacher attached to the group to advise and support. This teacher could directly or indirectly support discussions with parents. In addition, every registered provider must have 'due regard' to the Code of Practice (DfEE, 1994; 2001d) and have a member of staff responsible for SEN provision. As special educational needs coordinator (SENCO), he/she would be involved in any discussions with parents and have experience of dealing with such situations.

## Parental resistance to acceptance

Having identified special needs, practitioners must be prepared for parental resistance to acceptance for a variety of reasons:

- Parents may be shocked and believe categorically that their child is just a little delayed or lazy and will 'catch up' in time.
- They may have friends who have undergone negative experiences of such situations and who relay their own 'horror' stories and warnings.
- Parents may not be able to fully comprehend the information or appreciate the importance of the issues raised.
- Parents may be fully aware of the issues but be unable to come to terms with the reality of the situation.

As the mother of an autistic son recalls, the period between diagnosis and intervention was immensely difficult:

> Dr X saw Graham twice. At the end of the second session, she told us that perhaps he had a speech delay with a 'difficult personality' (my theory at the time) or perhaps was 'somewhere along the autistic spectrum', gave us a referral to a local mental health early intervention centre and left in a hurry. She never spoke to us again and did not furnish us with a copy of her assessment. More than five years later I'm still bitter over the callous way the diagnosing doctor treated us. (Internet 2)

His mother then pursued a private diagnosis which took considerable time and effort. Once a diagnosis of autism had been given she recalls that:

> There was at least six months where I could not talk about Autism without crying. I remember the day after he was diagnosed; I went to the local shopping mall. In the middle of Eaton's (a large Canadian department store), I started to cry when I saw a boy the same age. (Internet 2)

## Preparation for initial discussion meetings

It is pertinent to prepare for initial meetings with parents and attempt to pre-empt difficult situations that may arise. When planning, the following list could be used:

- Parents should be informed in advance of:
  - who will attend and why
  - any reports to be discussed
  - possible referrals
  - possible meeting outcomes, which should reduce the uncertainty for parents.
- Evidence from observations should be used to support discussions.
- The child's strengths and weaknesses should be highlighted.
- Parental consent should be gained for any referrals to additional professionals.
- Information discussed should be flexible to accommodate parental reactions.
- Practitioners should put parents at ease within this potentially difficult situation and encourage them to contribute throughout.
- The meeting should conclude with a discussion of plans of action, Individual Education Plans (if appropriate) and details of future meetings.
- Recording is necessary for future reference.

Throughout the meeting the views and concerns of the parents must be heard, as they know their child best. Parental information and observations should enhance the assessment process, by adding another perspective on the child. Combined with information from the attending professionals, the meeting, as a whole, should then be in a position to draw informed conclusions.

## The importance of the initial meeting

Practitioners should remember that the success or failure of the initial meeting will set the scene for subsequent meetings and discussions. Every attempt should therefore be made to ensure an agreeable outcome or the child's difficulties could be exacerbated by delays in parental consent, withdrawal of the child from the provision or parents' future avoidance of any subsequent conversations, informal or otherwise. Mallet concludes:

> Very often, when your child has 'special' needs (i.e. additional to those generally expected), you have contact with a great number of professionals. It is every parent's experience that some can be enabling and empowering, empathetic and supportive, while others are not. In practice what counts is attitude and the style of working which this leads to. (Mallet, 1997: 30)

Positive interactive partnerships between parents and professionals also conform to the guidance within the Children Act 1989 (DoH, 1991) and the Code of Practice (DfEE 2001d; Internet 3) that promotes partnerships and partnership schemes.

Home visits can be extremely informative and work positively for both parents and professionals, but it is acknowledged that they are time-consuming and require cover for members of staff unless they are undertaken 'after hours'. However, the benefits of initial or continuing discussions within the home setting can help to break down potential barriers, allowing parents more freedom of speech, increased time for clarifying issues and a feeling of control within the situation.

## Parental issues following diagnosis

Following initial assessment and/or diagnosis additional issues concerning parents may emerge, bringing their own difficulties and problems:

- possible increase over time of the range of professionals inputting with one child and his/her family
- possible increase in appointments
- reactions from family, friends, neighbours and local placements
- ongoing meetings, discussions, reports and assessments
- possible placement outside of the immediate neighbourhood
- longer-term effects on individual family members.

Practitioners must consider carefully, at all stages, the implications of their comments, discussions and strategies on parents.

# Grandparents

Historically, grandparents have been closely involved with their grandchildren and, although family structures and working patterns have changed, many grandparents still play a major role in the lives of their grandchildren. Today some grandparents support the care of their grandchildren while parents work, and thus take on a greater part in the children's upbringing, spending the most time with them and supporting them through various key changes and stages. As professionals we may see grandparents regularly and parents infrequently, so we must consider issues pertinent to them as a part of our planning and policies.

## Initial acceptance of diagnosis

At the time of initial diagnosis grandparents will share many difficulties and concerns with the parents, but may also experience feelings relating to their concerns for the parent (their child) and the need to be supportive. If grandparents also have difficulties accepting the diagnosis then further complications may arise. As one mother reported: 'Graham's grandparents also found the diagnosis hard to accept. All of these feelings take time. Although the grief never goes away it does get easier to cope with' (Internet 2).

As with parents and siblings we should consider issues concerning grandparents, because they are highly significant in the life of the child with special needs. At the same time we must appreciate the individual family relationships that exist, as it is not always the case that parents and grandparents have a healthy, supportive relationship. In such instances practitioner involvement must be sensitive and follow primarily the views and wishes of the parents.

Grandparents and extended family members may unintentionally create additional pressures and concerns for parents, who are dealing with very real problems on a daily basis. Blamires, Robertson and Blamires suggest that:

> Further removed from the child than its parents, relatives may not see or may not wish to see the reality of the problems.
> It is not easy to continually point out real difficulties to grandparents anxious to dote over 'perfect' grandchildren, and it is not easy to decide how open to be about difficulties that may only worry relatives who will often then feel powerless to help. (Blamires, Robertson and Blamires, 1997: 19)

# Siblings

Siblings may share common concerns and difficulties with parents but also deserve individual consideration.

## *Problems accepting newborn siblings*

When a newborn baby arrives in a family, existing children will face considerable change. Basic changes such as reduced attention from parents may well cause difficulties for older siblings, but those can be avoided through careful planning and preparation on behalf of parents and extended family. Parents generally try to involve children before and after the expected birth to help alleviate potential difficulties. However, if the newborn is found to have special needs, circumstances may further change and new and very different issues may arise. A prolonged hospital stay may create a situation where an older sibling has to be cared for by relatives resulting in several or many moves between houses and interrupted attendance at nursery or school.

The position of a child within a family can also impact on their personality and development. The oldest sibling may be expected to assume the role of temporary carer and supporter to younger siblings, placing additional pressures and responsibilities on their shoulders, whereas a middle child could feel isolated as attentions are focused on the newborn baby and the oldest sibling in his/her new caring role.

The effects may be considerable (positive and negative) resulting in:

- jealousy
- aggression
- tantrums
- regression of skills learned
- lack of cooperation
- consideration
- cooperation
- love.

## Key issues for siblings of children with special needs

Carpenter (1997) summarises relevant research exploring the effects on siblings highlighting their complex needs. He identifies seven key concerns of siblings of young children with special needs which can be summarised as:

1 A need for age-appropriate *information* about the specific special need.
2 Feelings of *isolation* from a range of sources, including isolation from information that is given to other involved family members and isolation from siblings in other families experiencing similar difficulties and problems.
3 Perceived *guilt* at having caused the special need in some way or, at the time of leaving home themselves, guilt at no longer being able to support parents with the care of their sibling.
4 Feelings of *resentment* as the child with special needs commands more time and attention from parents.
5 Pressure felt to *achieve well*, to somehow make up for the possible reduced levels of expected achievement of the child with special needs.
6 Greater demands to help with the *care* of the child with special needs.
7 Concerns for their own *future* and that of the child with special needs.

At the same time, however, siblings of children with special needs may identify very positive opportunities arising from the situation. Empathy and a clear understanding of the issues faced may enhance personality as well as maturity. The National Autistic Society (NAS) offers a range of information to siblings, including recognition of the effects of growing up with a sibling with autism:

> Problems for younger people who have a sibling with autism can include teasing from other children, lack of privacy, disruption of home life and a feeling of resentment that the whole focus of the family is always on the autistic member. However, being a sibling of a person with autism is not necessarily all bad. Research has suggested that, although it can be a stressful experience at times, it does not in the long run necessarily have a negative effect on that person. Many have reported that learning to see the world through the eyes of their autistic sibling has been an enriching experience and taught them to become more tolerant of people's differences. (Internet 4)

## Supporting materials

The NAS website offers a range of publications for parents, siblings, family members and professionals alike, including storybooks to inform other children, such as Gorrod's (1997) *My Brother is Different*. Written in simple, age-appropriate language this book can be used within settings to help raise awareness and understanding with young children, parents and staff. This one example demonstrates the availability of useful resources and information for a wide range of special needs.

## Key issues for practitioners

As practitioners we must therefore address the specific issues relating to siblings through:

- acknowledging and respecting their roles and responsibilities
- ensuring that age-appropriate materials are available to provide information
- creating opportunities for them to meet with other siblings of children with special needs as well as ensuring they have ample opportunity to meet with their peers
- supporting parents in giving quality time to their children
- ensuring staff are aware of the specific needs of siblings.

If we really intend to support the families of the children we work with, then siblings must be included in our planning and discussions. Their needs may have similarities to their parents, but equally there will be separate issues to address.

---

### Case study

Andrew was the first and only child of Ian and Sarah and was diagnosed at birth with Down syndrome. Immediately, Sarah was moved to a side ward and experienced initial feelings of difference, isolation, anxiety and loss at the same time as an incredible love for her child. Acceptance of Andrew's condition took a little time for both parents. At this point, due to their own personalities and characteristics, they determined to provide the best possible opportunities for their son, supporting and helping him to achieve his maximum potential. They were linked with the local Down syndrome support group and immediately gained as much information as possible to inform themselves and thus help their son. From an early stage the extended family accepted the news and worked to support the family as much as possible, despite living over 200 miles away. Friends of the parents were generally accepting but there were those that, over a period of time, withdrew from contact.

Regular appointments were soon a feature of the family's life, including consultant paediatrician, GP, HV and Portage worker. This was in contrast to other families with a newborn child who would only attend the GP surgery when needed and would experience a few HV visits in the initial weeks only. Subsequently Ian and Sarah would attend the HV clinic on a regular basis for weight checks and advice. The Portage worker attended the house weekly to work with Andrew and Sarah within a developmental assessment and planning framework. Each week tasks would be set for Andrew and Sarah to work on. Immediately a commitment was needed to be at home for these as well as the HV and GP visits, in addition to driving 15 miles to attend appointments with the consultant paediatrician.

At the age of 2 years Andrew started part-time attendance at a local early years special needs unit and at the same time was enrolled in a private nursery school. Hence more professionals became involved: head of unit, staff at the unit, speech and language therapist, occupational therapist, head of nursery school and nursery staff. At this stage the head of the special needs unit became the key worker for Andrew and subsequently coordinated all input and chaired all review meetings to which all professionals and Andrew's parents were invited.

At age 2 years and six months Andrew was diagnosed with lymphatic leukaemia and was admitted to hospital. A range of treatments followed including chemotherapy, radiotherapy and intensive drug therapy, and his attendance at the special needs unit and nursery were temporarily halted. Throughout this period the range of professionals grew to include the local nurse from the Cancer and Leukaemia in Children (CLIC) charitable organisation, oncology team at the hospital including paediatric oncology consultants, plus the local CLIC support group with which the family became closely linked.

Periods of remission and relapse then followed for several years with intermittent attendance at hospitals and thus non-consistent placement attendance. Andrew's development, in all areas, would progress appropriately then regress, resulting in regular amendments to his individual education plans.

Despite all the difficulties incurred Andrew sustained attendance at the unit for long enough to undergo a statutory assessment of his special needs by the LEA, involving the introduction of an educational psychologist. A Formal Statement was produced just before Andrew's transfer to a local mainstream school at the age of 5 years and six months. This one-year delay in school entry was agreed by all parties as most appropriate for Andrew owing to the time spent in hospital and his condition. Prior to school entry Andrew's parents decided against the local mainstream school in favour of a school in the private sector.

A summary of involved professionals highlights a considerable range of professionals, each with their own agenda of meetings, appointments, expectations, support and advice:

Portage worker
Head of special needs unit
Nursery assistants
Head of nursery school
Staff at nursery school
Speech and language therapist
Paediatric oncology consultant
CLIC nurse
Radiology staff

Educational psychologist
Early years officer (LEA)
Local Down syndrome group
Local CLIC group
GP
HV
Occupational therapist
Oncology nurses and doctors
Paediatric consultant

The practicalities of managing such a network placed considerable pressure on parents.

### Parental issues arising, that impact on professional practice:

- Gathering of information was largely due to the determination of Andrew's parents, but not all parents would do this or be able to do this.
- Time management factors and need for transport.
- Difficulties when Andrew's mother needed to return to work and thus find a childminder who would be able to continue attending appointments.
- Andrew's father was working full time and was unable to attend every Portage session, which he would have preferred to do.
- Andrew's father wished to attend all appointments and thus needed an incredibly understanding and sympathetic boss who was amenable to flexibility. Would this apply to all employers?
- Need to understand and assimilate information imparted at meetings, reviews and informal discussions. Could all parents cope with this?
- Need for access to a telephone.
- Need for the parents to have the strength to cope with the emotive and traumatic diagnosis of leukaemia.
- Need for Andrew's parents to be able to deal with difficulties regarding school placement, including the negative comments and views of some local parents.
- Andrew's parents were able to have greater choice regarding Andrew's schools than many parents.
- Basic rights to be able to continue with a 'normal' family life.

### Practitioner issues arising:

- Careful and considerate management of the key worker system.
- Regular liaison between all parties, including parents.
- All involved professionals to be sympathetic, understanding and respectful.
- All professionals to understand and respect the roles and responsibilities of the other professionals involved.
- All professionals to ensure that both parents were equally well informed at every stage, especially Andrew's father.
- Professionals to take into consideration the needs of Andrew's extended family members.

Hopefully, this illustrative case study highlights some of the key issues raised earlier in the chapter and establishes some considerations for practitioners.

# Implications for practice

The ongoing support of families is important if we are to support the child with special needs. At times needs will change and require differing approaches and perhaps, different personnel to provide the most appropriate support. Knowledge and understanding of local support networks, statutory and non-statutory, is essential for professionals.

Individual family members may seek support from different sources or a combination of sources in order to deal with situations, concerns and issues. It may be that a mother will listen to the advice of the consultant paediatrician and then wish to debate the conversation with her closest friend to clarify her thoughts before discussing it with her husband. This may then affect the quality of the information passed on to the father. A parent may ask to bring a friend or family member to meetings and appointments to enable clarity of discussion, raise additional issues and concerns, and ensure accurate recollection afterwards. In the same vein it may simply be that a friend's physical presence is needed for support. As professionals we should be prepared to respect, discuss and accommodate, if possible, all parental requests regarding their own support networks involving friends, family members, local community groups, charitable organisations and work colleagues. In addition the advent of the Internet provides a plethora of information, including websites created by and intended for parents and other family members as well as those created by charitable organisations.

Research assists professionals in understanding parental perspectives and supports the view that we may not always know what families need or what is 'best' for them. We should support and advise in the most appropriate manner and accept the views and feelings of the parents we work with.

# Increase in numbers of children with special needs

At the start of the twenty-first century the increase in numbers of children with special needs places considerable pressures on early years practitioners. This is partly due to the advancements in medical science and technology over the years and the resultant increases in survival of previously fatal conditions. The current educational climate of inclusive education for all children with special needs also has major implications for practice. There is clearly a need for additional and ongoing training to understand, respect and provide effectively for the individual needs of family members, which in turn will help to support the child. The work of researchers such as Carpenter (2000), Dale (1996) and Herbert (1994) must be encouraged and supported to ensure that we understand parental and family perspectives with increasing greater depth.

Herbert's (1994: 91) studies of the separate views of mothers and fathers highlight six key implications for practice that could be easily used as a basis for training:

1 A need for initial and in-service training to include listening skills, current terminology and up-to-date information.
2 Improved coordination of services.
3 Accessibility of information.
4 Local networking of services available.
5 Services should be flexible to address differing needs.
6 The needs of each and every family member must be considered.

## Summary

Reflecting on the issues surrounding the families of children with special needs has, hopefully, highlighted the need to ensure that all family members are equally well supported. As practitioners we aim to provide the best, and must therefore continue to explore and research family perspectives to enable appropriate intervention and support. At all times we should consider:

- the family being central to the child's life
- a child's parents know them best
- family members, immediate and extended, and their impact on the child's life
- how well the family is functioning
- the possible negative and positive effects of individual families on their children
- how best to support each member of the family
- existing support systems within the family
- the relevant legislation and guidance regarding parents, parental partnerships and families of children with special needs
- our own working practices with regard to coordination of services and effective multidisciplinary working systems
- the sensitivity of the issues we are dealing with.

Historically, parents have not always been considered as partners in their children's development, care and education, but legislation and guidance now ensure practitioners view the family as central to every child's life. Through careful and sensitive consideration of individual needs, views and feelings we can empower family members and address their needs more effectively.

Throughout our planning, policy-making and practice we must consider and address, to the best of our ability, the needs of each family member. While the child must always be the key focus of our work, family members must always be considered. This will enhance our work with the child and help him/her to work towards achieving his/her full potential.

## Key issues

❖ The impact of a child with special needs on family members must be acknowledged.

❖ We should adapt our policies and practices to support the needs of family members.

❖ To provide effectively for young children with special needs we should ensure the needs of individual family members are also provided for.

❖ Practitioners should be familiar with local statutory, private and voluntary supporting agencies.

## Some suggestions for discussion

### Item 1

Focusing on one child with special needs you are working with consider how much knowledge you have regarding the following significant people:

- his/her mother
- his/her father
- his/her grandparents
- his/her siblings
- his/her extended family members
- the family's friends and social contacts.

Reflect on the feelings and views of each, their impact on the child, the impact of the child on each person and the interaction between them. Identify positive and negative issues.

### Item 2

Does your current practice support all the issues raised in item 1 above? In addition to those issues raised, reflect on:

- information – available in accessible format for all (mothers, fathers, grandparents and siblings)
- advice – is advice available, for each family member, from experienced and sensitive practitioners; are there facilities/rooms to accommodate private and sensitive discussions; is there access to advice from a variety of sources?
- support – knowledge of the full range of supporting services, including sibling support; understanding of the roles and responsibilities of professionals in other disciplines; familiarity with referral procedures; what

levels of coordination currently exist within the supporting network; can individuals, including parents, establish contact with other supporting agencies?

- meetings – do both parents attend meetings? If not, are the needs of both parents being met? Could changes be made?

### Item 3

Using your knowledge of one family you are currently supporting, list issues that have been raised within this chapter that may be impacting on their lives and reflect on how you provide support for these.

## 📖 Suggested further reading

Carpenter, B. (ed.) (1997) *Families in Context: Emerging Trends in Family Support and Early Intervention*. London: David Fulton.

Dale, N. (1996) *Working with Families of Children with Special Needs*. London: Routledge.

Hornby, G. (1995) *Working with Parents of Children with Special Needs*. London: Cassell.

# 3

## Partnerships with Parents

### Introduction

As the government continues to legislate for working partnerships with parents, this chapter explores the purposes, benefits and characteristics of partnerships with parents and discusses ways in which we can establish systems and processes to ensure that these work effectively. The issues surrounding parental partnerships in general share many commonalities with partnerships between parents of children with special needs and practitioners. Parental and professional perspectives are explored and examples of good practice discussed to tease out the factors we should all be addressing to ensure that partnerships are enabling for all parents. In addition, we discuss barriers to partnership, perceived or otherwise. David (1994: 10) echoes the need for effective partnerships and suggests ways forward: 'How workers are enabled to empower families, to work in partnership with them, to cater flexibly for what the families themselves identify as their needs seems to be the challenge for professional and voluntary agency managers for the 1990s.'

Partnerships with parents do not naturally evolve and early years workers should never presume to have empathy with, or understand, all parents. At best we can respect, listen and use the systems in place to support parents, ensuring they have total understanding of everything that occurs, are aware of their rights and feel able to contribute positively at all stages. If appropriate systems are not currently in place then they should be planned and established.

Partnerships should ideally comprise an equal balance between practitioners and parents, with both parties working towards the most appropriate outcomes to support children with special needs in achieving their full potential. Robson (1989: 126) explored equality within partnerships, highlighting the possible imbalance: 'A successful partnership is based on equality, whereby each partner recognises and benefits from the talents, skills, expertise and knowledge of the other. At times one partner may adopt a relatively passive role, in other situations a more active role.'

Through identifying features of good practice and exploring parental and practitioner perspectives we suggest ways forward in this time of increased recognition of the value of meaningful partnerships in the early years.

# Parental involvement

It may be suggested that in the pre-school phase, whatever the setting, parents are generally welcome at all times to visit, discuss their children's progress and participate in a range of activities within the group. This can be beneficial for all parties involved, particularly children as the skills and expertise of parents can be used within the group to enhance existing skills and expertise. However, on school entry the involvement of parents can sometimes diminish to invitations to assemblies, listening to children read and helping with fund-raising activities. As children then progress to the junior and secondary phases parental involvement diminishes further, creating a distance. Thus parental involvement and participation are susceptible to change as children progress through the educational phases. Rennie (1996: 197) identifies five distinct stages as a developmental progression of parental involvement within a setting that could be reflected on as planning and policy-making processes progress:

1 Confidence-building for all involved.
2 Awareness-raising and starting participation.
3 Real involvement.
4 Parent–teacher partnership.
5 Parents as co-educators.

As parents approach early years settings for the first time there already exists a common ground between them. They all have children of similar ages, are about to embark on attendance, have spent the previous few years nurturing and developing their children to the best of their ability and wish for their children to succeed. This common ground presents a bond between parents that can be positively used by the setting to the benefit of all, sharing experiences, discussing common problems and capitalising on personal skills. It is a starting point from which outstanding achievements can be realised if fostered within an ethos of positive partnership.

For most children the preceding years will have been spent at home with a parent/carer so the introduction to an early years setting can be traumatic. This is not only for the children but also the parents and, if the youngest child in the family is embarking on attendance, then it may be even harder for the parent/carer to accept. The feelings of no longer being needed to support the child in the same way can have quite severe effects and while all parents want to see their child settle in happily and confidently there can be a sense of ironic disappointment if the child does just that. All of a sudden it becomes apparent that the child is beginning a more independent life. For the child with special needs the transfer to an early years setting may be more problematic and require sensitive handling.

For children with special needs the parent/carer may feel even more protective and find it much harder to transfer their child's care over to others. It is therefore important that practitioners plan the induction process thoroughly in an attempt to eliminate, or at least diminish, possible anxieties. Familiarity with the child and his/her family can ease this process considerably, particularly if this is achieved via home visits and visits to the setting. Issues of concern, procedures, policies and information sharing can all be raised in a more informal manner prior to admission and this will, hopefully, be seen as a two-way process. The parent/carer has the most concise knowledge about the child including his/her likes and dislikes, progress to date, appointments attended, referrals made, reports written and friends. This can all be used to support the child's needs through the induction process and in future planning.

Practitioners should recognise and respect the depth and breadth of learning that parents have already undertaken with their children, which can be underestimated and undervalued. Parents have a tendency to see the early education of their children as 'nothing special' or describe it as 'what parents do', but parents are responsible for supporting their child's development and skill-learning such as walking, talking, toilet training, social skills, self-help skills, behaviour and playing. This prior learning, albeit unstructured and unplanned, has nevertheless taken place within the home and the parents should accept full credit for this.

## Parental issues affecting partnership

Many issues, such as low self-esteem, hours of employment, social deprivation and poverty and feelings of inadequacy, can affect parental involvement with professionals. These can affect the level and quality of parental involvement, and any of the issues may present one or more barriers to meaningful participation. Time can also be a critical factor, even for those parents who do not work during the day, as they may wish to support partnerships with several settings attended by their children or they may experience childcare difficulties for younger children.

## Quality of partnership

If, as practitioners, we strive to accommodate all parents in a meaningful way, we will also share the rewards. True partnership with parents will very much depend on the quality of the relationships and the perceived benefits to all parties involved. Inviting parents into the staff room of a setting to repair damaged equipment may be of little benefit and cannot be described as an effective partnership. Parental and professional roles should support each other in a 'complementary' manner as Beveridge comments:

> The concept of partnership is based on the recognition that parents and teachers have complementary contributions to make to children's education. Accordingly, it is central to the notion of partnership that schools should demonstrate that they not only listen to, but also value, parents' perspectives. Many teachers aim to do this, but it must be acknowledged that the parental experience of contact with the school can be far removed from the partnership ideal.
> (Beveridge, 1997: 56)

Dale (1996: 2) also raises the issue of the quality of partnership: 'the term "partnership" does not tell us a great deal about the extent of the cooperation and reciprocity between two or more partners, except to suggest that there is some form of mutual cooperation and influence'. As a simple example, a bilingual child may enter an early years setting. Although a non-English speaker, his/her mother can be encouraged to attend sessions to watch and participate, as she feels able. Initially she may choose to stay in the background helping with the setting up of activities, making drinks and washing up but, hopefully, over a period of time she can be encouraged to participate further. Eventually her English should begin to develop and her confidence be enhanced. In time she may feel more able to support the learning of staff and children alike by introducing new activities related to cooking, traditional stories, dress and religious festivals from her own country and culture, as well as adding to more general topic-based work. Opportunities could arise for the mother to participate in adult education classes, help in a crèche and have regular contact with a range of outside professionals. From this scenario everyone benefits, but only if the nursery is committed to working with parents. Draper and Duffy support this view concluding that:

> For many staff the opportunity to work in partnership adds a new dimension to their work. Practitioners can assume their experience of family life is the way it is and working with parents from diverse communities widens their views on families and family life. Differences can be shared, respected and explored. Home life provides many opportunities for learning the setting can build on. (Draper and Duffy, 2001: 149)

Partnerships with the parents of children with special needs may be compromised by the existence of special schools and units that prohibit or limit regular face-to-face contact with parents. At their most basic level partnerships begin with the establishing of relationships, but these take time and effort to plan and develop. In a mainstream setting parents will arrive on a more frequent and regular basis where meaningful interaction can develop naturally. If, however, your child is transported several or many miles away to attend a special facility, then this interaction is immediately compromised. If parents do not have transport then regular contact is further compromised. Thus it may be suggested that for special schools and units parental partnerships may need considerably more effort in planning and maintaining in order to succeed. However, the fact that parents are not in regular contact with a setting does not mean that practitioners should not make the effort to establish effective partnerships, as supported by Hurst:

> This does not prevent them from taking seriously parents' need to be kept informed and to have regular contact with the practitioner responsible for their children. It is the awareness of parents' needs and the willingness to be adaptable in developing ways of meeting these needs which are the most important. (Hurst, 1997: 108)

# Home-school liaison teachers and family centres

During the 1960s and 1970s there emerged an increased understanding of the influences of a range of factors on children's social development and, as a result, a greater awareness of social deprivation. In several counties new roles emerged to address these needs, such as home–school liaison teachers. More family centres were established, some funded by education departments and some by social services departments, to address the effects of social deprivation in specific localities and/or 'educational priority areas'.

Home–school liaison teachers were generally assigned to an infant/primary school and/or a family centre. Their roles included the breaking down of barriers between schools and families, encouraging attendance at early years settings, supporting local pre-school providers and responding directly to the needs of the families. Owing to the nature of the areas in which they worked, generally areas of poor housing, high unemployment and with very young parents, much of their work involved children and families with special needs, in the broadest sense. Therefore, special needs input, educational or otherwise, became a key feature of their work. In many instances the home–school liaison teacher acted as a mediator or enabler between the families and the systems and processes in place to help them, but invariably non-educational issues such as claiming appropriate child benefits would emerge. If, as in Chapter 2, we acknowledge the effects of the family on the child, then to enable a parent to resolve financial difficulties would reduce stress and pressure, and ultimately benefit the child. At such times the practitioner could advise and support, introducing the family to the appropriate department or agency that could best respond to their difficulties. Owing to budgetary restraints many of these roles were discontinued during the late 1980s or practitioners were absorbed within family centres. While many would reflect positively on the successes of these roles, an alternative viewpoint is offered by Edwards and Knight:

> It could be said that the attempts of the 1970s at encouraging parental involvement because of perceived deficits in the home environment rested on a set of assumptions about the supremacy of middle-class attitudes and values. An unkinder view would be the suggestion that early years practitioners as a group were struggling to be recognised as professionals and were therefore willing to take on parental involvement schemes ... (Edwards and Knight, 1994: 113)

However, having experienced at first hand such work in the 1970s and 1980s, I would raise several issues to establish debate. First, I would agree that early years professionals were, and still are to a degree, fighting the battle to gain respect for the value and importance of their work, along with an acknowledgement of their expertise, knowledge and skills. This battle has been long-standing and will probably continue into the future, although it is hoped that the recent government acknowledgement of the benefits of early years provision will help raise the profile of practitioners, as early years work is not the 'easy option' that some may suggest. Secondly, I consider that some excellent home–school partnerships were established at that time which still thrive today. As the direct result of the work of one such practitioner, the following are indicative of some of the initiatives established within a family centre, which have continued to grow and develop since the 1980s:

- Parental support groups – led by parents, including representation on governing bodies and LEA committees.
- Regular visits from representatives of outside agencies within the family centre to respond to parental and family needs.
- A parents' newsletter, written by, produced and distributed by parents.
- Parenting classes on a range of subjects from 'Understanding the curriculum' to 'Cooking on a budget'.
- Increased and positive use of a wide range of parental skills within the school.
- Increased attendance at parents' evenings and open events.
- Twice weekly, parent-run crèche.
- Increased input of local community within the school.

## Positive change or enforced change?

Practitioners are unlikely to sustain a philosophy that does not support individual families. An ethical question emerges, however, as to whether our particular knowledge and skills should empower us to enforce change on families, especially if this is in direct conflict with our commitment to respect all cultural backgrounds. If a child is at risk in any way then practitioners have a clear duty to intervene, but when we consider issues such as poor parenting skills, we must first debate what defines good, bad or inadequate parenting and justify our right to encourage change.

If we consider that a particular parenting style is unsatisfactory, then we should reflect carefully before encouraging change. There are families who are bringing up their children in the same way that they were brought up, so are repeating a learned parenting style. If this style does not harm the child in such a way as to demand action to prevent abuse, then should we suggest that improvements could be made? This action could be perceived as an insult to family members from previous generations and would possibly not support continued partnership.

## SureStart

The current government initiative to fund SureStart projects nationwide is a direct attempt to alleviate the effects of poverty and deprivation, and provide young children and their families with the means to improve the opportunities available to them. The total invested was £452 million over a three-year period.

This was intended to enable the creation of local SureStart groups, comprising parents and professionals from a variety of agencies working together to identify areas of provision that could be improved. The SureStart aim is to support parents initially, through access to professional expertise and knowledge, but then for the professionals to withdraw allowing the families to take responsibility and ownership. SureStart's philosophy relies on effective and collaborative partnership between local families and local professionals without which the aims cannot be achieved. The level of that partnership will very much depend on the individuals involved, the balance of power and the levels of input, respect and shared perspectives.

Practitioners have sometimes pinpointed parents as responsible or partly responsible for their child's difficulties. For example, practitioners may take the view that a child's behaviour difficulties are the direct result of home circumstances and/or parenting style. From this negative standpoint, to work on the behaviour difficulties in the isolation of the setting could have limited success. Unless meaningful interaction can be entered into with the parents in a supportive ethos, then progress may be limited. Only through a process of parents and practitioners working together will this situation be likely to improve having identified joint difficulties/goals.

## Characteristics of positive partnerships

So what are the key features and characteristics of positive partnerships? When defining principles of nursery education Goodall suggests that quality provision should include:

A partnership which:
- Acknowledges, celebrates and capitalises on parent or carer involvement, as the child's first educator;
- Is flexible, negotiated and responsive to the needs of individual parents and their families;
- Provides opportunities whereby nursery colleagues offer parents or carers a range of options;
- Is centred upon their own child, themselves, their families and their community;
- Allows them to become active partners in their child's education. (Goodall, 1997: 163)

These principles, while aimed at general nursery education, can equally be applied as a basis for good practice in any early years setting to the benefit of every child, whether he/she has special needs or otherwise.

The National Association of Special Educational Needs (Internet 1) offers eight key principles of effective practice for children with special needs in the early years, including one that focuses on partnerships: 'The fundamental rights and responsibilities of parents should be recognised and respected. They should be full partners in all aspects of assessment, provision and intervention. They should have access to all relevant information regarding their children and participate in all decisions affecting them.'

If we want partnerships with parents to be effective, supportive and of benefit to all parties, it is clear that we must view our work with parents as complementary. We should welcome parents into our settings at all times and ensure that our working practices respect the knowledge, skills and expertise that parents can share with us. A child is known best to his/her parents and their first-hand knowledge can benefit our work, and thus the child. In a simple example, if a parent tells us that their child is currently fascinated with dinosaurs, we can use this knowledge in our choice of activities and detailed planning. If a child is interested and motivated, he/she will be more likely to achieve success. It suggests that there is a link between the achievements and progress of the child and the effectiveness of the parent–practitioner partnership.

There is a wealth of research available highlighting the positive outcomes of effective parental partnerships. One such example is the study of Mortimore et al. (1988) identifying factors affecting school effectiveness. Although the study was written over a decade ago, the principles are still relevant today. Improved educational outcomes were used as a marker of school effectiveness, with the research concluding that increased parental links and interaction within the school helped to increase academic achievements and thus enhance overall school effectiveness. The QCA (1999: 19) documentation outlining the Early Learning Goals brings us up to date with current philosophy: 'Parents are children's first and most enduring educators. When parents and practitioners work together in early years settings, the results have a positive impact on the child's development and learning. Therefore, each setting should seek to develop an effective partnership with parents.'

Throughout the identification, assessment and reviewing processes related to special needs provision, parents have a right and a duty to participate fully. If the early years setting promotes positive partnerships from the outset, then parents and practitioners will be familiar with the stages of assessment and monitoring systems in place. Relevant information will have been shared with parents, their views considered and valued, and they would be fully aware of any action that was to be taken. Within a supportive environment parents would be aware of their rights and share in planning and provision.

Characteristics of effective partnerships could be:

- approachability, care and concern
- channels for two-way communication
- clarity and style of communication
- helping parents see what they may contribute
- providing opportunities for those contributions
- providing encouragement and support (adapted from Wolfendale, 1997: 64–7).

In addition I would suggest:

- providing accessible information about special provision
- keeping parents informed and updated
- trust and respect.

## Positive outcomes for practitioners

A feeling of mutual trust and respect should enhance practitioner confidence. Knowing that with input from parents they are maximising the learning opportunities for the child, and thus improving learning outcomes, should support staff motivational levels. When practitioners work alongside parents in a setting, they will be confident that parents understand the way in which they work and the pressures they may be under. This greater understanding could help when practitioners are discussing issues with the wider parental audience, as parents who have supported the work of the setting will have a greater awareness of the day-to-day reality.

Shared responsibilities in the setting can also help to alleviate practitioner workload as long as each role is carefully planned and parents are well prepared. Parents are not replacement practitioners but can support and enhance the work of the practitioner. The selection of tasks undertaken by the parents will reflect the practitioner's views on control, balance of power and the parent's capabilities, so tasks should be planned carefully to enhance work already taking place, support the children and benefit the parents.

Practitioners should gain increased knowledge about the children from the parents which will inform planning. A child's likes and dislikes, fears and worries, strengths and weaknesses may be viewed differently by parents and practitioners so the sharing of information can only be beneficial.

## Positive outcomes for parents

Through observing practitioners, parents may gain an improved understanding of the importance of providing appropriate activities and supporting children's learning, which could lead to improved support within the home and thus improved learning outcomes for the children. Playing a greater part in their child's learning and development will also increase parental confidence.

If we believe that all parents are eager to see their children progress and develop, then it follows that to have played a greater part in that progress will be incredibly motivating. Parents can feel proud of their input in the setting and the direct help and support they are giving both practitioners and children. As a result, self-confidence should be raised, and parental development and learning will have taken place.

## Positive outcomes for children

Arguably, the children will benefit most from effective partnerships, as they will feel part of a supportive network free of tensions between home and setting. Children are sensitive to conflict around them which can place them in a compromising position and indirectly affect their learning. In a simple example, a child who is naturally very fond of the practitioner could be upset overhearing his/her parents discussing conflict with the practitioner. The child could have divided loyalties and may be uncomfortable within the setting or even refuse to attend, or conversely be uncomfortable at home. The child's security could be severely compromised and, as young children need consistency and security, this is likely to have a negative effect.

Enhanced learning opportunities may emerge within the home situation, reinforcing the learning within the setting and, in some cases, parents will be enabled to participate more actively at home because of their enhanced confidence and their observations of setting activities. An effective parental partnership system should therefore lead to improved educational outcomes and achievement, and all parties will reap the benefits and rewards.

When focusing on children with special needs parental partnerships may present more obstacles but the benefits, especially to the children, cannot be stressed more, as suggested by Drifte (2001: 24): 'it is for the benefit of all concerned, but most particularly the children, that a sound and positive working relationship between home and educational setting is established and maintained'.

## Levels of partnership

Hopefully, the days are gone when practitioners were viewed as the 'expert professionals' that made all the decisions. Historically, there followed a period when parents were encouraged to play a greater part in their child's education and care, and we are continuing to move towards more empowering partnerships. However, there are still some parents who feel intimidated or uncomfortable interacting with professionals, for a wide variety of reasons. It may be that their own negative school experiences compromise their ability to work with professionals or that they still view practitioners as 'the experts', with whom they could not enter into purposeful discussions. Wolfendale (1989: 17) concluded: 'One of the most common reasons given by parents for not being involved in their child's pre-school centre is lack of confidence in the face of professional expertise.'

As previously mentioned, parental involvement within early years settings can be tremendously varied, ranging from annual concerts to full and total participation in the daily working life of the setting. As required by current legislation and guidance, all settings must identify the ways in which they involve parents. In addition, practitioners should ensure this is a process which supports real partnership and is not just a policy response to government requirements. Levels of partnership can be explored in terms of the balance of power between practitioners and parents. For a full and meaningful partnership to exist there should be equality between the parties, with the balance of power being equal. Both parties must therefore feel that their input is valued and reciprocated. At the stage of initial diagnosis of special needs, parents may need time to adjust and be unable to be effective partners, but with support and encouragement it should be anticipated that parents will be enabled and empowered to take a more active and equal part as time progresses.

While the philosophy and nature of early years settings often lend themselves more readily to parental involvement, settings invariably *expect* a level of participation from parents, which is clearly stated within the policy documents and information given to parents. This is possibly linked to the equality between parents and professionals in this phase, where many groups will have parental input in committees and the daily workings of the group will be open to all for scrutiny and discussion. As a rule, pre-school settings are less formal and have greater flexibility to accommodate visitors and parents. However, in some settings there still exists a certain level of professional control over the domain and, thus, power is reluctantly shared. In addition, planning, recording and delivering the Foundation Stage and/or the National Curriculum places considerable pressures on practitioners, who may argue that there simply is not enough time to become involved in parental partnership schemes requiring additional time, organisation and planning. So perhaps the level of parental participation is directly linked to the equality or inequality of power within the setting.

Hopefully, the days when schools had signs barring entrance to parents are gone, but as Rennie (1996: 1997) points out: 'Sadly, in 1996 a few schools retain such notices. Others have dispensed with them and yet retained the attitudes behind them.'

## Legislation and guidance

With specific relation to children with special needs the legislation and guidance that has evolved over the years has continued to emphasise parental rights, children's rights and the need for effective parental partnerships, although Paige-Smith (1997: 41) sees: 'education policy and practice restricting the rights of parents to participate in decision-making'.

The Warnock Report (DES, 1978) offered a complete chapter on parental partnerships and parental rights, with regard to children with special needs, emphasising the need for positive and equal partnerships with schools. A theme of parental involvement ran through the report which commented:

> The form and extent of parents' need for support will depend on a multiplicity of factors, including the nature and degree of their child's disability or disorder, his age, the family circumstances and, not least, the parents' own resources and independence. The support, however and wherever given, must be seen as taking place within a partnership between parents and members of the different services. (Ibid.: 161)

The subsequent Education Act of 1981 and circular 1/83 encouraged parental input in assessment processes and gave significant legal rights to parents. While the 1981 Act introduced the formal assessment process, it did not offer parents the right of redress if dissatisfied with any decisions or statements made relating to their child, unless there were factual errors. This was later addressed when SEN tribunals were introduced.

Although the 1981 Education Act reformulated special needs provision it was realised that the Act had not extended far enough and that problems and difficulties still existed, often centred around the differing expectations and priorities of parents and practitioners. As a result, a range of parental voluntary support groups emerged to campaign for continued improvements and to support parents in the short term. One such organisation is Network 81, established by two parents following the difficulties they had experienced with their own child's education. They were aware of their right to be involved in decision-making but found it hard to fight against a system that presented continuous bureaucratic obstacles to their input in the decision-making processes. Network 81 has continued to grow since first operating and offers a range of services for children with special needs and their parents. The group's aims are:

- To advance the education of children with special needs.
- To educate the parents of such children about all matters relating to the education of their children.
- To link up and support groups and individual parents of children with special educational needs.
- To raise awareness and publicise good practice in inclusive education.
- To encourage parents to take their rightful place in education policy-making.
- To promote parent-professional partnerships. (Internet 6)

The Code of Practice (DfEE, 1994) introduced a five-stage assessment model for the identification and assessment of special educational needs, outlined the key responsibilities of the role of SENCO and offered a basic principle relating to parental partnerships: 'Partnership between parents, pupils, schools, LEAs and other agencies is important' (ibid.: 1.2). The Code continued (ss 2:28–2:33) to outline requirements of providers, including registered early years providers, relating to parental partnership covering the areas of:

- SEN information needed for parents
- arrangements needed to ensure effective partnerships
- means of ensuring accessibility to information.

The Code of Practice introduced Individual Education Plans acting as a detailed working record of provision made to date and planned for the future. This was a result of significant parental lobbying following the 1981 Act as it was felt that such a record could be a shared document between practitioners and parents, giving parents the opportunity to see the targets that were being set for their child and to give them a say in the planning of those targets. There may be differing levels of parental involvement when the IEP is written as there will be those parents who wish to be fully involved and will discuss and debate issues with the SENCO, and those who appear disinterested. They perhaps feel that the planning of IEPs is for professionals as they lack the skills or expertise to understand the process or contribute to it. Smith's guidance for SENCOs suggests:

> If the parents are not actively involved, it is still important to communicate the content of the IEP so that they are informed of the areas of need identified as priorities. If possible, ask one of the parents to sign the form as this will help to raise the status of the IEP in their, and the child's, eyes. (Smith, 1996: 35)

So, although settings can claim in their documentation that parents are involved with the planning of IEPs, this may not indicate the depth or quality of that planning.

Following the introduction of the Code of Practice came the invitation from the DfEE in 1994 for LEAs to submit bids for Grants for Education, Support and Training (GEST) funding to establish Parent Partnership Schemes. Most LEAs applied and were successful in securing funding for a three-year period, to be reviewed annually.

Within the revised Code of Practice (DfES, 2001d) came a requirement for LEAs to have in place Parent Partnership Schemes and also to extend the remit of partnerships, as Emad (2000: 49) confirms: 'An important shift in the revised code of practice is the proposal to offer partnership services to all parents of children with SEN, not just those who have a statement or who are undergoing statutory assessment.'

The Children Act 1989 (DoH, 1991) also made reference to parental participation and partnerships by highlighting the rights and responsibilities of parents, and emphasising the need to take into account the child's wishes and feelings in any decision-making processes. The area of pupil participation in decision-making is highlighted within the Code of Practice (DfES, 2001d).

The fact that a whole chapter in the SEN Code of Practice (DfES, 2001d) is devoted to this area highlights the importance that is now placed on partnerships, which are seen as enabling and 'empowering' parents. The ethos of a shared responsibility is made clear:

> The work of the professionals can be more effective when parents are involved and account taken of their wishes, feelings and perspectives on their children's development. This is particularly so when a child has special educational needs. All parents of children with special educational needs should be treated as partners. (Ibid.: s. 2.2)

The Code continues to identify the responsibilities of LEAs and settings, plus the need for settings to involve parents fully from the initial identification of a child's difficulties and through the Early Years Action and Early Years Action Plus stages. However, if all settings have effective parental partnerships in place, then the transition to discussing a child's specific difficulties should be made easier, as mutual respect, understanding and the sharing of information would already exist. Communication should therefore be seen as a key feature of effective partnerships.

## Inspection requirements

Within the OFSTED inspection scheme, under which all registered providers are inspected, there is an expectation that all providers should be able to demonstrate their commitment to parental partnerships and to SEN policies. Thus, providers will need to have in place effective partnership arrangements and recording systems to ensure all parents are informed of the desire for a positive parent:provider partnership.

## Foundation Stage requirements

Within the Foundation Stage guidance (QCA, 2000: 9) is a clear acknowledgement of the need for effective parental partnerships in early years settings, which will be assessed as part of the inspection process: 'When parents and practitioners work together in early years settings, the results have a positive impact on the child's development and learning. Therefore, each setting should seek to develop an effective partnership with parents. A successful partnership needs a two-way flow of information, knowledge and expertise.'

The guidance offers nine features of good practice clearly highlighting the benefits to all parties, such as the sharing of information, expertise and the child's learning experiences.

## Parental involvement in observation, assessment and reviewing progress

When practitioners are observing children due to initial concerns over possible difficulties the child may be experiencing, it is important that parents are fully informed. It may be that once the concern has been discussed parents can offer explanations, such as bereavement in the family or family tensions, enabling concerns to be reassessed. If observations follow, then parents should be informed and involved at every stage. If mutual understanding exists at this point then, hopefully, any further action needed will be entered into in a framework of respect, with both parents and practitioners sharing the same goal.

If the child makes only limited, or no, progress then Early Years Action (DfES, 2001d: s. 4.24) would be entered into and again parents should be full participants in any discussions and decision-making that emerge: 'Settings should make sure that parents are as fully involved as possible with their child's education and should always be fully informed about how the setting is seeking to meet their child's needs.'

Parents can support the work of the practitioner by working at home with the child to ensure consistency of approach between home and setting and to support the progress of their child. If further intervention is required through Early Years Action Plus and statutory assessment, then parents should remain as partners throughout.

# Factors supporting positive partnerships

Having effective policies in place to support our work with parents and children with special needs is a key element of our work. So how can we ensure that policies respond to the needs of all parties and also satisfy legislative requirements?

## *Policies*

All registered providers, i.e. all maintained schools and all registered early years providers, must have in place SEN policies and written policies regarding existing parental partnerships. In addition there are expectations in place for all LEAs (QCA, 2000). Some LEAs may have outline policy documents available that can be accessed and adapted for individual settings. The LEA parent partnership officer and/or early years officers and/or early years forums would also be useful contacts for support and advice when drafting policies. There seems little benefit in reinventing the wheel when a host of documentation already exists that can readily be adapted.

Settings should include parents in the planning and reviewing of partnership policies to ensure that parental perspectives are considered fully. Practitioners should strive to create policies that empower parents and practitioners alike, to support the work of the setting, the parents and the child.

## *Creating or evaluating policies*

When formulating or reformulating policies all participating personnel should be involved to ensure every perspective is explored and to avoid making presumptions on behalf of unrepresented parties. Smith (1996: 52) recommends the following questions as a basic guideline for planning SEN policies which ensure parental partnership:

- How can we ensure that information relating to special needs reaches the parents who need it?
- Do parents feel that they can approach the school at any time if they have a concern?
- Do parents know who to contact about special needs?
- What channels do we use for communicating between home and school?
- How do we communicate with parents if we have a concern about their child?
- Do we have effective methods of gathering information from parents?
- Are parents actively involved in IEPs?
- Are review meetings organised in such a way which supports parental contribution?

The responses to these questions should give clear indications of existing gaps and ensure all relevant areas for consideration have been explored purposefully. At this point policies can begin to be formulated and planning for partnerships set up. All relevant parties should be totally committed to partnership and be motivated to employ their utmost to ensure success, as any resistance or concern about issues may compromise success before any partnership is established.

If policies are already in place then regular reviews are pertinent, again ensuring all parties are involved. Views regarding current policies can be invited and used as a basis for discussion to identify gaps, problems, concerns and ways forward. If possible or practical a worthwhile exercise could be to create a simple questionnaire for completion by staff and parents alike. This gives everyone the opportunity to reflect individually or with colleagues or friends and offer constructive comments in an anonymous manner which may encourage improved outcomes. The results or findings could then be circulated to all who participated and used as a basis for further discussions. If we do not seek parental views and respond to them, we are presuming we know their views and are excluding them from the process.

## *Reviewing existing policies*

As a setting it would be worth exploring precisely what information, support and participation is needed for parents from the setting and conversely, what information, support and participation is needed from parents. Discussions could include areas such as information, mutual support, participation opportunities, skill-sharing and teaching.

### *Information*
Information will pass between the two parties for mutual benefit, and obviously in the interests of the children. Settings should reflect on how information is shared regarding:

- the curriculum
- record-keeping systems
- planning
- identification of special needs
- monitoring progress
- the graduated response
- other local providers.

It may be useful for a member of staff or parent to collate such information as it emerges into a resource file that is readily accessible to all interested parties for reference and to support discussions. Conversely, staff can benefit from parental information about their children, the locality and the availability of resources that could prove useful to other parents. A noticeboard for open use by parents and staff alike can be a useful method of sharing information that encourages parents into the setting. Newsletters which encourage parental input are also a useful tool, especially if parents do not visit the setting regularly.

*Mutual support*
Simply offering parents a meeting place can encourage beneficial supportive discussions and the sharing of ideas. Parents of children with special needs may feel more comfortable talking to another parent who may share an understanding of the issues causing concern. Sharing common ground can be tremendously supportive and may help alleviate feelings of isolation and difference. Ideas, suggestions and sources of support could be shared and strong bonds formed that can enhance self-confidence for all parties, ultimately benefiting the children. Staff could also be involved in these meetings, if invited.

*Participation opportunities*
All parties need to be aware of existing participation opportunities and the readiness to welcome any new initiatives that may be suggested. Practitioners must also be ready to justify the existing range, or limitations, of existing participation as there may be parents who have experiences in other settings or new ideas that they would wish to be considered. An open, encouraging environment will ensure that those parents will be listened to and that their ideas will be welcomed. Parents will often come prepared to suggest an initiative having clearly thought it through in advance and having some or many of the required resources in hand. With minor effort on behalf of the setting, a very positive, parent led initiative could emerge.

*Skill-sharing*
Parents, staff and practitioners can all benefit from the sharing of knowledge, expertise and skills. Parents, staff and combined training sessions can be established, with all parties being encouraged to share skills. A whole range of sessions could be arranged on such aspects as behaviour management, surviving school holidays, immunisations, safety in the home, cooking with children, cooking from around the world, dealing with bureaucracy, local, child-friendly places to visit and purposeful play.

Skill-sharing could also extend to parents' skills being used within the setting, from gardening expertise to fluency in a foreign language. Parent to parent skill-sharing could evolve with parents establishing babysitting circles, social visits and so on. A vast range of opportunities exists.

*Teaching*
Parents can become real partners in the learning that takes place within the setting or within the home. Through a two-way interchange of ideas practitioners and parents can support the child's progress together. Problems can arise when there is clearly a lack of interaction between home and school that can result in a child's needs being compromised.

## Issues compromising partnership

It would be pertinent to initiate discussion relating to the issues that compromise or inhibit any expansion of parent partnership, to make all parties aware of issues from inside and outside of the setting that may appear problematic. Purposeful discussions may lead to the resolution of some issues, or at least to the planning of resolution, and an enhanced awareness of those that do not appear amenable to resolution. Debating these issues and any others that may emerge should enable a clarification of possible ways forward and would certainly benefit all as an awareness raising exercise. Policy documents could then be pulled together, including existing practices and an action plan for the future.

Practitioners should accept that not all parents will be keen and enthusiastic to enter a partnership but may feel nervous, lacking in confidence or even antagonistic, but all will have a strong emotional commitment to their child. Reports exist to suggest two distinct types of parents of children with special needs, involved and reluctant (Blamires, Robertson and Blamires, 1997). The initial and early contacts with parents are therefore vital to the future of the partnership, and practitioners should attempt to support all parents in becoming active and involved partners.

Legislation and bureaucracy can also create tensions for parents, so the LEA as well as the individual setting should strive to ease the situation through giving support and information. Guides to LEA special needs provision should be readily accessible to all parents and practitioners, and it would be helpful to involve parents in the design and format of such information as it needs to be constructive, easy to understand and in the parents' home language.

Local education authorities and individual settings must have clear policies and guidelines available to parents as well as policies for resolving conflict situations.

## In working practice

If we are committed to working with parents, we must acknowledge the benefits, examine our own working practices and recognise that this area of work does not simply happen but that we need to plan, establish and monitor partnerships to ensure positive outcomes are experienced by parents, children and practitioners.

When preparing to welcome new children into our settings parents should be given information regarding:

- the setting
- how practitioners will plan for, monitor and review their child
- which professionals will be involved
- which professionals may be involved in the future
- the roles and responsibilities of professionals

- the requirements of the SEN Code of Practice (DfES, 2001d)
- how they (the parents) can support the work of the setting.

Once children are established within the setting we should continue to ensure that parents are active participants in their child's progress through informing them regularly of the child's activities, successes, concerns, any changes that may be occurring in the planning and implementing of provision, and how they can help within the home situation. Equally, parents should feel able to inform the setting of activities, successes, concerns and changes. Parents should feel that they are not only involved with their child's setting but are real and active partners, taking a shared responsibility.

## Summary

If the children we work with are to be given the best opportunities to reach their full potential, then practitioners need to work together with parents and other professionals to ensure that this becomes a reality. We cannot do this without parental support, nor should we wish to. If we recognise the benefits of effective parental partnerships then it follows that we should establish, monitor and review our working practices to reflect this philosophy. As a starting point we should assess:

- how welcoming our setting is to *all* parents and children
- how involved we want parents to become
- our induction and settling in procedures
- the parental partnership policy
- our information-sharing processes
- if parents understand the roles and responsibilities of all those involved with their child
- how involved parents are in decision-making
- the information that we expect parents to share with us
- the information we expect to share with parents
- the record-keeping systems
- how well staff members deal with parents
- if staff members are always available to discuss issues with parents
- whether there is somewhere for such discussions to take place
- how we expect parents to work with their child in the home
- how aware parents are of supporting agencies
- how well parents are prepared for and supported in review meetings.

While not an exhaustive list, an exploration of the issues would be a useful starting point for reflection on current practices and moving towards improved practices. Dale concludes:

What makes it so hard to evaluate is that the real cost can only be assessed through establishing the cost of its absence: of families who are frustrated and dissatisfied and fail to be helped by the services on offer and therefore perceive themselves as unsupported. Partnership practice has a price – but can we as a society afford or justify the alternative? (Dale, 1996: 307)

---

### Key issues

❖ Parents should be respected and their feelings and contributions valued.
❖ Practitioners should acknowledge the benefits of effective, meaningful partnerships.
❖ Practitioners should work towards empowering parents.
❖ Practitioners should review existing partnership policies and ensure that practices reflect policies.
❖ Partnerships cannot be assumed; they need to be planned, established and reviewed regularly.
❖ The success or failure of partnerships will depend on the quality of the relationships and the equality within those relationships.

---

## Some suggestions for discussion

### Item 1

Brainstorm the benefits of parental partnerships to parents, children with special needs and practitioners, as perceived by the staff.

### Item 2

Discuss what is expected of parents and the setting within a partnership. Discuss how parents are informed of setting expectations. Discuss how staff can evaluate parental expectations.

### Item 3

Examine the setting's existing parental partnership policy and discuss:

- Are all parents given equal opportunities to participate?
- Are we using every opportunity to welcome parents before their child begins attendance?

How do we encourage the reluctant parents to become involved in (a) the setting and (b) their child's provision?

- What information is shared with parents?

- How appropriate is the format of information shared?
- How and where do we discuss issues of concern with parents?
- How do we prepare parents for review meetings?
- What opportunities exist for parents to be a part of the decision-making processes within the setting?
- If parents do not attend meetings and open days, what steps are taken to follow up?
- Does the setting listen to and support parental initiatives?
- How do staff deal with parental conflict/disagreement?

### Item 4

Consider the usefulness of surveying parents to assess parental perspectives on the effectiveness of your partnership systems.

What questions might you ask parents? Make a list and sample it on a small number of parents.

## 📖 Suggested further reading

Blamires, M., Robertson, C. and Blamires, J. (1997) *Parent–Teacher Partnership. Practical Approaches to Meet Special Educational Needs*. London: David Fulton.

Draper, L. and Duffy, B. (2001) 'Working with parents', in G. Pugh, (ed.), *Contemporary Issues in the Early Years*, 3rd edn. London: Paul Chapman.

Wolfendale, S. (ed.) (1997) *Working with Parents of SEN Children after the Code of Practice*. London: David Fulton.

# 4

---

# Interagency Working

## Introduction

Now, more than ever before, early years practitioners need to work together with colleagues from other disciplines and agencies to support their work with children and their families. Government legislation and guidance promote working across agencies in a proactive and 'seamless' manner but this presents many challenges for practitioners and policy-makers at local and national levels. Awareness and understanding of the roles and responsibilities of colleagues in other agencies is vital if we are to work together effectively as, only then, can the knowledge, expertise and skills of each participant (including the parents) be used to full advantage. Pugh (2001: 180) suggests: 'the explicitly multi-disciplinary nature of government initiatives in recent years and their focus on co-ordination and integration of early years services require something more than benign co-operation across existing professions. These initiatives require a truly multi-disciplinary response.'

This chapter identifies the need for, and benefits of, interagency working and highlights factors that enhance or constrain effective collaboration between professionals. In turn, this leads our discussions into issues relating directly to practice and possible ways forward for the future.

## Definitions and models

Terminology has changed considerably over the years and a range of terms exists to describe professionals from different agencies working together. These include multidisciplinary, multiprofessional, multiagency, interdisciplinary, interagency, transdisciplinary and transagency. At times these terms have been used in an interchangeable manner but the development of each term has been specific to the philosophies of the time.

### Multidisciplinary, multiprofessional and multiagency working

The terms multidisciplinary, multiprofessional and multiagency are somewhat simplistic as they indicate more than one professional or agency working with a child but do not imply working together across professional boundaries. In the simplest form each professional provides expertise and the child then moves on to the next professional. Professionals are seen as working in discrete and separate ways and information sharing may be limited.

## Interdisciplinary and interagency working

Within the interdisciplinary and interagency model we are progressing from a system in which professionals work in isolation with a child and his/her family to one in which professionals still work in parallel but more cooperation exists. There is an increased acknowledgement of the need for professional skills from a range of theoretical perspectives needing to work together to support the needs of the child. One discipline or professional is seen to be insufficient to provide for all the needs of the family and child but professionals are still largely bound by parents passing on relevant information from other professionals. At this stage, systems are still working on a skills-based response to needs rather than a child- and family-centred approach.

## Transdisciplinary and transagency working

The transdisciplinary or transagency approach developed in response to the recognition that areas of child development are inextricably linked and, thus, professionals cannot provide effectively without working across disciplines. This model also encompasses the needs of the family as well as the child as it supports the wide range of factors that can impact on a child's life, in much the same way as indicated by Bronfenbrenner's (1979) ecological system. The sharing of information and decision-making is deemed fundamental. This model is therefore dependent on professionals implementing a key-worker system whereby one professional will take responsibility for coordinating and managing provision for the child and his/her family. The family needs are thus supported by having only one contact source for information. Case conferences and progress review meetings are also central to this process, with all professionals, the parents and the child (if appropriate) coming together to discuss progress, comment on provision and make plans for the short and long term.

Research indicates that the transdisciplinary model of working is the most effective, supporting current philosophies (Carpenter, 1997; Mortimer, 2001). However at this current time legislation and guidance discuss and use the term 'interagency' working, so for this reason this term will be used throughout this book.

Whichever model is adopted the latest guidance within the SEN Code of Practice (DfES, 2001d, s. 10.1) highlights the need to work together: 'Meeting the special educational needs of individual children requires flexible working on the part of the statutory agencies. They need to communicate and agree policies and protocols that ensure there is a "seamless" service.'

## Historical developments

It is only since the 1970s that interagency work has become established and moved forwards. Possibly the two earliest and most influential legislative documents to support interagency work were the Court Report (Court, 1976) and the Warnock Report (DES, 1978).

The Court Report highlighted the importance of parental and professional roles, emphasising the need for practitioners to work with parents in the interests of the child and for practitioners to gain support and specialist guidance from other professionals. This philosophy was instrumental in the development of 'multidisciplinary' (as opposed to interagency) teams to support the processes of diagnosis and provision for children with special educational needs.

The Warnock Report further supported the development of 'inter-professional' working, suggesting that: 'The development of close working relations between professionals in the different services concerned with children and young people with special needs is central to many of the recommendations in this report' (DES, 1978: s. 16.1). The Warnock Report clearly indicated the need for interprofessional working throughout the stages of identification, assessment, monitoring and reviewing provision for children with special needs. The issue of interprofessional training within the early years was also identified as critical for effective provision in enabling professionals to further their knowledge and understanding of areas of 'common concern'.

The concept of 'interagency' working was further supported in the Education Act (DES, 1981) and the Children Act (DoH, 1991), with the latter suggesting the need for coordination of services at three levels:

- policy-making
- day-to-day operation
- between staff working in different settings.

Within the Children Act was a clear acknowledgement of the value of sharing skills and expertise:

> A co-ordinated approach helps to create an environment where people with different qualifications and experience can share skills and expertise and ideas in a positive way. It is important for all departments within a local authority to find ways of encouraging staff to work with this in mind, so that all the appropriate skills are available in all settings. (DOH, 1991: s. 1.16)

The Act was followed in 1991 by a guide for 'Interagency cooperation for the protection of children from abuse' (Home Office, Department of Health, Department of Education and Science and the Welsh Office, 1991) and, although this clearly related to child protection cases, it was another move towards collaborative working practices.

The Education Act (DfEE, 1993) and the guidance that followed in the form of the *Code of Practice on the Identification and Assessment of Special Educational Needs*

(DfEE, 1994), continued the move towards increased and more effective interagency working practices: 'Effective action on behalf of children with special educational needs will often depend upon close cooperation between schools, LEAs, the health services and the social services departments of local authorities' (ibid.: s. 2:38). The involvement of professionals from a range of disciplines to support the staged assessment of special educational needs within schools was seen to be the most effective way to ensure appropriate provision.

Interagency working was later supported through the development of Early Years Development and Childcare Partnerships in the late 1990s, whereby representatives from all agencies working with, or having a working interest in, young children worked together to plan and oversee provision in the local authority.

The most recent legislation and guidance with a focus on interagency working is the Special Educational Needs and Disability Discrimination Act (DfES, 2001c). The accompanying SEN Code of Practice (DfES, 2001d) includes a whole chapter devoted to working with other agencies with the key objective: 'to provide integrated, high quality, holistic support focused on the needs of the child' (ibid.: s. 10:4).

## Progression to date

So, how far have we progressed and to what benefit? From the preceding historical reflection it would seem that we have consistently moved towards improved interagency working but very recently McConkey reflected on the work of Gulliford since the 1960s and presented quite a damning picture of progression:

> It truly has been a road 'less travelled' as each service system has forged its own highway in trying to reduce the disabling effects of an intellectual impairment and the inevitable social consequences that it brings. Worse still, at times they have worked competitively rather than cooperatively, blaming one another for perceived shortcomings. And perhaps most seriously of all, they have worked in ignorance of one another's values, priorities and achievements. (McConkey, 2002: 3)

There are clearly areas where progression has been very positive:

- interagency assessments prior to statementing
- development of Early Years Partnerships
- setting up of more interagency early years centres, such as jointly funded Family Centres and Early Excellence Centres
- setting up of SureStart projects
- increased interagency training.

However, it may also be suggested that there are still key issues to be addressed if we wish to secure continued progression, such as:

- increased understanding and awareness of the roles and responsibilities of other professionals
- expansion of the key worker scheme
- joint funding
- joint training
- joint decision-making at all levels
- joint policies
- rationalisation of professional differences
- consideration of merging of roles and responsibilities, including shared or joint planning.

# The need for interagency working

When children attend our early years settings it is our responsibility to provide appropriate educational, personal and social activities to support their overall development. It is our aim to ensure they all achieve their full potential, but children with special needs and/or special educational needs will require more individualised opportunities to encourage progression. For some children this will require input from several or many professionals and thus there becomes a need for professionals to work together. David echoes this view:

> Their (the children's) teachers must often work with other professionals, and volunteers who are in some way connected with children and their families in order to understand children's difficulties, find ways of helping them and help children to learn effectively.
>
> It must be recognised that teachers of young children are not isolated and autonomous professionals, they work with a range of people who all contribute services for under-fives and their families. (David, 1994: 45)

The following case study highlights several key issues.

### Case study

Jodie was referred to a local pre-school special needs unit at aged 3 years and 3 months presenting with developmental delay. The report received by the head of the unit from the consultant paediatrician indicated that Jodie had originally been referred by her health visitor and was particularly delayed in the areas of cognitive and social development. In addition there were family difficulties in that both her parents were drug and alcohol abusers and had recently parted. There was a history of domestic violence. Following this the mother had left her husband and moved from another county to her current address.

As Jodie began to settle within the unit it became apparent that her difficulties lay predominantly in the areas of social and emotional development, and other difficulties stemmed from these difficulties as well as a lack of appropriate learning opportunities. Once staff encouraged her and showed her how to play, her development took off at a considerable pace. A setback occurred when her father moved into the house and levels of drug and alcohol abuse rose once again. At this stage the local supporting agency for drug and alcohol abusers and their families was introduced with a view to supporting the parents with their difficulties. It was also at this time that the social services department became involved, to support the family and work towards improving the family situation for all members.

Within a year Jodie was performing at an age-appropriate level in the areas of language and communication, cognitive and creative skills, and at the same time her self-esteem was considerably enhanced.

At all times the agencies involved maintained regular contact and the head of the pre-school unit acted as key worker to ensure effective coordination of services, monitor progress, call regular progress review meetings and act as the one focal point of contact for the family. Outside professionals working with the family used rooms at the unit for meetings with the family. The head of the unit was selected as the key worker because she had most regular contact with the family.

## Key issues

- Fundamentally, the difficulties experienced by Jodie were attributable to her parents' difficulties. This is a clear indication of the effects of the environment on a child and his/her development.
- As the family had no transport the local special needs unit became the central focus of provision.
- There was a need for the professionals to share information, knowledge and skills to ensure an understanding of roles and responsibilities.
- Without a supportive network of agencies and professionals Jodie's difficulties would have been exacerbated, as her parents did not consider using pre-school provision until it became a part of their rehabilitation programme.
- The range of professionals involved spanned all agencies, including the voluntary sector, and depended on effective interagency collaboration and coordination.
- As the head of the unit had not previously dealt with issues of drug and alcohol dependency she had to address this lack of knowledge to support the parents and thus, indirectly, Jodie.

This case study shows that professionals from health, social services, education and the voluntary sector, each with their own theoretical frameworks and philosophies, needed to work together to support the needs of the family members, including Jodie. The case study explored in Chapter 2 required input from a far greater number of professionals and the coordination of such a large group of professionals is a mammoth task requiring careful planning and organisation. In an early years setting there may be many children experiencing difficulties, so the coordination becomes magnified and it should be remembered that this is only one aspect of the practitioner's role. Demands are thus considerable.

If we continue to consider the child holistically as part of our setting, their family, the local community and beyond, we need to work towards the 'seamless' provision of services that is being called for. We must work together in a collaborative manner, sharing expertise, information and skills which need to be managed in a way that addresses implications for families. Parents should not be responsible for passing on information from one professional to another, it is the responsibility of the professionals. As Wall concluded:

> effective co-operation and collaboration must exist to provide a clearly defined response to individual needs. For this to be achieved all personnel involved must understand and respect each other's role. While this may seem a tremendous task it must be remembered that teachers have a knowledge of the workings of most of the outside agencies they are likely to deal with, but perhaps a deeper understanding combined with local policies for working together would benefit all. (Wall, 1996: 84)

## Understanding the roles of other professionals

To work in an interagency manner with colleagues from other disciplines will demand knowledge and understanding of their roles and responsibilities. Practitioners need to be clear on how another professional can complement and support their own provision for a child and in what precise ways, and how and when this support will take place. Clarity is needed on who will be responsible for coordinating the support so that each professional involved and the parents are fully aware of what has already taken place, what has been agreed upon, what progress has been made, what short- and long-term plans are in place and how provision is monitored.

Working with other professionals will be an essential aspect of the early years practitioner's role and, therefore, the need to establish effective working practices must be included within our planning and policies. The need to work together to understand the child holistically is summarised by Drifte:

> Working with other agencies is an integral part of supporting children with special educational needs (SEN) and their parents. This cooperative approach also provides valuable support to the practitioner, who can benefit from access to information and records that focus on a different aspect of the child's development. The practitioner can also benefit from advice and suggestions about the management of special educational needs. (Drifte, 2001: 41)

In the case study in this chapter we saw that Jodie's parents were working with the social worker, health visitor and drug and alcohol abuse worker. To ensure clarity of provision the head of the special needs unit, as key worker, needed to be aware of:

- the specific difficulties experienced by Jodie, her parents and siblings
- the input offered by each involved professional
- appointments attended by the family
- further referrals made
- organising and managing review meetings
- assessments and reports written.

Having such knowledge enabled her to ensure all parties were updated with information. Sometimes confusions arise or misconceptions exist because of a lack of coordination and collaboration which can compound a child's difficulties, as suggested by McFarlane (1993: 125): 'Knowledge of other professions' responsibilities tends to be gathered "on the move" rather than in a studied way, and is often as a result partial or superficial.'

## Skills and qualities needed

Working within an interagency framework requires certain skills and abilities and, clearly, a commitment to the principles and benefits of working in this manner is fundamental. If professionals believe strongly that inter-agency working benefits all, but most importantly the children, then hopefully they will be able to respond positively to demands on time and working practices despite constraining influences. Interagency working is still developing and there will necessarily be trials and tribulations for a considerable time to come. Committed professionals will be able to deal with these issues.

A desire to work more effectively with colleagues from other disciplines is required, as opposed to having a duty to work with colleagues from other disciplines. Those professionals who are interested in the workings of other disciplines and are less protective of their own discipline, expertise and skills will benefit positively from the experiences of increasing their knowledge and skills, both professionally and personally. Professionals must also be prepared to challenge their own philosophies and practices in the light of new information gained over time. This will, in turn, support their abilities to accommodate other perspectives.

## Professionals involved

Early years practitioners may work with any of the following professionals.

### *Education department*

The *educational psychologist* (EP) will:

- be a qualified teacher who has undertaken additional training in educational psychology
- support the identification, assessment and monitoring of specific difficulties
- suggest appropriate intervention strategies
- advise on local provision
- complete reports for statutory assessment
- offer training
- work with parents.

The *early years SEN support/advisory teacher* will:

- usually be a qualified teacher with SEN experience and expertise
- support local early years providers regarding specific children
- support staff in planning and providing appropriate opportunities to support specific needs
- offer staff training
- advise on local specialist provision
- support referrals to other specialists
- contribute to the statutory assessment process
- work with parents.

Most counties have the benefit of *specialist support teams* covering the areas of language impairment, visual impairment and hearing impairment. In addition, many counties offer behaviour support teams to work with individual children, groups of children and practitioners. Support team staff will generally be experienced teachers who may hold additional qualifications in their specific field. In addition, support staff may include nursery nurses (NNEBs) and learning support assistants (LSAs).

*Visual/hearing/language impairment and behaviour support teachers* will:

- advise practitioners on specific needs of individual children
- suggest exercises, strategies and appropriate learning opportunities for individual children
- advise on specialist equipment/resources needed
- liaise with parents
- assess and monitor provision for individual children
- refer children to other specialists as appropriate
- offer advice, support and training to practitioners and parents
- sometimes contribute to the statutory assessment process.

## Health department

The *general practitioner* (GP) will:

- take responsibility for family health needs
- identify and provide for medical needs/problems

- refer individual children to other specialists for specific medical assessments or treatment
- liaise with health visitors, practitioners and parents.

The *health visitor* (HV) will:

- provide primary health care for children under school age
- monitor children developmentally at regular intervals prior to school entry and identify and assess special needs when appropriate
- be informed when a child with special needs or medical problems is born
- offer support, guidance and advice to parents and professionals
- refer individual children to other specialists when appropriate
- advise on local provision and supporting agencies
- contribute to the statutory assessment process.

The *paediatrician and consultant paediatrician* will:

- monitor medical conditions in individual children
- refer individual children to other specialists when appropriate
- liaise with practitioners, other professionals and parents
- undertake a detailed developmental assessment if a child is failing HV developmental checks
- offer early diagnosis and suggest appropriate intervention and placement for children causing concern
- contribute medical information to the statutory assessment process.

The *school health* service:

Once children enter school general health surveillance becomes the responsibility of the *school health service* and, predominantly, the school nurse. School nurses will:

- advise staff on the medical needs of individual children
- offer basic hearing and vision tests
- offer child health advice and information to staff
- support referrals to other agencies.

The *speech and language therapist* (SLT) will:

- suggest exercises, strategies and appropriate learning opportunities for individual children with speech, language and communication difficulties
- work with individual children regarding their specific needs
- liaise with practitioners and parents
- refer children to other specialists if appropriate
- offer diagnoses of specific language impairments/disorders
- contribute information to the statutory assessment process
- monitor the speech and language development of specific children
- offer support and training to practitioners and parents.

The *physiotherapist*:
Some *physiotherapists* specialise in paediatric working and will:

- assess and diagnose physical difficulties experienced by young children
- suggest exercises, strategies and appropriate learning opportunities for individual children with physical difficulties
- contribute information to the statutory assessment process
- offer advice and support to practitioners and parents
- advise on specialist equipment/resources needed
- refer children to other specialists as appropriate.

The *occupational therapist* (OT) will:

- support children with physical difficulties to achieve independence
- assess fine and gross motor skills
- suggest exercises, strategies and appropriate learning opportunities for individual children
- advise practitioners on specific needs of individual children
- contribute information to the statutory assessment process
- advise on specialist equipment/resources needed
- refer children to other specialists as appropriate
- offer advice and support to practitioners and parents.

The *audiologist and opthalmologist* will:

- assess children's hearing/vision to identify possible problems
- suggest exercises, strategies and appropriate learning opportunities for individual children with hearing/visual problems
- contribute information to the statutory assessment process
- advise practitioners/parents on individual children's needs
- advise on specialist equipment/resources needed
- refer children to other specialists as appropriate.

The *clinical psychologist*:

There is some overlap between the roles and responsibilities of the educational psychologist and the *clinical psychologist*, but clearly their underpinning philosophies will differ due to their different training and work contexts, i.e. education or health. For these reasons referrals will depend on issues such as the structure of local services and division of key responsibilities. As an example it may be that a clinical psychologist would be responsible for the diagnosis of attention deficit hyperactivity disorder (ADHD) in one county but in the neighbouring county the educational psychologist would diagnose. In general, clinical psychologists will:

- advise and support families experiencing difficulties
- undertake developmental assessments

- suggest strategies and appropriate experiences for individual children, siblings and/or parents
- contribute information to the statutory assessment process
- advise and support practitioners on individual cases
- monitor provision for individual children/families
- offer family/child therapy
- refer children to other specialists as appropriate.

The *child mental health* team comprises a range of professionals that may include consultant psychiatrists, child psychiatric nurses, child psychiatrists, psychotherapists, counsellors and outreach workers. They can provide:

- assessments and diagnoses
- individual or small group therapy sessions
- within home support and advice
- reports to support the statutory assessment process
- support and advice to practitioners
- referrals to other agencies.

## Social services department

Practitioners within the SSD will have generic skills but usually work in specialist teams such as child protection, children with disabilities and children and family services. Social workers aim to enable families to help themselves, using professional expertise and resources. If a family is identified as experiencing difficulties providing appropriately for their children, then social workers can assess the situation and offer guidance and support, but with the aim that their services will be reduced over a suitable period of time and withdrawn at some point in the future. In such instances families can self-refer and thus ask specifically for help. In other cases it may be that the family is reported as being of concern and the social worker(s) will visit the home to offer support and discuss issues and ways forwards if the parents cooperate.

The *social worker* will:

- offer assessments of family situations and subsequent support
- refer to other agencies/provision
- support local child protection procedures
- monitor children and/or families
- advise parents on the range of local supporting agencies
- contribute to the statutory assessment process
- offer direct therapeutic intervention with children.

## Voluntary supporting agencies

Voluntary agencies are not directly funded by the local authority and are often registered as charitable organisations, having applied for and gained charitable status. They can be locally and/or nationally based and focus on generic or specialised areas, e.g. National Association of Special Educational Needs (NASEN – Internet 5) and National Autistic Society (NAS – Internet 7).

Voluntary agencies can offer all or some of the following to practitioners and parents alike:

* information, helplines and advice
* publications, from leaflets to books and videos
* local support groups, networked nationwide in some instances
* respite care in the local area
* training and resources
* advocacy services
* campaigning for awareness and improved services
* special schools (boarding and day pupils)
* holiday clubs
* research databases
* links to other agencies and services (local and/or national)
* representation on local and/or national committees.

### Portage

Portage (Internet 8) is a home visiting service for families of pre-school children with special needs, funded in some areas by the local health authority and in others by education. Usually following a referral from the health visitor or consultant paediatrician, a portage worker will visit the family to assess the child's needs using a detailed developmental checklist. From this initial assessment of needs both short- and long-term targets can be set with the worker visiting the home to work with the child and parent, supporting and monitoring progress based on strategies guided by the developmental checklist. It is anticipated that through initially working with the parent, the worker will, in time, be able to reduce input levels as the parent takes the lead in their child's provision. The parent will complete record sheets and discuss progress with the portage worker, before subsequent targets are jointly devised and planned.

## Working together

To work effectively together all practitioners must understand and respect each other's roles, and any barriers to collaborative working practices must be removed. Having a thorough working knowledge of colleagues from other disciplines will ultimately enhance the provision we offer the children and families we work with. This level of awareness cannot readily be achieved through a collaborative meeting or training session, although these will certainly contribute positively. Through regularly working alongside our colleagues, asking questions, joint decision-making and joint planning we should be able to increase our knowledge of their philosophies and working practices, as well as the constraints they work under. As Read and Rees (2000: 45) conclude: 'Teams that have been working together over time develop their own forms of verbal shorthand to share ideas and suggestions, and are able to ground their discussion in an understanding formed through day-to-day communication and awareness of each other's views.'

If time could be made available then half a day or a whole day spent shadowing another professional will assist understanding considerably. Having the opportunity at first hand to see a colleague working through a normal day will inform greatly, as issues and questions will arise naturally and increased awareness and understanding would occur. If this can be combined with joint training then provision should be enhanced. Local early years networks and fora would support such developments. As a past example, one practitioner had spent time seeking respite care for a family only to find that the attached social worker was doing exactly the same. With practitioner time being under constant pressure this could have been avoided through greater collaboration and information sharing.

Welton suggested three ways forwards to ensure collaborative working:

> Firstly, by raising the general professional sensitivity to the need for collaboration and joint action to meet children's needs. Demonstrating how by working with other professionals, a social worker, medical doctor, or teacher can provide more effectively for their client's needs. Secondly, through the development of informal contacts between members of each profession and service. Thirdly, through the development of formal systems of welfare coordination at policy making, administrative and professional levels. (Welton, 1985: 75)

## The role of the SENCO

Working together to provide for children's individual needs is required throughout the processes of Early Years Action and Action Plus, as detailed in the Code of Practice:

> The SENCO should be responsible for:
> - Ensuring liaison with parents and other professionals in respect of children with special educational needs.
> - Advising other practitioners in the setting.
> - Ensuring that Individual Education Plans are in place.
> - Ensuring that relevant background information about individual children with special educational needs is collected, recorded and updated. (DfES, 2001d: s. 4.15)

If interventions within the setting do not provide effectively for a child's needs, then outside professionals will be introduced to support the identification, assessment and intervention stages. Knowledge, understanding and awareness of the full range of additional agencies and the roles of relevant colleagues will thus be essential throughout this process. If the assessment process moves forwards to the more formal statutory assessment of needs, then the SENCO must have involved relevant professionals to ensure that the child's needs in all areas have been fully investigated. This will provide the local authority with a clear picture of the child in a holistic way, enabling them to reach a decision. The parents and any professionals and agencies involved with the child and his/her family must be consulted, so the SENCO's role is 'central and crucial' (Drifte, 2001). Reports submitted will not necessarily just relate to areas of development such as cognitive and speech and language skills but may also need to assess additional factors or situations impacting on the child's progress. In the case study previously explored, reports were required from the social worker and drug and alcohol abuse worker in addition to the educational psychologist, speech and language therapist and SENCO. This enabled all influencing factors to be considered prior to decision-making about subsequent intervention strategies and specific provision requirements. Drifte (2001: 48) supports the notion of the centrality of the SENCO role: 'the SENCO has to collect and collate all the records relating to the child, from the earliest stage of concern, with vigilance, to ensure that the LEA has all the necessary information required to make a decision regarding assessment'.

In addition, the SENCO must ensure that information regarding the full range of services within the locality is available to all parents. Information relating to the staged approach, from identification of special educational needs through to formal assessment, should be given to parents as well as the contact details for the local Parent Partnership scheme.

## Planning and coordination in early years settings

Perhaps the most important consideration will be the recording systems maintained within settings as these will be fundamental to future provision. In this age of accountability, perhaps more so than ever before, we must ensure that while records should always be thorough, they should not be too cumbersome to maintain. Ease of access to records must be considered, so professionals and parents alike can interpret them in an accessible way.

The SENCO should ensure that each professional is fully aware of the roles and responsibilities of his/her colleagues within the setting, which can be supported through regular staff meetings. In addition, settings should have available a central list of agencies within the locality that can be accessed to support the setting's provision. Since the evolution of Early Years Development and Childcare Partnerships authorities now have a comprehensive list available to parents and professionals alike, but such lists need regular updating to include new and changing details, and may need tailoring to meet the requirements of individual settings.

The key-worker system, whereby one practitioner within a setting takes responsibility for the provision of a group of individual children, will remove some of the responsibility for planning and record-keeping from the SENCO as each practitioner will be responsible for the maintenance of the records for their own key-worker children, with the SENCO taking a more supervisory role. Regular progress reviews will then update practitioners, outside professionals/agencies and parents as to progress achieved and referrals made, over the past few months. The key-worker will be selected as the most appropriate member of staff to work with the child, their family and other professionals, and success will depend partly on the trust and honesty established within the relationship. The key worker will make sure records are updated and liaise regularly with parents, the SENCO and professionals.

Previously, the relationship between professionals and parents would have been one in which the professionals 'imparted' knowledge and skills to parents but, currently, we are working towards a more family-centred approach which acknowledges the parents as partners, crucial members of the interagency team and a key influence on the child. Carpenter (2000: 140) expands on this: 'The family-centred approach is not a panacea; it will not instantly bring about quality services, but it will reposition the family at the heart of service-delivery as the most informed source of knowledge about the child and its family.'

## *Children with medical needs*

As more and more children with medical needs are included within mainstream settings additional consideration needs to be made as practitioners will need to liaise with a wider range of professionals. The current guidance for educating children and young people with medical needs (DfES, 2001a) refers to children from statutory school age to age 19, but although direct reference is not made to children under 5 years of age it could be suggested that the recommendations would indicate good practice for pre-school practitioners. This joint approach by the DfES and the Department of Health (DfES, 2001a: 4) acknowledges: 'the important part that both health and education play in the well being of children and young people. For pupils recovering from trauma or illness, a teacher can play a vital part in the recovery process because education is seen as a normal childhood activity.'

While working to ensure educational continuity for the child, it is clear that interagency collaboration will be essential for all involved and this may involve early years practitioners working with professionals whose roles and responsibilities are vastly different from their own. These could be health professionals, home-teaching tutors, hospital tutors and/or therapists. It will therefore be necessary for practitioners to enhance their current knowledge and skill levels to support the child and his/her family appropriately. Liaison with medical personnel may be time-consuming but will be essential, and time must be made to ensure regular contact and continuity of provision for parents and professionals alike. The guidance (DfES, 2001a: 23) suggests: 'Adequate time for liaison between agencies is needed to ensure successful working together. LEA's should consider staffing policies which provide the necessary flexibility to enable effective liaison ...'

# Factors affecting collaboration

Possibly the most recent study to examine interagency working was conducted by the National Foundation for Educational Research (NFER, Internet 9) on behalf of the Local Government Association. The report (Atkinson et al., 2002: ii), which includes an examination of 30 initiatives is highly recommended for further reading and comprises: 'analysis and discussion of the different types, or models, of multi-agency activity; the rationale for their development; agencies' and individuals' involvement in multi-agency activities, their roles and professional backgrounds; the impact of multi-agency activities; and the challenges and key factors in their success'.

Relating specifically to the factors affecting collaboration, the report highlighted five key areas as consistent challenges to effective interagency working systems:

- funding and resources
- roles and responsibilities
- competing priorities
- communication
- professional and agency cultures and management.

These findings concur with similar conclusions drawn by Wolfendale (1997) and Roffey (2001) and also link closely to McConkey's (2002) summary of Gulliford's work on the 'less-travelled road'.

# Issues supporting future progression

## *Joint funding*

Funding continues to be an ongoing pressure for practitioners and until extended joint funding policies at local and national levels are in place then problems will remain. A frequently raised issue is that of the provision of speech and language therapy within early years settings. The ongoing debate surrounds whether the local education or health department should pay for this service, but hopefully with the advent of Early Years Development and Childcare Partnerships and interagency Early Years Centres, more joint funding will emerge and the problem will hopefully diminish. As a result of the National Childcare Strategy, central government funding became available for Early Excellence Centres able to demonstrate high-quality, interagency working in the early years, another positive move forwards in the funding debate.

Local politicians should appreciate the short- and long-term benefits of joint policies and funding to enhance the range of provision they support and to reduce tensions, especially for practitioners working at ground level. It would be hoped that an increase in joint funding initiatives would support interagency working and be seen by practitioners as clear leadership and positive management.

## Unification of services

The effects of funding disputes will directly impact on practitioners, all of whom want to deliver the most appropriate provision to individual children but may feel compromised by local policies and funding arrangements. Perhaps here it is appropriate to promote early years or children's authorities that are funded as one and comprise education, health, social services and all other agencies working with children, rather than separate and discrete, profession-focused departments. The current Early Years Development and Childcare Partnerships are a step in the right direction comprising representatives from a range of disciplines, agencies and parents, but each of these has their own professional base within one department (e.g. health or education). They are not, as yet, part of the same fund-holding administration.

## Resources and training

In the current climate of supporting inclusion, additional funding issues arise for practitioners and local authorities. Settings may need additional resources, material and human, to provide for the needs of individual children or simply to extend current resources to account for greater diversity. There is also a need for ongoing training to ensure practitioners have the necessary skills and knowledge to provide for all children's needs within today's settings, if we are expecting mainstream practitioners to accommodate an expanding range of individual needs. As an example, it could be argued that very specialised knowledge is required to understand and provide appropriately for a young autistic child. If that knowledge does not exist, then practitioners could inadvertently be compromising the child's development. In addition, practitioners should have knowledge of local supporting agencies and professionals trained in such a specialised field to advise and support and perhaps offer staff training. In such a case there would be an ideal opportunity for such training to be of an interagency nature.

## Joint planning for individual needs

Practitioners should always use joint planning of the provision for individual children to avoid situations, which still exist today, wherein the 'specialist' undertakes their assessments or intervention devoid of reference to the everyday provision within the setting and/or the family. Any input must be seen as a part of a complete package of provision, with components supporting and complementing each other, not working independently. Through regular meetings to discuss future targets and strategies to be used, joint discussions should occur to provide coherent provision linked to each aspect of the child's life.

## Training for interagency working

It should be remembered that professionals are rarely trained for interagency working, so, without training sessions planned to cater for professionals from a range of disciplines, the professional and personal skills needed may not exist or develop. It could be suggested that training sessions which are jointly planned, delivered by a range of professionals, attended by a range of professionals and which allow time for discussions would be the most effective. Such training would ensure that opportunities arose to discuss differing perspectives and profession-specific issues, which should lead to enhanced understanding of differing roles and the issues constraining or enhancing the work.

## Differing professional cultures

Each discipline will have specialised philosophies, policies and working practices but these do not need to be totally diverse and practitioners do not need to 'protect' their own professional culture. Through sharing our perspectives and aims, greater awareness and understanding, combined with mutual respect should emerge. As the Atkinson et al. (2002: 225) report revealed: 'This study of multi-agency activity has highlighted once again the complexity and also potential of "joining up" services. It has revealed the investment needed, in terms of finance, time and staff resources to develop new ways of working and inter-agency collaboration.'

## Organisational structures

Organisational structures and effective communication structures need to be established, based upon interagency philosophies. As more and more funding opportunities arise we must ensure that the existing diverse range of early years provision does not become even more diverse but that we establish systems and processes that bring a unified approach nearer.

## Referral systems

Currently referral systems are predominantly profession based, depending on the professional identifying or diagnosing. For example, if the health visitor identifies a child's difficulty then a referral to the consultant paediatrician may follow, both clearly health authority based. Recommendations may include attendance at an early years setting which could be education based, so perhaps there is an opportunity for greater centralisation of the referral system.

In many areas there will be local interagency teams which meet to jointly plan future provision for individual children following the initial diagnostic process. With input from the full range of professionals, conflicting issues can be dealt with at an early stage thus reducing time and ensuring more appropriate provision. However, professional boundaries and budgets may still impede this process.

In Gloucestershire the current referral system for young children with special needs is a good example of effective interagency working combined with parental participation. When a professional is specifically concerned about the level of a child's difficulties, they can refer the child to the local panel for early years. In addition, the parents themselves can refer their own child to the same panel, which meets monthly. The panel is led by an educational psychologist and comprises the child's parents, paediatricians, the pre-school liaison officer, a portage worker and a representative from the family centres, opportunity centres and early years centres. The child will be discussed and decisions and recommendations made regarding either a referral to another professional and/or recommending a specific placement or setting that can provide for his/her needs. In turn, the professional or setting the child has been referred to may undertake a home visit to begin the process of provision.

The Code of Practice (DfES, 2001d) does not appear directly to address the issue of referral systems in the chapter entitled 'Working in partnership with other agencies'. It focuses briefly on general principles of interagency working but then progresses to explore each department separately. The Code of Practice does, however, encourage 'collaboration and effective communication systems at management and practitioner levels' (DfES, 2001d: s. 10:4).

## Individual professional skills

We are now seeing a range of professionals with considerably extended skills. Further skills have been developed within their own professional discipline alongside the development of knowledge and expertise regarding roles and responsibilities that would previously have been deemed outside their remit. If we wish to continue moving forwards with interagency work then such highly skilled professionals with diverse working backgrounds across disciplines will support the 'blurring' of professional boundaries. Within the UK we are very much profession led as our initial training is specialised within one discipline, but we are now seeing the continued emergence of early childhood qualifications that are very much interdisciplinary and offer students training across the disciplines. Perhaps this philosophy should be extended to support wider interagency initial training. The Atkinson et al. report supports this view through its identification of:

> a 'new and hybrid professional' who has personal experience and knowledge of other agencies, including, importantly, these services' cultures, structures, discourse and priorities. This understanding would seem to be a vital *sine qua non* for successful interagency collaboration. It may be that such familiarity needs to be offered to many others during initial training and in continuing professional development. (Atkinson et al., 2002: 225)

## Summary

Interagency working has developed considerably but issues and barriers to effective working still exist. The benefits to children, parents, families, early years practitioners and professionals from all disciplines are clear, but currently we see a range of approaches. Changes should continue at ground level, local authority and national levels to ensure the 'seamless' service we are striving for and to unify approaches.

With greater collaboration and cooperation between practitioners we will enhance the service we offer to parents and children alike. Parents of children with special needs already have a range of difficulties and challenges to face, but with a more unified approach to provision and effective use of the key-worker system we can, hopefully, support their needs more effectively.

Working more collaboratively with colleagues will extend our own skills and expertise, enable us to understand differing professional perspectives, roles and responsibilities, and improve our interventions with children. Our personal and professional gains will also be considerable. However, commitment and belief in the positive outcomes of interagency working from national policy level will be needed to ensure success.

---

### Key issues

- ❖ Practitioners should acknowledge the benefits of interagency working.
- ❖ Positive commitment to interagency working is needed from policy level to practitioner level.
- ❖ Areas still requiring development would include joint funding, planning and decision-making, resources, training, and organisational structures.
- ❖ Respect between colleagues from differing disciplines is essential to help remove professional boundaries.
- ❖ Time management must allow for regular liaison roles.

## Some suggestions for discussion

### Item 1

Examine the working practices within your setting and determine if your systems support a multiagency, interagency or transdisciplinary approach. Reflect on the outcome and attempt to define how effective this approach is for the parents, staff and children.

### Item 2

Does your current workplace have a directory of agencies that can be contacted for advice and/or support? If not, consider the value of such a document and how you might create it. Discuss the information for inclusion – should it be a list of names and telephone numbers or could it offer more detailed entries to inform parents, visiting professionals and staff?

### Item 3

Consider a training session in an area already identified as a training need. Could this be enhanced through interagency delivery and opened up to colleagues from other disciplines? Can you identify changes this might make to the training experience and the outcomes?

### Item 4

If your setting is part of a local interagency forum, seek the views on possible joint training with your colleagues in the future. If outcomes are supportive then identify possible ways of moving forwards.

### Item 5

Identify the strengths and constraints of your current interagency working practices and attempt to highlight possible ways forwards.

## Suggested further reading

Atkinson, M., Wilkin, A., Stott, A., Doherty, P. and Kinder, K. (2002) *Multi-Agency Working: A Detailed Study*. Slough: NFER.

David, T. (ed.) (1994) *Working Together for Young Children: Multi-professionalism in Action*. London: Routledge.

Mortimer, H. (2001) *Special Needs and Early Years Provision*. London: Continuum. (Chapter 6.)

# 5

## Observation and Assessment

### Introduction

As part of the ongoing recording and monitoring system within early years settings, the usefulness and power of observation and assessment are sometimes overlooked as they may be deemed time-consuming when there is already a shortage of time to complete the other tasks required by agencies such as the government, parents, governors or committee and local educational authorities. However, observation can enable:

- informed planning
- informed understanding of a child's current competence levels
- reflection on the appropriateness of provision
- sharing of information with other parties
- assessment of specific children, groups, interactions, the learning environment and staff.

The Foundation Stage guidance (QCA, 2000) and Code of Practice (DfES, 2001d) acknowledge the value of observation and assessment, and place requirements on all early years practitioners to ensure these are part of the ongoing teaching and learning process. Thus practitioners need to have a clear understanding of the purposes and benefits, combined with practical examples, both of which are offered in this chapter.

In order to identify a child's current competence levels, we rely on observation of skills mastered which then informs our future planning. For children experiencing difficulties we should strive towards early identification, diagnosis of specific difficulties and the introduction of appropriate intervention strategies. None of these can take place without prior observation and assessment of the current situation.

Observation and assessment processes can also be used to identify the effectiveness of the setting, specific areas of the setting, specific activities and the practitioner. Arguably, to see the children progress and be happy is every practitioner's ultimate aim and one that gives us tremendous satisfaction and reward. We therefore need to be prepared to examine our own practices closely to ensure that we are supporting and not compounding children's learning opportunities inadvertently. If we aim to provide appropriately for all children within our settings, then we should be prepared to capitalise on the value and practical usefulness of observational approaches and ensure observation is a regular activity.

Purposeful observation offers benefits to practitioners, parents and children, and is a positive way of responding to the needs of all children, not just those experiencing difficulties, and my own experience supports this view. For those children experiencing special needs we should ensure that we focus on assessing the child and not the difficulties being experienced. In the case of an autistic child, for example, while practitioners need to understand the effects and implications of autism, we should focus on the child's current skills, strengths, weaknesses, likes and dislikes which will inform planning. The autism is secondary. With each child we are thus increasing our knowledge and considering each child as individual and unique.

We usually observe children when they are involved in their everyday activities, but there may be occasions when we need to set up specific activities to support a specific observation. However we look at it, observation and assessment should be an integral part of every early years establishment.

## Children's rights, legislation and guidance

The Warnock Report (DES, 1978) emphasised the importance of effective assessment through initial, more informal, assessments through to the stages preceding formal assessment and the production of a statement of special educational needs. Early identification of special educational needs was also deemed essential within the report, acknowledging that: 'all professionals who come into contact with young children must be helped, through their training, to identify those showing signs of having special needs or problems, and to appreciate the educational implications of their special needs' (ibid.: s. 4.17).

Observations will clearly support the processes of early identification and appropriate intervention. The Education Act (DES, 1981) adopted many of the Warnock Report's key areas and thus continued the underlying philosophy of early identification and provision, supported by ongoing observation and assessments.

### *Children's rights*

The United Nations Convention on the Rights of the Child acknowledges the rights of all children to education which should be free in the primary phase. It continues to state that:

The education of the child shall be directed to:
(a) The development of the child's personality, talents and mental and physical abilities to their fullest potential;
(b) The development of respect for human rights and fundamental freedoms;

(c) The development of respect for the child's parents, his or her own cultural identity, language and values, for the national values of the country in which the child is living, the country from which he or she may originate, and for civilizations different from his or her own;

(d) The preparation of the child for responsible life in a free society;

(e) The development of respect for the natural environment. (Internet 10: art. 29)

While it may not be explicit in the Convention, within the UK it could be suggested that to provide an education as thus defined it would be necessary to establish observation and assessment to ensure individual development to the fullest potential.

## Listening to the child

The Children Act (DoH, 1991) supports the importance of listening to the child, which is echoed in the Code of Practice (DfES, 2001d). This is an important consideration as it is often presumed that very young children are incapable of contributing to discussions regarding their education and learning, when in reality they have valid opinions which can inform practitioners. Children can complete simple questionnaires and respond to questions about the areas of learning they are involved in. Such information can then be used in planning and should be included in the reports compiled. If children are capable of contributing to the process of assessment then their views should be valued and respected. The Code of Practice also echoes the importance and value of consulting with children, concluding that:

> Ascertaining the child's views may not always be easy. Very young children and those with severe communication difficulties, for example, may present a significant challenge for education, health and other professionals. But the principle of seeking and taking into account the ascertainable views of the child or young person is an important one. (DfES, 2001d: s. 3.3)

## Practitioner requirements

Within the Early Learning Goals document (QCA, 1999: 5) practitioner responsibilities for observation and assessment processes are defined as: 'Practitioners must be able to observe and respond appropriately to children, informed by a knowledge of how children develop and learn'. This requirement is discussed alongside the need for practitioners to offer a 'well-planned and well organized learning environment' and 'well-planned, purposeful activity and appropriate intervention' (ibid.). So the value of observation begins to emerge as clearly linked to the learning environment as well as to individual children.

Through observing the children and/or the learning environment we can revise plans and, perhaps, changes to the environment, to improve provision. Subsequent observations will further inform, so the process is a continuing cycle.

The *Curriculum Guidance for the Foundation Stage* (QCA, 2000) recognises the importance of observation and assessment in relation to effective teaching and learning in early years settings. Practitioners are advised that: 'Assessment gives insight into children's interests, achievements and possible difficulties in their learning from which the next steps in learning and teaching can be planned. It also helps ensure early identification of special educational needs and particular abilities' (ibid.: 24). So practitioners should identify current performance levels in order to plan the next steps to ensure progression for all children and should not be focusing solely on identifying weaknesses and/or difficulties.

With particular reference to children with special needs, observation and assessment will be a part of our everyday work at each stage of provision. When initial concerns are raised, observation can help to clarify thinking and identify specific areas of difficulties as well as strengths, which can both be used to inform subsequent planning. At the stages of Early Years Action and Early Years Action Plus, observation will continue to play an important role, ensuring progression and monitoring the effectiveness of intervention strategies in place.

## Baseline assessments

Since September 1998 reception class teachers have been required to undertake baseline assessments of young children within the first seven weeks of starting school. We will see later, however, that this process is currently undergoing change. Guidance for schools via the DfES circular 6/98 stated that:

> The assessment should cover as a minimum the basic skills of speaking and listening, reading, writing, mathematics and personal and social development. Teachers will be able to use the information from the baseline assessments to plan their teaching to match individual children's needs. Over time, schools will be able to judge children's progress against this baseline. (Internet 11)

Since their inception, baseline assessments have been the subject of much debate, raising a concern regarding their appropriateness so soon after children enter the more formal school situation. For some children it will take considerably longer than seven weeks to adjust to their new environment and, thus, it was suggested that the results could represent an inaccurate picture of a child's current competences. No standard assessment scale was offered but accredited schemes were identified for teachers, resulting in an array of formats and a general lack of consistency nationwide. In addition, a narrow perspective band of 'subject areas' was assessed with little evidence of an holistic approach.

A subsequent QCA consultation document (Internet 12) on baseline assessments has resulted in changes planned for September 2002, when a new 'Foundation Stage Profile' will be introduced. This will be 'a new national assessment for the end of the foundation stage' (Internet 12) and it is hoped that the documentation and guidance will support an holistic early years philosophy, not rely totally on a one-off snapshot picture. It is clearly hoped that a revised system will eradicate some of the issues of concern, but there are still many early years specialists who remain concerned about the need for and value of formal assessments on very young children, as Pugh (2001: 74) summarises: 'Clearly, the only sensible move would be for baseline assessment in the early years of the 2000s to meet its demise, in favour of ongoing teacher assessment – fully supported by rich and challenging professional development.'

### *Ongoing observations and assessments*

Assessment, informed by observation, is a key feature within the Code of Practice (DfES, 2001d) stating that both are fundamental to effective and appropriate provision for children with special needs. Practitioner monitoring forms the basis of ongoing provision using baseline assessment outcomes, regular observational records, outcomes relating to the National Literacy and Numeracy objectives, key stage performance indicators and standardised assessments (ibid.: s. 5.13).

If provision for special needs progresses throughout the stages of Early Action, Early Action Plus, School Action and School Action Plus, outcomes and interventions will rely heavily on the observational processes built into the setting's practices. If a statement of special educational need follows, then observation and assessment will continue to play a major role in the work of practitioners. This will inform ongoing planning and interventions plus the annual review meeting where a range of assessment outcomes will be discussed as objective evidence of progress made and areas of difficulty being experienced. With this information professionals and parents can make informed decisions about the future.

The abilities required to be an effective observer are not necessarily inherent and training should be available to practitioners covering:

- purposes and values of observation and assessment
- principles of observation and assessment
- range of observational methods available
- considerations required prior to observing
- adapting teaching, individual education plans and planning as a result of observations
- need to involve parents and children.

The need for and requirements regarding observation and assessment are now clear, but a more detailed examination of some of the above areas will deepen understanding and awareness.

## Purposes and values of observation and assessment

In any early years settings children will be busy throughout the session or day, involved in a variety of child-led and adult-led activities. Practitioners provide appropriate learning experiences to foster and encourage children's development across the range of skill areas and undertake informal observations regularly. Within the working day it is often difficult for practitioners to be able to stand back and observe a child or a group, in a planned way as sufficient numbers of adults need to be present to ensure that the observer can be freed from their responsibilities and focus entirely on the observational process. Perhaps as practitioners our greatest reward is to watch children playing at and learning what interests them and marvel at their enthusiasm and natural curiosity, but through careful and systematic observation we can ensure we maximise the potential of the learning environment for all attending children and thus maximise their progress. Pugh supports the importance of observation and assessment concluding that:

> Observation and assessment are the essential tools of watching and learning by which we can both establish the progress that has already been made and explore the future – the learning that is still embryonic. The role of the adult in paying careful and informed attention to children's learning and reflecting upon it is crucial to the enhancement of children's future learning. (Pugh, 2001: 70)

If a child begins at an early years setting with identified special needs, then practitioners will need to communicate with parents to establish which professionals have been involved to date, gather information from any previous assessments and/or reports, plus, perhaps most importantly, the nature of the child's difficulties and the implications for the child within the setting. Ideally this should take place during a home visit when the parent(s) and child are in their own environment which would be reassuring and hopefully give the child confidence in the situation with a professional or, as for many families, yet another professional.

With all the information to hand practitioners can then begin to plan appropriate learning experiences for the child and, as their knowledge of the child develops, more information will emerge that can be used in planning to ensure the maximising of the learning opportunities and the environment.

Ireton devised the Child Development Inventories and Teacher's Observation Guide and suggested that:

> Young children's development is best appreciated by observing them in action in their everyday environments at home and in preschool. To make best use of their observations teachers need a systematic approach to observing what each child is doing. Observation guides, child development charts, and summary sheets are helpful tools for teachers. (Internet 13)

As previously mentioned, *observations can help to clarify a child's current levels of performance and skills mastered*, but it should be remembered that if interventions and provision are to be amended in the light of the observations then practitioners should not assume that if a child has not mastered a skill that he/she is incapable of doing so. We must check that the task is child appropriate (exactly at the right level to move the child forwards, thus stretching his/her knowledge and skills but without the risk of failure); capitalises on the child's interests; that as practitioners we are supportive and encourage positive reinforcement; that difficulties such as a child's emotional development and/or self-concept are not prohibiting the child from accessing the task; that the room encourages support and learning for that individual child and that our classroom management skills are effective. Perhaps this may seem an impossible task, but it could make the difference between success or failure for many children.

As an illustrative example: if a large group of young children is given the same worksheet to complete, then the child for whom the task is too difficult or too easy may become bored and restless. This may result in task-avoidance strategies or the manifestation of unacceptable behaviours. Two conclusions can be drawn from this scenario:

- the child has behaviour problems, or
- the task is inappropriate for the child.

Interpretation (or misinterpretation) of this simple example will clearly have significant effects on the child, practitioner and future planning. Therefore the skills of the observer, combined with their knowledge of the child and the setting will be paramount.

*Observations can be shared with parents* to discuss progress made and to consider parental observations from outside the setting. A child may demonstrate skills at home, but not in the setting, for a variety of reasons, including self-confidence. This information will help the practitioner to create a 'holistic' picture of the child. In addition, parents and practitioners can work together to maximise progress.

It may be that a child is reluctant to participate in dressing up due to issues of gender and/or culture, so the practitioner should seek information from discussions with parents. Information gained will then enable greater understanding on the part of the practitioner and setting, combined with an acknowledgement and respect of these important family factors. A child whose grandfather is seriously ill in hospital may be distressed with stories about doctors and/or role-play. With practitioner understanding these needs can easily be supported.

*Observational outcomes will also be shared with a range of supporting agencies* working with the child and the family. At progress review meetings or annual reviews for statements, evidence from all parties will be needed to inform further decision-making. Observational evidence will support this process with clear indicators of progress made, the child's likes and dislikes and strengths and weaknesses. When combined with reports from the child's parents and other professionals working with the child, the holistic picture can again emerge and inform decisions and planning.

Observations can be undertaken on:

- individual children – focusing on one or more specific areas of development or progress, e.g. social interactions
- groups of children – to focus on one or more area, e.g. abilities to share and take turns

- the whole group – to assess whether all children have mastered one skill, e.g. jumping with two feet together
- an area of the room – to assess whether the area is well used, appropriately used and what interactions occur there
- a practitioner – to assess an area of professional skill, e.g. appropriateness of interactions with the children.

Evidence from such observations could be included within a report for a meeting with parents and/or outside agencies as a way of sharing information about the child and his/her progress.

Thus the purposes and values of observation and assessment can be summarised as to:

- develop our own understanding of children's current competence levels (to assist with individual planning)
- reflect on the appropriateness of provision (tasks securing failure for some children, mismatch of curriculum)
- inform planning (organisation of room, session)
- inform others (parents/carers, outside professionals, staff)
- assess interactions (adult:child; child:child; adult:adult; child:adult)
- assess specific events (behaviour, speech and language, physical development, social interactions etc.)
- assess staff (performance, interactions with children, supporting children with activities etc.).

Information gathered can then to be used in our monitoring, evaluations and future planning, as Woods summarises:

> With the insight from the observations we are better equipped to:
> - devise optimum environments to promote the holistic development of each child and respond to his/her needs;
> - take appropriate action if any aspect of a child's development, behaviour, health or well-being causes us concern and does not appear to be within the range typical for his/her age;
> - interact more sensitively with children and form happy relationships with them;
> - monitor, evaluate and improve the provision we make for children, i.e. the care we give, the curriculum we devise and the outcomes we achieve. (Woods, 1998: 16)

# Principles of observation

The principles of effective and purposeful observation and assessment processes are interlinked with their purpose. If we have a clear understanding of the purpose of our intended observations then that will be our guiding principle. Bowers suggests useful key factors on which to base our decision regarding whether to observe, what and how to observe:

- Why do I need this information? What is the purpose of my efforts?
- Based on what I need to know, what kind of information will be helpful? Test scores? Written records? Works found in portfolios?
- How often and when do I need to collect such information, and how can I best assure the information is accurate and valid?

In addition, any method used should be selected for its appropriateness for the children on whom it will be used. Two important criteria are developmental appropriateness, e.g. 'Is it designed for the age of child I'm testing?' and cultural appropriateness, e.g. 'Is it relevant to the background and daily circumstances of the child?' (Internet 14)

As well as our own observational skills we have available to us a range of checklists and assessments that can be used by early years practitioners, for example the Portage developmental checklist (Bluma et al., 1976), the PreSchool Behaviour Checklist (McGuire and Richman, 1988), Playladders (Mortimer, 2000) and Griffiths Developmental Scale (Griffiths, 1970). These checklists can be used as they stand or, as in many instances, sections can be taken out as they are most appropriate to the individual setting and situation, in a 'mix and match' approach.

Before undertaking observations practitioners should ensure they have reflected on ethical issues, such as gaining permission from the child's parents and considering the responsibilities of the observer. Any parent has a right to refuse permission but this will be unlikely if the purposes and potential benefits are explained thoroughly as most parents will be supportive of initiatives that will encourage progress. The responsibilities of the observer would include consideration of the safety of the children, confidentiality, appropriate behaviour and perhaps, most importantly, entering the process with an open mind. If practitioners have preconceived ideas and/or expectations of the outcomes then there is be risk that outcomes will be affected, or worse, invalid.

The principles for observing and assessing can be summarised as the need for practitioners to:

- be clear on the need for and purpose of assessing
- ensure the appropriateness for the child
- ensure the process is meaningful
- consider ethical issues
- ensure the validity of outcomes
- use appropriate observational methods for the child and the setting
- consider the timing of the observation as children can perform differently in mornings to afternoons, and Mondays to Fridays
- ensure there is adequate staffing to free the observer from additional responsibilities if necessary
- be clear on how the outcomes will be disseminated, and to whom.

Perhaps the key to effective assessment is an understanding of the observational process as a whole, with thorough planning being central. Practitioners will need to work through the following stages:

1 Decide on the need and purpose.
2 Plan the process.
3 Be clear on ethical issues.
4 Begin assessment.
5 Reflect on outcomes.
6 Decide ways forward as supported by outcomes.
7 Adjust planning appropriately.
8 Monitor progress.

This process may resolve the issues under examination, in which case observations will cease to be needed or, if not, practitioners will need to revise the process. The effectiveness of the process will depend on careful planning and implementation, resulting in outcomes that positively inform future practices to the benefit of the child(ren), practitioners and parents alike.

## Methods of assessment 1 – observations

For most practitioners observation is a feature of everyday working life and practitioners can often be found with a notebook and pen close to hand to jot down unplanned observations that can be added to normal recording systems at a later time. However, as previously discussed, specific observations should be planned. Prior to beginning the observation practitioners should work through the stages outlined in the previous section and, as a part of this process, the most appropriate observational method should be selected from the range available. It will also be helpful to produce a cover sheet including such details as:

- child's name
- child's age
- date
- name of observer
- the specific setting or area of setting
- permissions gained
- aims and purpose of observation
- start and finish times.

Using a cover sheet attached to records of observations can be added to a child's general records as evidence to staff, parents and outside professionals of actions undertaken by the setting to evaluate an individual child's performance. When working with children with special needs records are crucial to enable all parties access to the information. When seeking the support and advice of outside professionals such evidence will provide accessible and useful information.

## Time sampling

This can be defined as the observer making a note of the child's actions and inter-actions at regular intervals over a set period of time. It may be that practitioners are concerned about the amount of time a child spends at the sand tray and the time sampling approach will enable collation of evidence. It may be that the child is observed every ten minutes throughout a session of three hours, on a Tuesday morning and a Thursday afternoon, giving over 36 recorded entries during the period. At each ten-minute interval the observer will note exactly where the child is in the room, or simply place a tick or cross on the record sheet to indicate whether he/she is at the sand tray or not. The outcomes of such an observation will clarify to the staff (and others) the amount of time spent at sand play and action can be considered. Perhaps removing the sand tray from the activities available to the children two or three days a week will encourage increased involvement in alternative activities. So, through this relatively straightforward approach the child's opportunities, and thus potential, can be extended. If staff are also concerned about the child's interactions with others, then the process can record with whom he/she is interacting and the nature of the interaction.

Time sampling is also useful to investigate aspects of the learning environment. For example, staff at the setting may be concerned about the lack of use made of the book corner and a time-sampling approach can be used in the same way as in the example above, to note if there are children using the book corner or not at the preset intervals. If results indicate that the book corner is used for a minimum amount of session time, then the staff can devise ways to make alter-ations to encourage greater usage. Similarly, if the quality of language used in the book corner is a concern, then this can be recorded at the same time intervals.

Devereux (1996: 83) identifies the key uses of time sampling as: 'particularly useful for tracking children's activities and interactions over a period of time, for building up a picture of particular children, and for appraising the value and use of equipment'.

## Event/frequency sampling

Event or frequency sampling is useful when practitioners wish to clarify their understanding of a specific event as it records the frequency of an event. As an example, if we are observing a child's unacceptable behaviour, for example hitting another child, the information can be used as a baseline. A programme or strategies can be implemented to reduce this behaviour and possibly encour-age an alternative behaviour. Then at a later date the observations can be repeated, hopefully to highlight the improvement in behaviours demonstrated and success of the intervention. Recording can take the form of a simple tick sheet to indicate the number of times the behaviour occurs or more details can be included, such as time of day, antecedents, consequences, whether an adult was present and so on. Additional information will enable more individualised strategies to be introduced. For example, if the child only hits one other child when that child interferes with his/her play, practitioners would need to consider which child the strategies should be aimed at. Results of the initial observation can be presented within a report as a simple table of 'scores' or as a graph or chart (Figure 5.1):

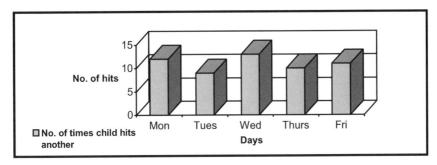

**Figure 5.1** Baseline observations

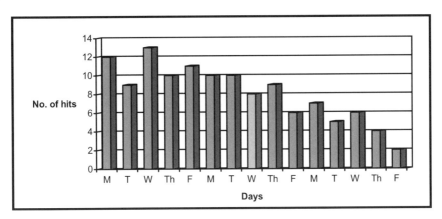

**Figure 5.2** Baseline and intervention observations

When strategies have been implemented graphical representation clearly summarises the process, as in Figure 5.2, where the first week was the period of baseline measurement and during the second and third weeks the intervention strategies were in place. The outcome of the process is that the number of times the child hit another is successfully being reduced.

## Illustrative example

The results of such observations can inform practice greatly, as in my own experience a child's hitting out and anger was observed by event sampling, but in addition to recording the number of times the child hit out at another the antecedents were noted. It became clear that the child reacted this way when the group was asked to tidy up and he was in the middle of a task or project, such as building a garage from bricks and another child began clearing the equipment away. The strategy that supported this child was to speak to him five minutes before tidying up time and decide on how to store or protect his work until later, if not finished. Incidents of hitting out and anger reduced dramatically. A significant discovery was made through the observational process and the learning environment was successfully adapted to suit his individual needs with very little effort from anyone.

Time sampling and event sampling are both relatively straightforward to undertake and give precise data to work with, however, finding the time to complete observations within a busy setting may not be so easy, as additional staff may need to be brought in to cover. In addition it is not easy to remain detached from the children and focus solely on the observations in hand and the children themselves may make it difficult by constantly asking you to help or support them, as you would usually do during the session. Children are not used to staff members sitting on the perimeter of the room and writing, instead of playing and working with them.

## Focused or target child observations

A full, detailed written record of a child's movements during a predetermined time can offer practitioners a full account of:

- which specific activities the child has selected
- which area(s) of the learning environment he/she has been working in
- with whom he/she has interacted
- with whom he/she has spoken
- evidence of expressive language used.

While observing a child in this way it is useful to have a watch nearby and to note the time at frequent intervals, clarifying the exact time spent at each activity. To ease notation, codes can be evolved which should be written on the record sheet for clarity of understanding by others. Possible codes could include:

| | |
|---|---|
| TC = target child | A1, A2, A3 ... = adults |
| B1, B2, B3 ... = another boy | AC = art corner |
| G1, G2, G3 ... = another girl | HC = home corner |
| ST = sand tray | P = cooperative play |
| BP = brick play | SP = solitary play |
| BC = book corner | PP = parallel play |
| PT = puzzle table | |

As a result of the observations strategies can be implemented to promote changes for the child, the practitioners and/or the setting.

## *Illustrative example*

Through the process of focused observation minor changes were made to the learning environment and planning for a three-and-a-half-year-old boy, Adam. Adam was generally perceived to be lacking in application to tasks other than cars, lorries and train play, and had a tendency to run from one end of the room to the other regardless of who or what was blocking his way. He had been referred to an early years special needs unit as the local pre-school group could not cope with his 'disruptive behaviour'. While these behaviours could be deemed age appropriate for a two-year-old, they were clearly impeding his opportunities to access the learning environment in a meaningful way. The observation over a 45-minute period was repeated three times during one week and identified the following key issues:

- Adam spent his time flitting between activities, but rarely settled to any activity for more than three/four minutes at a time. (This could also be represented in graphical form – see Figures 5.3 and 5.4.)
- Adam did not once walk around the room – each time he got up to move elsewhere, he ran.
- Adam mostly avoided all table-top activities such as puzzles, sharing or turn-taking games, cutting and sticking, art, colouring or writing-based activities.
- Adam resisted attempts by adults to participate in table-top activities.
- At any time that Adam remained at a table-top activity he needed immediate success or he was unable to cope and would leave the table.
- Adam needed to be in control of any activity he was involved in and did not appear aware of interrupting other children's play and sometimes annoying the children.
- Adam's speech and language skills were advanced for his age.

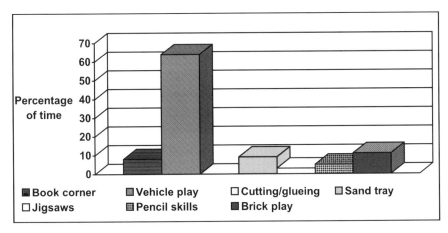

**Figure 5.3** Baseline observations – percentage of time spent at each activity.

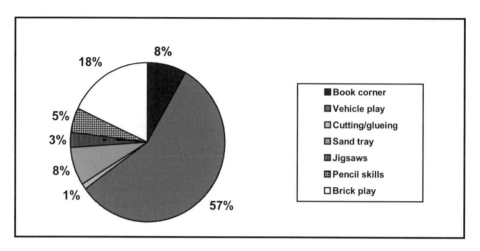

**Figure 5.4** Baseline observations – percentage of time spent at each activity.

Through these and subsequent observations designed to focus more specifically on certain aspects of Adam's performance the following key issues were highlighted:

• Adam did not have the necessary skills to participate successfully in the table-top activities.
• Adam's social skills were delayed or he was demonstrating inappropriate social skills.
• Adam felt a need to run between activities.
• Adam particularly enjoyed activities involving a range of vehicles.
• Adam demonstrated good imaginative skills in his vehicle play.
• Adam demonstrated good creative skills in his building with bricks or Duplo – but these mostly centred on roads, rails, tunnels and bridges.

As a result the staff discussed Adam's progress with his parents to suggest possible ways forward. The following strategies were employed:

• The layout of tables in the room was changed to limit free running space.
• Whole-group and small-group activities were planned into the curriculum around a theme of 'fast and slow vehicles'. This had a dual purpose of capitalising on Adam's love of vehicles and also exploring slow and fast movements.
• One-to-one activities were planned and introduced to help develop Adam's skills required for the successful completion of table-top activities, such as turn-taking, sharing, achieving success and patience. This was supported by increased praise as positive reward.
• Role-plays and stories were used to develop Adam's awareness of appropriate and inappropriate social interactions, with adults and Adam's peers acting as positive role models.

Adam's behaviour and progress within the group situation improved consistently and in some areas surpassed expectations. It became apparent to the staff that he had somehow 'missed' some stages of skill development and simply needed steps to be retraced and strategies introduced. For example, it was soon clear that rather than not having the patience to complete a jigsaw, he simply did not know how to tackle the task. The steps needed to complete a jigsaw were introduced to Adam in small stages to ensure success, and within weeks he had advanced from six-piece jigsaws to 50+ pieces – a very pleasing outcome for the staff and Adam's parents alike.

It was the carefully planned and instigated processes of observation that enabled this structured response to Adam's very individual needs yet many of the activities implemented were also of benefit to the other children in the group. Through the sharing of information with parents at every stage of the process, changes were also implemented within the home that further supported Adam's development. The information gathered was further shared with Adam's health visitor at his progress review meeting so all parties involved were informed and able to support the process.

## Sociograms

Continuing to assess Adam, a sociogram could have been used to develop greater understanding of Adam's social interactions. A record would have been established and observations carried out for a set period of time to note, for example who he shared time with, the nature of the interactions and what verbal interactions took place. Again this could be represented graphically if desired and even reflect gender relationships or type of play Adam was involved in (Figure 5.5). While a sociogram can clearly focus on one particular area of development, practitioners should note that children's friendships and favoured playmates can fluctuate on a fairly regular basis and this should be reflected in any interpretation of the data.

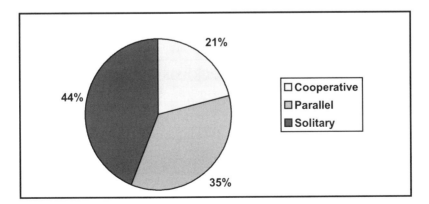

**Figure 5.5** Types of play

## *Movement/tracking charts*

These are a rapid method of noting a child's movements during a set period and can be easily interpreted. Starting with a basic sketch of the room layout, arrows and times can be added to indicate a child's movements between activities so that conclusions can be drawn about how many activities are approached and the length of time spent at each. If subsequent movement charts are taken at different times of the day and the week then a fuller picture will emerge, but as can be seen in Figure 5.6, the mass of arrows can be very difficult to interpret easily and if the times were added onto this chart it would appear even more muddled. If we reflect on Adam (previously highlighted) and his difficulty with rapid and brief times spent at activities the chart would have been very confusing. In addition, the same information can be elicited from a target child/focused observation.

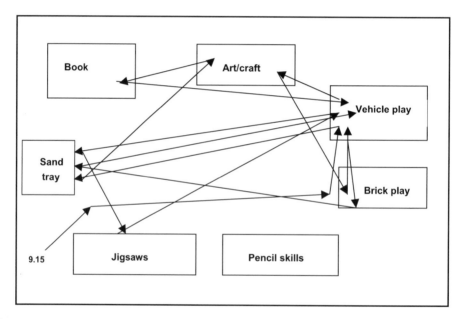

**Figure 5.6** Movement sample chart

# Methods of assessment 2 – checklists and questionnaires

Checklists are often the preferred choice of early years practitioners and are viewed by some as easier to implement and interpret. However, certain considerations should be reflected upon before relying on checklists for assessment evidence. First, checklists only offer a snapshot picture of what a child can do, on that day and at that particular time, and tend to note achieved milestones. So, for those children experiencing complex special needs, by nature of the large gaps, they equally represent the skills a child has not mastered. If the checklists do not cover, for example, every physical skill, then only those checked can be commented on. A checklist may indicate that a child can hop, jump, run and catch a large ball at 2 metres but may not show whether the child can pedal a tricycle. Caution should therefore be employed in the interpretation of outcomes if a thorough understanding of a child's development is required as opposed to a snapshot picture. Within the philosophy of holistic provision for young children checklists can be interpreted as more like a preordained assessment check that clearly does not fit with an holistic philosophy. Secondly, checklists are created around a sequential approach to development and assume that all children will proceed through the defined stages in much the same systematic order. Practitioners working with young children with special needs, or any early years children, will be aware that not all children progress this way. However, despite reservations, developmental checklists are used within many early years settings and do have some usefulness, for example, baseline assessments.

Usually presented in tabular form checklists are generally easy to interpret and therefore accessible to all, but they can also be represented pictorially so the children themselves can be involved in recording their own progress (see Figures 5.7 and 5.8).

| NAME | Hops X4 | Jumps from 50 cm | Climbs 6 steps | | |
|---|---|---|---|---|---|
| Ian | | | √ | | |
| Mark | e | √ | √ | | |
| Michael | | √ | √ | | |
| Kate | | e | √ | | |
| Tracy | e | √ | √ | | |
| Samantha | | √ | √ | | |
| Rowan | e | e | √ | | |
| | | | | | |
| | | | | | |

**Figure 5.7**  An example of a tabular checklist, (**e** = emerging skill)

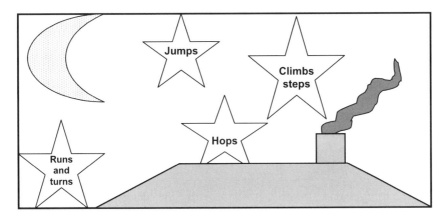

**Figure 5.8**  An example of a pictorial checklist

Strategies needed to support children who need to develop particular skills further can be devised and implemented using the evidence from the checklists which can be updated regularly as part of an ongoing monitoring process.

Some local authorities may have their own checklists, either self-created or taken from a standardised checklist, for use within all registered settings or within special needs settings. Portage workers base all their work on the portage developmental checklists (Bluma et al., 1976) covering all skill areas and breaking down tasks into achievable steps to ensure success. Health visitors and speech and language therapists will use their own specific checklists or screening tools to monitor children's progress. Mortimer (2000) has devised the Playladders checklists, originally created for use in early years settings and using existing checklists as a foundation. They are designed to avoid the developmental checklist approach in favour of approaching observation and assessment from the realities of children's activities. Mortimer summarises the process:

> Early years educators are encouraged to play alongside the child as part of their regular activities within a group of children. By observing how a child is playing, it becomes easy to visualize and record the stage on the playladder later, once the children have left. Play thus proceeds uninterrupted by the assessment and recording. Once the play behaviour is recorded on the checklist, a 'next step on the ladder' is suggested, and this new skill can be encouraged or taught at a future play session. (Mortimer, 2001: 125)

Mortimer's particular approach fits in well with the Foundation Stage's breaking down of steps into achievable targets to ensure success for all children.

# Methods of assessment 3 – observing through play

Much debating continues surrounding the difference between play and learning, but current thinking supports the view that learning through play, with appropriate support or 'scaffolding' by adults, is an ongoing process in which all young children participate, be it the baby who places everything into his/her mouth as part of early discovery, or the child who struggles to build a bridge to pass trains under and, through a process of elimination combined with trial and error, learns about shape, size, balance and develops fine motor skills. If we therefore accept that much learning transpires from play situations then it seems sensible to find ways of recording evidence through observing children at play.

One of the problems with observing play is objectivity. As adults we may assume we understand what a child is doing and learning in a play situation, but it may be difficult to assess progress and record it in a meaningful manner. Moyles suggests:

> The problem appears to be that human beings are all unique and all perceive situations in different ways, depending upon their own experiences, expectation, attitudes and values and, therefore, interpretation of what individuals

observe and what they assess as progress will be different from person to person as we each operate our own selection systems. (Moyles, 1989: 101)

Perhaps the key is to be clear on our intended learning outcomes for play-based activities and from this we should be able to identify if outcomes have been met or not, thus informing future planning. If, for example, a setting is working within a theme or topic entitled 'Travel', then the activities will have been planned and the early learning goals to be addressed identified. One activity may involve planning and building a railway station, with accompanying railway lines, buildings and interconnecting roads. There will be a range of learning objectives that such an activity will support and, once these have been identified, outcomes can be matched against them. Record sheets can be devised to note the learning objectives and evidence of the children's outcomes that can then inform future planning. Observational methods can be selected according to their appropriateness for the task.

Practitioners support a child's learning through skilfully intervening to encourage progression to the next stage of learning. This lies within a Vygotskian philosophy that suggests children have a 'zone of proximal development' indicating their learning potential, with adult support. This philosophy encouraged further research into the effects of adult input on the development of young children. It should be remembered that practitioners, often feeling pressured by legislation and requirements, may feel inclined to direct or lead children's play, learning, progress and development too much by telling them what to do next or informing them how to overcome obstacles they are facing without giving them the time and opportunity to discover solutions for themselves. Perhaps more useful and practical learning will take place through a child's own process of trial and error and elimination. Identifying the problem and trying to discover ways around it can often produce more lasting knowledge and skills.

Practitioners can play alongside a child and then use the Playladders approach to recording, or take notes throughout the period, which can be transcribed in more detail later if required. Alternatively, an adult can observe a child playing with another adult and make detailed observations. Sometimes this approach has the benefit of enabling greater objectivity and can highlight issues surrounding the practitioner and his/her approach, as opposed to the child's development. Subsequent observational records can then be shared with parents and other practitioners at progress review meetings. In addition, discussions after the observation could highlight different adult interpretations of the same event.

Play therapy, for children with specific difficulties, has become an increasingly favoured approach, particularly when providing for children who have been abused or those experiencing emotional, social and/or behavioural difficulties. Play therapy requires the support of highly trained play therapists who have specialist skills in this area and is not for use by the unqualified practitioner, although play in general may be perceived as a therapeutic approach as well as a learning experience.

# Methods of assessment 4 – involving the children

Since the Children Act (DoH, 1991) children have had a right to be heard, but perhaps there is an assumption that very young children are not mature enough, knowledgeable or verbally capable of contributing anything of value to our observations and assessments. It must also be acknowledged that there are discrete differences between listening to and truly hearing and understanding what a child is saying. The Code of Practice (DfES, 2001d: s. 3.2) clearly highlights the importance of involving children in decision-making processes at every stage of their provision: '(The children) should, where possible, participate in all the decision-making processes that occur in education including the setting of learning targets and contributing to IEP's, discussion about choice of schools, contributing to the assessment of their needs and to the annual review and transition processes.'

For very young children with special needs difficulties may occur due to limited verbal skills and recording skills, but ways can be developed by which children can be empowered and feel a part of the process. Knowing a child's likes and dislikes can enable more successful progress through heightened motivation for the child to participate, so it would be of greater use to plan activities that the child would prefer, to achieve targets, than to continually present them with tasks they do not particularly enjoy. As we saw earlier Adam's likes and dislikes were identified and used successfully within future planning, benefiting all the children in his setting.

For very young children likes and dislikes can be discovered through simple pictorial records, which can be added to the child's records and shared with parents and other practitioners. Simple drawings or photographs of a range of common activities can be presented alongside three faces – one happy, one indifferent and one sad. The activity can be discussed with the child and then he/she could colour in the appropriate face to indicate preferences. To ensure understanding, an adult could complete a similar chart alongside the child, making sure that the child is not simply copying the adult's selections. With the advent of information technology (IT) and the extensive IT skills of many practitioners, the production of such charts would be straightforward, but children are generally quite happy with an adult's attempts at drawing, however limited and inaccurate they may be. If practitioners do not feel able to produce a recording sheet then there may be a parent or friend of the setting who is willing to help. It should not, however, be forgotten that children have a tendency to want to please the adult and may give the responses they think the adult wants to hear.

Young children can also be involved in progress recording through progress books, collecting and presenting evidence of their work in portfolios, responding to interviews (to identify their likes, dislikes, views) and through the self-completion of charts as previously described. In my own experience, sticker books (made from sugar paper) were a successful way of involving children as they helped to make their own book and they were allowed to enter at least one smile each time they attended, with an adult adding the reason for this success. When supporting children with behavioural, social, emotional and/or self-esteem diffi-culties, many smiles were added on a daily basis to celebrate achievements (no matter how small) and to encourage continued progress and effort.

Circle time can be a valuable tool to facilitate listening to others and even chil-dren with limited or no communication skills or withdrawn children can still participate, albeit in a different way. If appropriate, the practitioner can tell the group what the child has achieved and how much effort they have made. This way all children can be positively rewarded through the respect of being heard and their efforts being acknowledged and valued.

## Methods of assessment 5 – children's behaviour

Children demonstrating unacceptable behaviours can be supported in early years settings through observation and appropriate interventions. While approaches to behaviour difficulties will be discussed in greater detail in Chapter 7, there are a few key points relevant here.

First, it should be remembered that children develop and learn inappropriate behaviours, they are not born with them, and, secondly, the behaviours are the problem and not the child. If a child is persistently told he/she is naughty or unkind then the self-fulfilling prophecy can allow that child to remain naughty or unkind, and it may well be that the negative adult responses received are exactly the reinforcement necessary for the child to continue demonstrating the same behaviours.

In my own experience I have received many children into the special needs setting with behavioural problems. If we are not careful, practitioner expectations can severely compromise our responses to the child. If we are convinced the child will continually 'be a handful', 'be naughty', 'be difficult' and achieve little, then our provision may well reflect this. Through detailed observations over a period of time intervention strategies can be designed and put in place to reduce the unacceptable behaviours and increase acceptable behaviours. It may be that a combination of event sampling, time sampling and target-child observations are undertaken to give a detailed overview of the child's current difficulties and the issues surrounding them. The outcomes could highlight problems with practi-tioners, the setting, the tasks and/or the behaviours, and each should be carefully reflected upon before intervention strategies are devised. In addition, the child should be considered within the wider context and all the possible causal factors leading to the behaviours identified. Some of these may well be beyond our control or intervention, but most we will be able to address.

Links between behavioural difficulties, academic achievement and low self-concept have been highlighted consistently over several decades, as summarised by Lambley:

Pupils who lack success in learning often react to failure by non-involvement strategies. Their withdrawal of effort can show in various forms: total lack of motivation and retreat into dullness and laziness; avoidance strategies (such as distraction, fidgeting, day-dreaming) or resistance to the learning task expressed in actions such as antagonistic and aggressive behaviour. (Lambley, 1993: 86)

At all times, practitioners must be prepared to examine all possible causal factors including their own practices and appropriateness of the tasks offered to the child to support a child experiencing behaviour difficulties. Observation will play a key role in this process.

## Profiling

Profiles of young children and their progress are commonplace in early years settings. Each child will have individual records kept including:

- basic information and details
- entry profile
- previous involvement with other professionals
- intervention strategies employed
- stages of Early Years Action or Early Years Action Plus
- parental information gathered
- records of progress review meetings.

In addition, evidence of work undertaken and progress made will generally be kept, linked to the early learning goals, which may include photographic, video or audiotape records.

Many early years settings will undertake a home visit before a child begins attendance, during which the parent will be asked basic information about their child. This should include the child's fears, self-confidence, likes and dislikes and self-help skills which will help the practitioner to prepare for the child's entry, thus making the transition as smooth as possible for the parent(s) as well as the child. For children with special needs the information would extend to cover copies of previous assessments or referrals and details relating to the child's particular areas of difficulty and the specific implications this may have for the setting and the planning of activities. This will be the start of the child's profile of development.

As time progresses, a child's profile will naturally increase considerably in size, but will contain a thorough and detailed catalogue of past, current and future progress made and all plans and strategies that have been implemented. In today's climate of inclusive 'educare', practitioners who have identified a child as experiencing difficulties will have the profile to inform any outside professional who may become involved. This will be a complete and informative record on which to base discussions. When discussing progress or issues with parents, having the child's work as evidence to support points being made should support a clearer understanding. Such profiles are also a method of satisfying the requirements of the Foundation Stage as they log each child's progress in an accessible manner.

# Summary

The purposes and values of effective observations as part of an ongoing assessment process have been highlighted, indicating that all practitioners have a duty and responsibility to monitor the progress of each child in a way that is accessible to parents, children and other professionals. A range of observational methods has been offered for consideration, with clear guidelines as to the practical and ethical issues that must be taken into account before embarking upon any such process. Effective observation will greatly inform practice and ultimately benefit the child, ensuring that the plans and interventions that follow have been informed through an examination of a range of information relating to the child's current levels of performance and considering all factors that may compound or enhance future progress.

Practitioners with a thorough knowledge of child development should undertake child observations and assessments to monitor progress. If children are experiencing difficulties, or additional difficulties, then observations will support early identification and appropriate intervention. If a practitioner needs to refer a child to an outside professional, or discuss progress with parents, then evidence of observations and assessments undertaken will support those discussions.

It should be stressed that observations must be based around the child, within the child's world, and take into account all possible influencing factors on the child's progress and development. The more natural the observational setting, the more natural the responses of the child are likely to be. Effective observations and assessments should continue as an ongoing, cyclical process to ensure the most appropriate provision is made available to our youngest, and perhaps most vulnerable, children. If early identification is viewed as essential, then observations and assessments should be deemed equally as essential.

---

### Key issues

* ❖ Observations and assessments are a part of everyday working practice.
* ❖ Practitioners will need a thorough knowledge of child development and observational methods to undertake and evaluate observations.
* ❖ Observations should have a clear purpose, be manageable and inform planning.
* ❖ Children and parents should be involved in the process.

---

## Some suggestions for discussion

### Item 1

Reflect on one child within your setting that is causing concern. List the reasons for this concern and try to identify the most appropriate observational method to enable clarification and subsequent interventions.

### Item 2

Reflect on the layout of your main activity room and discuss how observations of learning areas may help to develop an improved learning environment for the children in your setting. Identify one area of the activity room that you would consider would benefit from change. Identify how you would observe and what outcomes you might expect. Implement the observation and compare the outcomes with your anticipated outcomes.

### Item 3

Are the parents aware of ongoing observations and assessments that take place? If not, how could this situation be improved, to ensure all parents are included in the process?

### Item 4

Discuss this question as a staff: Does your assessment process have a clear purpose or is it undertaken to satisfy government requirements?

## 📖 Suggested further reading

Hobart, C., and Frankel, J. (1994) *A Practical Guide to Child Observation and Assessment,* 2nd edn. Cheltenham: Stanley Thornes.

Mortimer, H. (2001) *Special Needs and Early Years Provision.* London: Continuum. (Chapter 8.)

Moyles, J. (1989) *Just Playing? The Role and Status of Play in Early Childhood Education.* Milton Keynes: Open University Press. (Chapter 7.)

# 6

## Programmes of Intervention

## Introduction

In the preceding chapter we considered the need for regular observations and assessments within our work with children with special needs. To be meaningful, observations need to inform our planning and any intervention programmes or strategies we wish to put in place to support progress.

It is now widely acknowledged that early intervention is essential to ensure all children are given opportunities to achieve their full potential. In this chapter a range of intervention programmes that could be used in an early years setting to respond to the identified needs of a child or children are examined. Programmes and suggestions for supporting children with speech and language difficulties and children with autistic spectrum disorders are explored in detail as exemplars to demonstrate how and why programmes could be individually tailored to meet specific needs. This is achieved partly through description and partly through case studies, and leads to a discussion of issues and practical and realistic strategies for practitioner use.

## Definitions

An intervention is an interaction between two people to bring about change and, therefore, early years practitioners undertake interventions each time they are working with children. Interventions may be short, medium or long term and will be planned carefully to ensure effectiveness and appropriateness. In the scenario where children enter a new setting, some may find parental separation distressing. The supportiveness of staff and encouragement to participate in the range of activities available will be planned in the adult's mind before action is taken. Even if it may not have been planned in a formal way, through normal recording systems, this support is nevertheless an intervention strategy.

At the other end of the scale we could consider a child with severe autism who has long-term and very specific needs. Interventions for this child will be discussed in advance and committed to paper through short-, medium- and long-term goals and plans, which will form the child's IEP. This will be monitored and reviewed regularly, with parental and outside professional input and discussions, and will be informed by observations and assessments undertaken. Any interventions will have considered the needs of the child and the best use of resources (human as well as learning materials) to encourage progress. One-to-one adult support will not always be necessary but will be considered as part of the planning process. As the Code of Practice (DfES, 2001d: s. 4.26) suggests: 'The key lies in effective individualised arrangements for learning and teaching.'

## Effective interventions

### *Key features*

As previously outlined, interventions are part of a cyclical process and cannot exist on their own (see Figure 6.1).

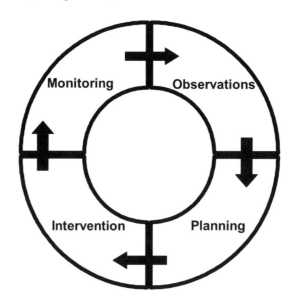

**Figure 6.1** Intervention as part of a cyclical process

In today's inclusive climate all practitioners will be working towards providing appropriate opportunities for each child within their setting, so adapting tasks to suit individual needs is an integral aspect of the practitioner's role. Considering children with special needs as somehow different from this can exclude them and is not, therefore, inclusive.

To ensure our adaptations are effective, practitioners need to be clear of their intentions and should therefore consider the following questions:

- Why is adaptation necessary?
- What are you aiming to achieve?
- How will you measure the success or effectiveness?

- How will this be planned and executed?
- Is this a short-, medium- or long-term adaptation?
- How will the adaptations and outcomes be recorded and where?
- Who will need to be informed?

With the new child who is experiencing difficulties separating from his/her parent, the adaptation or intervention will hopefully be relatively short term and will need little prior planning and organisation, nevertheless there is a need to record the events in the child's profile or records as this difficulty in adapting to a new situation may be indicative of other social and/or emotional difficulties. In the future, if subsequent difficulties arise, the information recorded may be pertinent and help practitioners and parents to understand the new situation and thus inform any new interventions deemed necessary.

As practitioners need to be accountable to parents, other professionals and the government (local and national), the recording of any interventions to show effectiveness (or otherwise) is a requirement, not simply a suggestion. Through consistent monitoring and evaluation of intervention strategies employed, practitioners will be able to satisfy these requirements, which will be indicative of the effects of the interventions used.

## Legislation and guidance

The new inclusive schooling statutory guidance offers the following structure for practitioners implicitly acknowledging the role of effective observation and intervention:

> in planning and teaching the National Curriculum teachers have a responsibility for:
> - setting suitable learning opportunities;
> - responding to pupils' diverse learning needs; and
> - overcoming potential barriers to learning and assessment for individuals and groups of pupils. (DfES, 2001b: 4)

Linked to the Code of Practice (DfES, 2001d) the inclusive schooling document offers guidance for children over statutory school age, but it could be suggested that the guidance is indicative of good practice and is therefore relevant to working in the pre-school phase. The graduated response within the Code of Practice also highlights the importance of effective observation, assessment and intervention for children experiencing difficulties:

> Children making slower progress may include those who are learning English as an additional language or who have particular learning difficulties. It should not be assumed that children who are making slower progress must, therefore, have special educational needs. But such children will need carefully differentiated learning opportunities to help them progress and regular and frequent careful monitoring of their progress. (DfES, 2001d: s. 4.8)

In the same vein, *The Early Learning Goals* highlight the need for practitioners to offer: 'Well planned, purposeful activity and appropriate intervention to children' (QCA, 1999: 5). Also emphasised is the need for partnerships with parents, so an awareness and recognition of the need to involve parents at all stages of the intervention process is necessary. Parents may be able to support the intervention suggested by the setting within the home and, through regular feedback, progress at each setting can be monitored. This would again fit in with the holistic view of provision.

Throughout the current legislation and guidance, we are reminded of the cyclical process of observation, planning, intervention and monitoring outlined previously and the manner in which each element is embedded within the others. These are not separate and discrete but part of the ongoing working practices of early years practitioners.

The features of effective interventions can be summarised as:

• part of an ongoing, cyclical process
• responding appropriately to legislation and guidance
• responding appropriately to individual needs
• having measurable outcomes
• involving and informing parents and other professionals.

## Differentiating the curriculum

When practitioners adapt or 'differentiate' the curriculum for individual children they will use the information gained from observations and assessments to inform subsequent planning. Using a child's known likes and dislikes, appropriate resources and materials can be incorporated that will motivate the child. In a similar way, knowing a child's preferred learning style can inform planning. If these aspects are combined with knowledge of the appropriate level at which individual steps need to be taken to ensure success and progress, then intervention should be effective. In previous chapters Adam was introduced, whose special needs were supported through interventions that reflected each of the above issues and were meaningful and offered him success. Systematic recording at each stage enabled clarity of understanding for all adults within and outside the setting, and transferring details into progress review reports was then a straightforward process. The recording also enabled another adult to continue with the work if Adam's key worker was absent.

Setting appropriate targets or teaching objectives will be essential when differentiating the curriculum for an individual child and, again, these can be shared with and supported by parents. Webster and McConnell offer practical suggestions for working with speech and language difficulties and support the importance of clear objectives:

There are several good reasons to set down a clear profile of teaching objectives. In the first place, there may be many professionals, other than teachers, involved with the child and objectives should be agreed upon through discussion so that targets to aim for are clear to all concerned. Secondly identification of what it is hoped the child will learn provides a framework for evaluating progress over time. (Webster and McConnell, 1987: 164)

Using Adam's situation as an exemplar, the following teaching objectives and strategies were developed to support the development of his jigsaw skills:

Aim: For Adam to complete a six-piece puzzle unaided by half-term.
Strategies:

- To sit with an adult for up to five minutes to work on jigsaws.
- Every positive response to be rewarded verbally by the adult.
- On completion of his time maximum, to be given sticker.
- The adult to explain each stage prior to commencing.
- Adam to undertake as much of the task as he is able, with the adult withdrawing physical support as his skills develop.
- Adam to share his successes at circle time and take a jigsaw home to work on with his parents.

This step-by-step approach was discussed by staff at a meeting with Adam's parents and they were able to support the intervention within the home. They also appreciated their involvement and were able to transfer the skills they developed at the planning and intervention stages into other learning areas within the home with great success. Their response was very positive for Adam but, perhaps as importantly, for themselves as they felt supported in their desire to encourage their son's progress and informed staff that their new-found abilities were useful in so many other areas of home life, improving life for the whole family. They concluded: 'It was so easy once they showed us how to break it down into steps.'

The Foundation Stage guidance (QCA, 2000) clearly breaks down learning for each of the six areas of learning into 'stepping stones' which are good examples indicating how tasks can be divided into manageable sections for the child. However, it must be remembered that practitioners may need to break down stages even further for children with special needs, as their individual requirements may demand more graduated stepping stones to develop some skills. The SEN Toolkit (DfES, 2001e) was produced for use alongside the SEN Code of Practice (DfES, 2001d) and section 5 offers a wealth of accessible information for practitioners regarding managing individual education plans. Included within the Toolkit (DfES, 2001e) is the suggestion of using SMART (Specific, Measurable, Achievable, Relevant and Time bound) targets within IEPs. To suggest a target of: 'Adam will improve his ability with jigsaws' is neither specific, measurable, achievable, relevant or time bound. However the target could be rephrased to satisfy the SMART target criteria: 'By half-term Adam will be able to complete a six-piece jigsaw.' All targets should be formulated as SMART targets if possible.

## Individual Education Plans

If a child's difficulties have not responded to initial intervention strategies, then the graduated response outlined within the Code of Practice (DfES, 2001d) will commence with Early Years Action. At this stage information will be collected from parents and any other professionals involved with the child, and practitioners, along with the SENCO, will be in an informed position to suggest ways forward. Formalising future plans will involve the creation of an IEP which will be drawn up in accordance with the requirements of the Code of Practice (DfES, 2001d: s. 4.27): 'this (the IEP) should include information about the short-term targets set for the child, the teaching strategies and the provision to be put in place, when the plan is to be reviewed, and the outcome of the action taken'.

The IEP will make it clear to all involved exactly how the curriculum is being adapted to accommodate the individual difficulties of the child. It should be noted that the IEP relates only to those adaptations that are different from or otherwise additional to the curriculum offered to all the children. However, this approach has a sense of 'remediation' about it as we are veering towards compensating for the child's problems as opposed to enabling them access to the curriculum. It could be suggested that such a backward step in thinking and practice would be detrimental to the progress of SEN provision. If inclusion is the way forward, we do not want to regress to remediation packages. The SEN Toolkit suggests:

> The IEP should include information about:
> • the short-term targets set for and by the pupil
> • the teaching strategies to be used
> • the provision to be put in place
> • when the plan is reviewed
> • success and/or exit criteria
> • outcomes (to be recorded when IEP is reviewed). (DfES, 2001e: 7)

While there is no set format for IEPs, which should be clear and to the point, they should identify what and how progress is to be achieved. The format can be individual to the setting, created by a group of local settings through the local early years forum or network or set by the LEA. Using the expertise and skills of a greater range of practitioners can save reinventing the wheel and incorporate an increased diversity of experience. In addition, a combined IEP format would produce consistency for feeder schools. A key issue regarding the management of IEPs is that of being achievable and manageable. They should not become paper exercises that take SENCOs away from their crucial work with the children and staff. The SEN Toolkit suggests:

the procedures for devising IEP's and reviewing them must be manageable. The IEP should be considered within the context of the overall class management of all pupils and staff.

Timeslots for delivery of the IEP should be realistic and integral to classroom and curriculum planning.

All IEP's must be achievable for both the pupil and the teacher. Targets should be in small steps so that success is clearly visible to the pupil, the parents and the teacher. (DfES, 2001e: s. 5, p. 8)

All IEPs should be reviewed 'regularly', identifying the outcomes of the previous IEP and preparing SMART targets for the subsequent IEP, if one is needed. The Advisory Centre for Education (ACE, 2002: 11) suggests that reviews should occur 'at least three times a year'.

Reverting back to Adam and his avoidance of table-top activities, difficulties concentrating at circle time and his tendency to run up and down the room, his IEP could be as follows.

---

### Sample Individual Education Plan

*Name:*   Adam

*Nature of difficulty:* Referred by local playgroup, staff found his inability to focus on his tasks and his tendency to run around the room despite obstacles, too disruptive to the group. Adam likes to control his play situations and spends most of his time involved in floor play with vehicles, sand tray play and brick play. He demonstrates good imaginative and concentration skills whilst engaged in activities of his choice. He finds it difficult to concentrate on a circle time activity, such as a story and rhymes, for more than three or four minutes.

*Targets:*
1  Adam will be able to complete a six-piece jigsaw unaided.
2  Adam will be able to sit and focus on a circle time activity for a minimum of five minutes.
3  Adam will not run around the room between the activities.

*Methods:*
1  Transport and buildings puzzles (four to 12 pieces) will be purchased for use with Adam. Each session Adam will be encouraged to sit with an adult to break down the skills of completing a jigsaw. Positive verbal encouragement will be used consistently. At the completion of each session Adam will be given a sticker and his efforts will be shared with the whole group at circle time. Adam's parents will be shown his work. Adam's sticker chart will have spaces for ten stickers and when completed he will be allowed to take it home. Adam will be allowed to take one jigsaw of his choice home each time he attends.
2  Rhymes and short stories with clear pictures involving farms, building sites and

continued over

┌─ continued from previous page ─────────────────────────────

vehicles will be used each circle time session. At the end of the story Adam will share with the group his work of the day. Adam will be positively rewarded throughout for his attention skills and sitting appropriately. Adam will sit near the front to ensure he can see the pictures clearly and that he can see and hear any positive reinforcement (verbal and/or body language) from the adult. Adam will be given a sticker at the end of each circle time. Any minor incidents will be ignored unless they interfere with the participation of other children.

3  The activity room will be reorganised to limit free running spaces. Music and movement times will focus on a topic of fast and slow to emphasise different and appropriate movements at different times. An adult will remain near to Adam to encourage and support.

*Review date:* This IEP will be reviewed in six weeks time.

*Parental input:* This IEP was prepared and discussed with Adam's parents on ................. They support the targets and will praise him appropriately to reinforce the praise and encouragement received within the group. They will follow up at home the work with jigsaws and using stories to encourage his attention skills. Adam will be given 'his special time' after he has had his bath but after his younger sibling has gone to bed.

*Review date:* This IEP will be reviewed in six weeks' time.

## Specific intervention programmes 1 – speech and language difficulties

Unless specially trained or qualified in the field of speech and language, early years practitioners are not expected to make a diagnosis or devise a specialist programme for a child with speech and language difficulties. If a child requires such specialised support, then the practitioner's role is to enable a referral. This would involve discussing concerns with parents and, depending on local arrangements, either contacting the health visitor to request a home visit to discuss the issue further or suggesting the parents contact the health visitor directly. In my own experience many parents are happy for the practitioner to make the contact.

If speech and language delay is a concern, the child may be referred for a full hearing assessment at the local hospital. If hearing is cleared and there are no other issues that could be causing the speech and language delay, then a referral to the local speech and language therapist may follow. After an initial assessment, a report is produced and the early years setting is, hopefully, included on the circulation list to receive a copy. If the early years setting is a multiagency setting then a speech and language therapist may already be working in the centre, either full time, part time or on a visiting basis. In this case the whole referral process can be dealt with within the setting. It should be noted, however, that the availability and regularity of appointments of speech and language therapists will vary across the country, and sometimes within areas.

## Definitions and terminology

Early years practitioners should be aware of the following terms as they may appear in speech and therapy reports:

- *Comprehension of speech* – relates to a child's ability to understand language. Some children with speech and language difficulties become experts at lip reading and using clues from the environment as well as visual and body language clues, and may be able to respond appropriately, thus concealing underlying difficulties. Early years practitioners are naturally, and quite rightly, experienced at giving a range of indicative clues when interacting with children. So if we ask a child to throw a used tissue into the bin we will probably have:

  – offered the question 'Will you please?' with our facial expression as well as verbalising the request
  – offered a screwed up tissue to the child. Where else would it go but the bin?
  – pointed towards the rubbish bin.

  The child would therefore not have had to understand a single word uttered to complete the task successfully.
- *Expressive language* – ability to use language appropriately in a range of situations.
- *Articulation* – physical muscle use of the mouth, tongue, teeth, nose and breathing, all of which are necessary to produce sounds.
- *Phonology* – comprises the individual sounds that combine to make words.
- *Syntax* – combining of words into phrases and later, sentences appropriately.
- *Intonation* – raising and lowering of voice in different parts of sentences and phrases to emphasise.

## Impact of speech and language difficulties

Speech and language skills are a necessary requirement for development in areas of cognitive, social, emotional and self-concept development and, of necessity, are the medium used mostly within early years settings to deliver the curriculum. Without these skills children's development will be compromised. Some children will be frustrated at their inability or limited ability to communicate as well as their peers and may withdraw within themselves and away from any interactions to avoid further frustration. They may have been repeatedly told they 'don't listen' or 'never listen' so may give up trying. Very young children can at times be very supportive of their peers who are experiencing difficulties but a few may be unkind and insensitive. Such children could be supported in their approaches to others. Levels of frustration may result in unacceptable behaviours within the home and/or setting and it would be futile to spend time focusing on the behaviour difficulties without first attempting to alleviate the underlying cause – the speech and language difficulty. Webster and McConnell (1987: 12) suggest that: 'We should not underestimate the deep and pervasive influence of language difficulties upon the child's development.'

## Assessments

A range of assessment materials is available for speech and language therapists to use, and some which early years practitioners can be trained to use. In some areas the Derbyshire Language Scheme (Knowles and Masidlover, 1982) is used by a range of early years settings but such schemes should not be used without the child receiving a speech and language assessment nor by untrained practitioners. Trained practitioners can use the Derbyshire Language Scheme's Rapid Screening Test to give a current level of comprehension and expression for a child, and a wide range of appropriate activities is offered to foster and encourage the development of skills. Webster and McConnell (1987) offer a detailed review of speech and language tests and assessment materials in general use.

Arguably, the most effective knowledge early years practitioners have is that of 'normal' language development. With this knowledge and their working experiences they are generally well placed to identify difficulties, or potential difficulties, and respond appropriately. Closer observations of a child over a period could focus on their social interactions, self-concept development and speech and language skills, with the evidence made available to support referrals if needed.

## Intervention strategies within early years setting

Some children experiencing speech and language difficulties will have difficulties in other areas as well, and may require special school provision or language unit provision. However, with the current move towards an inclusive education system, most children will remain in their local provision and be ably supported by the practitioners therein. If a child is undergoing regular sessions with a speech and language therapist then working together will enable the early years setting to support the work being done in therapy sessions. It may be that the speech and language therapist will send, via the parents, tasks that can be undertaken within the setting to support the specialised work in the therapy sessions. Coordination in this way, among parents, setting and therapist provides the most comprehensive support for the child. In addition the speech and language therapist may visit the setting on a regular basis to discuss progress and next steps with staff. This again is beneficial to all, particularly if the parents are involved. Perhaps the most appropriate suggestion for supporting children with communication difficulties is to encourage and support effective communication skills, not to correct but to model language and to support and minimise the effects of the difficulties on the child. Spenceley (2000: 51) suggests hints and tips for practitioners:

- Speak slowly and clearly.
- Simplify your speech.
- Give instructions in the order in which they are to be carried out.
- Repeat key words and information.
- Expand simple utterances (eg child: 'teddy chair'; adult: 'yes, teddy is sitting on the chair')
- Model correct use (eg child: 'teddy falled over'; adult: 'yes, teddy fell over, didn't he?') (Spenceley, 2000: 51)

Once the practitioner knows which specific areas of the child's development require support within the setting, then an IEP can be drawn up to clarify the provision, the arrangements required and the teaching strategies. It may be that the speech and language therapist has recommended work on memory skills, attention skills and free conversation during small toy play, all of which can readily be achieved within the setting. Using the therapist's suggestions three or four targets can be established and future planning can be adapted to begin supportive work. The IEP will ensure monitoring is consistent and progress review meetings will involve feedback and further discussions between the practitioners, parents and therapist.

## *Makaton*

Makaton is an additional resource available for use with children experiencing communication difficulties. Usually suggested and established by a child's speech and language therapist, training is available in most parts of the country for early years practitioners. Makaton uses a combination of speech and gestures or signs which are supported by a standard line drawn picture. The underlying philosophy is that we all use gestures and other visual clues when we communicate, so, for those experiencing difficulties with expressive language, Makaton can give additional support and structure to enable communication without the need to verbalise. However, practitioners themselves do use verbal language to accompany the use of the signs and/or pictures as a model. In my experience Makaton enables communication and thus increases self-confidence as it relieves the frustrations of not being able to verbalise and communicate in the same way as others. While some may suggest that replacing verbalisation with signs and pictures removes the need and desire to speak, evidence to date supports the opposite. In my own experience Makaton relieves the child's frustration and removes the focus on expressive language. Over time the child's expressive language begins to develop. Makaton can be used easily within any setting and ideally should be introduced within the home situation at the same time, which clearly depends on parental support and willingness to participate.

Words, signs and symbols are introduced in a gradual and progressive manner beginning with the obvious mummy, daddy, drink, biscuit, please and thank you, and subsequently additional words are introduced.

## Specific intervention programmes 2 – autistic spectrum disorders

As with communication difficulties, practitioners need to have a sound basic awareness of the effects of autistic spectrum disorders and the implications for the learning environment if they are to provide effectively for young children with autism. An understanding of the effects on the individual members of the child's family would also be beneficial. Without a basic knowledge practitioners can inadvertently severely compound the child's difficulties and in the early days of working with autistic children I now know that, despite my best efforts, I did not have sufficient knowledge or understanding of autism to provide effectively. At that point I realised I had to research for myself to improve provision and support the progress of autistic children. I would strongly recommend that any early years practitioner who is expecting a child on the autistic spectrum into his/her setting should spend time exploring the National Autistic Society website (Internet 4) containing a wealth of accessible, practical and up-to-date information on all aspects of autistic spectrum disorders as well as a useful publications list. The NAS also offers short courses nationwide, which are very informative.

Within an inclusive educational philosophy, combined with the increase in children diagnosed with an autistic spectrum disorder, mainstream settings can expect to provide for children with such difficulties. The Code of Practice, for the first time, makes specific reference to autistic spectrum disorders and acknowledges the type of support that may be needed:

These children may require some, or all, of the following:
- flexible teaching arrangements
- help in acquiring, comprehending and using language
- help in articulation
- help in acquiring literacy skills
- help in using augmentative and alternative means of communication
- help to use different means of communication confidently and competently for a range of purposes, including formal situations
- help in organizing and coordinating oral and written language
- support to compensate for the impact of a communication difficulty on learning in English as a additional language
- help in expressing, comprehending and using their own language, where English is not the first language. (DfES, 2001d: s. 7.56)

## *Definitions and terminology*

Autism is now acknowledged as a lifelong condition and, although appropriate educational and social provision can improve some autistic behaviours, some characteristics will remain throughout the child's life. Primarily, autism affects social, imaginative and communication development but autistic children can have additional learning difficulties, as well as an area of expertise, such as drawing, music or mathematical calculations. Autistic children may appear disinterested in the learning environment and/or the people within it and will have great difficulty establishing friendships, as they do not see a need to interact with others. They will not, in general, be alert and interested in any activity except their own ritualistic behaviours, such as repetitively rolling a train up and down a table for long periods of time.

Kanner, in 1943, first presented the term 'autism' which was followed, in 1944, by Asperger's description of high-functioning autistic behaviours that are now known as Asperger's syndrome. In between the severe autistic diagnosis and that of Asperger's lies a spectrum containing a range of autistic disorders of varying severity.

The three key difficulties associated with autistic spectrum disorders form the triad of impairments (see Figure 6.2).

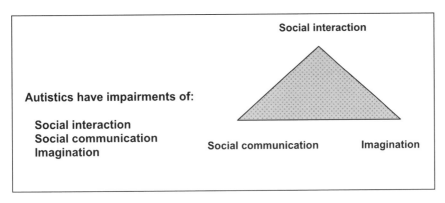

**Figure 6.2**  Triad of impairments

To provide for children with autism practitioners should attempt to understand the child's view of the world through autistic eyes. We can all acknowledge that children generally develop great curiosity about the world around them, but for autistic children this is not the case. We cannot presume to bring the child fully into 'our world' as he/she will not understand it, but should consider the need to access the 'autistic world' and with that understanding we can plan and provide appropriate and stimulating activities for the child. The early years setting will simply not make sense to a child with autism, and he/she will not be capable of making sense of it without specific help and support.

## Impact of autism

The characteristics of autism have been highlighted but some of the resulting effects on the child in an early years setting would be some or all of (depending on the severity of autism) the following:

- Appears aloof and disinterested.
- Does not interact with others.
- Does not attempt to communicate.
- Does not respond to his/her name or other verbal comments.
- Avoids eye contact.
- Does not sit down for circle time or snack time.
- May place hands over ears.
- May rock back and forth and/or flap hands vigorously.
- May scream.
- Does not demonstrate imaginative skills.
- May stare at lights.
- May demonstrate unusual and obsessive behaviours.
- May not understand a sequence of events or routine easily.
- May be insensitive to pain.
- May be hypersensitive to sounds, tastes and textures.
- May resist trying new experiences.
- May become highly distressed at unexpected changes to routine.

If we pause to consider the impact of these effects on a child (a) within the early years setting and (b) within the home, we will begin to have an understanding of the impact of autism.

## Diagnosis and assessments

To diagnose autism is complex and specialised and is not undertaken by early years practitioners. Depending on the local arrangements, the clinical psychologist, educational psychologist, consultant paediatrician or a local specialist child development centre or autistic unit undertakes the diagnosis and make recommendations regarding provision. Early diagnosis is helpful to ensure appropriate support is available as early as possible and any planned interventions can begin. Currently, a range of diagnostic assessments and checklists exists, including:

- Diagnostic and Statistical Manual of Mental Disorders IV – DSM-IV (American Psychiatric Association, 1994)
- Childhood Autism Rating Scale – CARS (Schopler, Reichler and Rochen-Renner, 1988)
- Pre-linguistic Autism Diagnostic Observation Schedule – PL-ADOS (Di Lavore, Lord and Rutter, 1995)
- Checklist for Autism in Toddlers – CHAT (Baron-Cohen, Allen and Gillberg, 1992).

Assessments informing the diagnosis should be thorough, detailed and of an interagency nature including:

- detailed history of development
- any relevant medical information
- evaluation of progress to date from parents and any professionals working with the child and/or family
- assessments of all developmental areas.

## Intervention strategies and specific approaches

There is a range of specific intervention approaches available to the practitioner and in my own experience it may be that you choose to use some elements from more than one approach, in an eclectic manner. Some strategies will be common to more than one approach and will suit the practitioner and the needs of the individual child. As a general rule the following can be used.

### General strategies

As a broad general rule structure within the learning environment will probably support the child with autism very successfully, helping with understanding, increased learning potential and encouraging independence. Structure can be achieved through:

1 Sticking to routines to ensure consistency.
2 Visual routines: using photographs or simple pictures attached to a board or display. As each task is completed the child will remove it from the board and place it in the 'finished' box. The child will always know what comes next.
3 Visual labels with accompanying words on all resources and learning materials combined with organisational structure will encourage independence.
4 Work systems where each task to be completed by the child is placed in a tray or basket and placed on the left-hand side of the worktable. The child will soon learn to work in this order through the tasks and place them on the right hand side of the table when completed. This will encourage independent learning. Tasks must be explicit as the child will not be able to assume what you want them to do.

### Other strategies

1 Extend imaginative play. If the autistic child is obsessed by trains, vehicles and wheels you will find there is a tendency to identify any vehicles and circular shaped objects that could rotate, even in materials where you cannot see it. This can be used by modelling and extension of the child's existing and possibly obsessive play routines through playing alongside the child (not with the child who may react negatively to your close presence).

This could simply be imitating the child's play. As the child allows you to continue you can demonstrate an extension to the current play routines. Through repeated modelling the child will hopefully begin to imitate and 'allow' you to become more involved as he/she begins to realise that play and fun can be a shared experience.

2  Be vigilant of potentially unsafe situations and play. A child who is obsessed with hinges and locks may repeatedly open and shut a door onto the fingers of his/her other hand, apparently oblivious to any pain.

3  Help the child to understand what you are asking by presenting only that which is necessary. A child presented with a table covered in round inter-connecting shapes may be overpowered by the visual stimulation of so many and simply leave the table to escape or cover their eyes or ears to block out the sensation. If you are working on connecting three pieces together then only present three pieces.

4  Offer a quiet area for one-to-one work that is free from stimulation and dis-traction to enable greater concentration.

5  Talk slowly and in simple language when working near or with the child to offer examples of good language. Repetition of common words and phrases will eventually pay dividends and support communication development.

6  Encourage eye contact by tilting the child's head towards you or touching the child to indicate that communication is a two way interaction.

7  Be aware of the autistic child's possible sensitivity to touch. Whereas you may naturally offer physical comfort to a child who has fallen over or is dis-tressed, to pick up and hug an autistic child may increase the distress.

8  Have consistent routines within the setting, as autistic children need the structure and familiarity more than their peers.

9  If the child will only join in snack time if he/she has the same chair, in the same place (possibly away from the table) and must have the same type of snack and cup, then so be it. The benefits of limited participation in this social activity will allow access to role models of social interaction, social skills and language skills.

10  Exaggerate your use of bodily, facial and hand gestures to encourage aware-ness and understanding of gestures.

11  Avoid using phrases and idioms, as autistic children understand literal not implied meanings. 'Jump in the bath' means exactly that!

It should be noted that immediate responses and/or progress are unlikely, but for the child with less severe autistic difficulties then progress could be more rapid.

### Specific approaches

The *Lovaas* approach is an intensive behavioural approach aiming to teach behaviours and skills through intensive one-to-one teaching situations. The child will be physically encouraged to give eye-to-eye contact and the correct responses will be encouraged and rewarded if successful. The types of skills taught in this way with young children will range from basic sitting and attending, to identifying a picture from verbal clues, matching objects and the combining of two building blocks to begin understanding of 'building' with bricks. The system is very regimented and is viewed, by some, as placing the children in the receiving position as opposed to involving them in real and exploratory activity. The transference of skills may be compounded by the rigidity of the programme in that a child may be able to build bricks in one situation but not in a different environment. Trevarthen et al. (1998: 224) echo these concerns: 'But this is not a fully satisfactory method for learning mutual participation, even for a pre-schooler with autism. Behaviour shaping puts the child in a receiving position that may offer security, but may also establish rigidity, and close off interest in novelty or change.'

The Lovaas approach will focus teaching sessions on:

- establishing eye contact
- developing imitative verbal and play skills through repeated modelling.

The intensive sessions with the trainer or therapist will be for up to 40 hours every week, so realistically this is not an approach that can be readily applied within an early years setting or solely by the parents in the home. In my experience the Lovaas approach is predominantly used within the home and is not combined with attendance at a local early years setting. A team of therapists will be used to ensure continuity and they will follow a planned programme devised following baseline observations and assessments.

The *Treatment and Education of Autistic and Related Communication Handicapped Children* (TEACCH) approach offers a programme that can continue from pre-school until adulthood, with the principles applied and adapted to different situations and activities as appropriate. Thus skills can be supported that can then be transferred into the home and, at a later stage, into the work situation. Following development of the approach at the University of North Carolina, the system has been accepted by many local workplaces where staff work alongside the professionals from the TEACCH team to support the autistic adults working within the businesses. The jobs undertaken by the autistic adults can be adapted according to their individual needs and levels of development. The principles of the approach are based on the following:

- structured teaching, routine and organisation
- left-to-right work systems
- communication teaching
- visual representation
- stress reduction
- social skills training.

The TEACCH principles can be adapted for use in early years settings once training has been undertaken or under the guidance of a trained professional, but the key ideas of structure and routine can be, and are, widely used.

The *Picture Exchange Communication System* (PECS) approach to developing communication skills is often used to support the TEACCH programme as it offers a structured system enabling non-verbal children to initiate their own 'conversations' and thus gain independence. The system relies on the child handing a picture card to an adult to indicate a need, and by receiving the desired item reinforcement occurs. Generally the process begins with children asking for a biscuit or drink; the child can be given a picture of the biscuit or drink and, initially, be physically helped to place the picture card into the adult's hand. The adult then responds with a clear verbal model of the question and the item is handed to the child. As the child becomes familiar with the system, options and choices can be introduced so the child is making real, positive decisions. According to Cumine, Leach and Stevenson (2000: 46): 'This approach was specifically developed with the needs of young children with autism in mind. It was recognised that these children require highly structured intervention to develop the language and social skills needed for communication.'

The *Structure; Positive approaches and expectations; Empathy; Low arousal environments, and Links with parents* (SPELL) approach was developed by the National Autistic Society in the UK to address the individual and different learning needs of children and is used within the National Autistic Society's own schools around the country. The curriculum focuses on skills in communication, social skills and imagination (the triad of impairments) and structure is again the key for supporting children's learning. The approach centres on an understanding of and response to the child's autistic world with low arousal learning environments in each class or group. Close parental and professional links are important to the success of the approach.

The *Auditory Integration Training* (AIT) approach works on the principle that there is a sensory imbalance which can be supported through music, via headphones, which is modulated through the complete pitch range as difficulties exist in processing auditory information, compounding the child's abilities to develop meaningful speech and language skills. A specialist practitioner will visit the home for one-hour inputs on a daily basis for ten days and it is said that the therapy enables learning, speech development and general progress to be made.

*The Son Rise programme* (Options therapy): parents need to travel to America for specialised training in this approach which they can then continue when they return home, supported by emails, telephone calls and video exchanges. It is a child-centred approach which encourages the child to play in his/her own way, developing his/her own explorations without confrontations or adult direction.

On returning home the family needs to set up a separate playroom for the activities and arrange a team of helpers or volunteers that can work for seven or eight hours a day, seven days a week, so demands are considerable. The programme is regularly reviewed, with volunteers participating in evaluations of video recordings made and the planning of future targets.

The *Higashi approach* (Daily Life Therapy) is based on whole-group work, not individual teaching situations, and focuses on stabilising the emotions of autistic children, encouraging physical activity to stimulate the brain and promote strength, which in turn enables social relationships and thus the ability of autistic children to accept other people around them and as part of their lives. The approach continues 24 hours a day, so when the children return to their accommodation blocks the principles are still applied. Reports indicate that substantial improvements are made with children's self-help skills, self-confidence and socialisation. The curriculum offered to the children comprises predominantly physical exercise, arts, language, mathematics and science.

---

### *Case study*

Ben was referred to an early years special needs unit by his health visitor and was described as demonstrating 'autistic type behaviours'. He was currently awaiting a full developmental assessment by the consultant paediatrician. A home visit was made at which both parents were present to discuss Ben's individual needs and to identify the key issues from their perspective. They had researched Ben's difficulties, felt sure he was autistic and were able to accept this. The behaviours certainly fitted within the autistic spectrum. It was agreed that Ben would commence attendance and that the staff would observe and assess him over the first few weeks before meeting again with his parents to discuss the outcomes and suggestions for the future. It was hoped that by this time he would have had his appointment with the consultant paediatrician and the report would be able to inform our discussions.

The observations and assessments identified the following issues:

- Ben did not interact with anyone and would remove himself from potentially interactive situations.
- Ben demonstrated obsessive and ritualistic play routines with his tractor, which always had to be within his sight. If he could not see his tractor he would become distressed.
- While rolling his tractor back and forth along the window sill he would watch the traffic pass by and became very excited and animated when a fire engine passed.
- Ben would not join the group for snacks or circle time and would become distressed if encouraged.
- Ben could identify rotational qualities in any object and could become fixated with it.
- When Ben picked up something new to him he would explore it with his hands and mouth for two or three minutes before playing with it or discarding it.
- Ben would spend up to ten minutes flicking through books (from left to right, and turning pages appropriately) looking for tractors. When he found one he would slide the book along the floor to simulate vehicle movement.

- Ben was oblivious to the usual noises within the room but would become very distressed if a child cried or the fire alarm went off, rocking his body, flapping his hands and shutting his eyes very tightly.
- Ben enjoyed rolling his tractor down the slide but did not want to try himself.

*NB: These outcomes are in detail to illustrate points to the reader. Any written records would be more succinct.*

- The observational outcomes were discussed by staff and Ben's parents who felt they summed up Ben accurately. The following strategies were agreed, to be reviewed after six weeks. In addition a daily diary was passed between parents and staff.
- Ben's key worker was to spend two or three minutes, at least four times each session, playing alongside Ben at the window sill, imitating his play and making comments about the passing traffic. The length and time, frequency and level of interaction to be adapted according to Ben's responses.
- Key worker to introduce alternative vehicles into her window sill play and begin rolling vehicles on a table placed by the window.
- On the table would be one or two four-piece jigsaws – one of a tractor and one of a fire engine, plus a book about a farm. At the key worker's discretion she would complete a jigsaw, describing what she was doing and/or describe the pictures in the book.
- At snack time the key worker sat at a separate table away from the group with a snack and a drink, plus the same for Ben. Initially he would be allowed to remove his snack and eat/drink it elsewhere but he would be encouraged to join her.
- For the first six weeks the unit requested that no fire drills took place on the days Ben attended.

At the review six weeks later it was noted that Ben would now watch the key worker completing the jigsaws and listen to her talking about the book, although he would not join her at the table. He now played alongside her with the vehicles and occasionally offered her a specific vehicle to indicate he wanted her to play. Two days before the review he had shared snack time seated at the table next to his key worker, provided she did not look at him or talk directly to him.

Staff and parents were very pleased with this considerable progress and activities were continued and extended over the coming weeks and months, with short- and long-term targets included in his IEPs. By the end of his second term at the unit Ben was successfully undertaking one-to-one work with his key worker at a table using a structured teaching approach (as per the TEACCH programme), he was using visual timetables and had begin to communicate using the PECS system. The same strategies and principles were used within the home situation and regular progress reviews took place involving parents, staff and other professionals.

# Summary

Throughout this chapter we have emphasised the need for practitioners to provide appropriately for the individual needs of young children through a cyclical approach incorporating observations, planning, interventions and monitoring. Individual Education Plans will clarify the arrangements made and include short- and long-term targets established to ensure progress. These IEPs should be reviewed regularly and partnerships with parents should be encouraged at each and every stage. The breaking down of tasks into small steps or 'stepping stones' is essential for meaningful task setting that will ensure success and thus progress for the child.

We have examined scenarios involving provision for children with speech and language difficulties and autistic spectrum disorders in some detail and, through this, the principles of assessing children and formulating targets which directly respond to their individual needs have been emphasised. The case study of Ben does not actually include the word 'autism' in the setting's planning as the condition is not really viewed as the key issue, rather that understanding and responding to Ben's individual needs are the key issue, taking into account his preferences, likes and dislikes. However, it could be suggested that, without a sound understanding of the impact of autism, the targets formulated would not necessarily have been appropriate for him. So, while the possibility of 'autism' was not an issue for the staff, prior knowledge of autism was indeed necessary for Ben's intervention programme.

While a range of approaches has been discussed it must be clarified that no single approach will necessarily offer all the answers for all the children. Practitioners will often use elements from a variety of approaches to provide most effectively for children's individual, and often changing, needs. Specific programmes have been introduced throughout the chapter and a list of corresponding websites follows for those wishing to gain additional information.

---

### Key issues

❖ Any intervention should begin at the child's current stage of development and progress in small steps, reflect individual needs and take into account any contributing factors.
❖ Regular evaluations and monitoring are needed.
❖ IEPs comprising SMART targets are needed.
❖ Parental partnerships and interagency working are essential for effective intervention.

## Some suggestions for discussion

### Item 1

Examine your setting's process for identifying and providing for individual needs. Does your current procedure fit in with the cyclical model suggested within this chapter? If not, discuss where differences occur and consider whether changes could be made.

### Item 2

Within the inclusive educational climate discuss the confidence levels among staff members to provide effectively for any difficulties that a child may present. Does this highlight any training needs? If so, how could these be addressed?

### Item 3

Consider the setting's recording systems for observations, assessments and IEPs. Are these manageable, practical and accessible to all?

### Item 4

Try out the formulation of SMART targets. Consider one child experiencing difficulties within your setting and using existing observational outcomes create SMART targets that could be included in an IEP. Reflect on how these targets could then be fitted in to your current planning documentation.

## Suggested further reading

Cumine, V., Leach, J. and Stevenson, G. (2000) *Autism in the Early Years: A Practical Guide.* London: David Fulton. (Chapter 4.)

Mortimer, H. (2001) *Special Needs and Early Years Provision.* London: Continuum. (Chapter 9.)

Webster, A., and McConnell, C. (1987) *Special Needs in Ordinary Schools: Children with Speech and Language Difficulties.* London: Cassell. (Chapter 5.)

## Useful contacts

ACE (Advisory Centre for Education)
🖳 www.ace-ed.org.uk
☎ 0909 800 5793 (Advice line) ☎ 020 7354 8318 (Business line)

Afasic (Representing children and young adults with communication impairments)
🖳 www.afasic.org.uk
☎ 0845 355 5577 (Helpline) ☎ 020 7490 9410 (Administration)

Higashi approach
🖳 www.bostonhigashi.org

ICAN (Children with speech and language impairments)
🖳 www.ican.org.uk    ☎ 0870 010 4066

Makaton
🖳 www.makaton.org    ☎ 01276 61390

NAS (National Autistic Society)
🖳 www.nas.org.uk    ☎ 020 7833 2299

PEACH (Parents for the Early Intervention of Autism in Children)
🖳 www.peach.org.uk    ☎ 01344 882248

PECS (Picture Exchange Communication System)
🖳 www.pecs.com    ☎ 01273 728888

Son Rise programme
🖳 www.son-rise.org

TEACCH (Treatment and Education of Autistic and Related Communication Handicapped Children)
🖳 www.teacch.com

# 7

## Responding to the Affective Needs of Young Children

## Introduction

Research evidence clearly identifies links between low self-esteem, social, emotional and behavioural problems and learning difficulties, therefore it is essential that all early years practitioners acknowledge and address the affective needs of individual children alongside any additional difficulties displayed. Charlton and Jones highlight the importance of this area:

> whether or not time is allocated to work on children's affective functioning too often depends on adventitious encounters with teachers who have been converted to the need to address such areas. It is time – as a profession – that we all recognised, for example, the need to give adequate time to 'working on the self'. It is iniquitous for us not to undertake this task. As educators, are we called upon to educate the 'whole' child? If not, who looks after the neglected parts? (Charlton and Jones, 1990: 149)

A range of potential causal factors exists, including the setting and home, and to provide effectively these should be explored. If a child is experiencing affective problems, then until these are addressed it may be futile attempting to provide learning opportunities related to the curriculum as his/her ability to access opportunities may be impaired. It is also important to acknowledge the role practitioners can play in compounding or supporting a child's affective development and for practitioners to be prepared critically to analyse their own practices.

Through an examination of research and theory this chapter will highlight some key issues and suggest ways in which practitioners can support the 'whole child' through an exploration of affective development. Social, emotional and behavioural development will be explored as will the importance of the self-concept. In addition, as many more early years settings are dealing with children experiencing behaviour difficulties, practitioners will be guided through the process of observation, planning an intervention and evaluating the effectiveness of that intervention, combined with practical strategies for use within any early years setting.

# Definitions and terminology

What is affective development? A personal reflection should help create an understanding of the range of issues covered by the terms 'affective development' and 'affective needs'.

At secondary school I recall enjoying English language and particularly creative writing, but when transferring to a new class with a new teacher I persistently received low marks. For one piece of homework I put in tremendous effort in an attempt to satisfy and please the teacher and also to improve my grades. I eagerly awaited the return of the marked work with quiet confidence and was, first, disappointed as the return date was delayed by two weeks due to 'excessive teacher workload' and on eventual return my work had a strong red line through every page with 'FAIL – You have obviously totally missed the point. I am very disappointed as I was told you were a good pupil'. The reader will be able to judge my reaction, but two key issues arise:

- The fact that I recall this incident with such clarity over 30 years later highlights the impact it had.
- Areas affected: social (embarrassed to share my mark with peers and disappointed to have to tell my parents), emotional, self-confidence, self-esteem and motivation to try in the future.

A range of factors can affect our current and future performances including levels of self-concept, confidence, ability to succeed and learn, motivation, emotions and social competence. It is these areas that relate to affective development. If we consistently meet failure then we are less likely to risk trying new challenges for fear of further failure(s). If we are confident about ourselves as individuals and learners then we are more likely to succeed. All these factors are interrelated.

Children with special needs may already find success more difficult to achieve or may have difficulties with issues of confidence and/or self-concept related to their individual needs. Therefore, while it is essential to address affective development with all young children, those with special needs may need additional and individualised consideration.

Until quite recently affective development has not been evident within curriculum documents and guidance but, as suggested, if these are overlooked it may be pointless working on a curriculum as the child's abilities to access that curriculum may be severely compromised. Practitioners should acknowledge the affective needs of young children and respond to them appropriately, thus enabling successful and confident individuals and learners who can maximise the potential of the learning opportunities presented to them. Within the Foundation Stage the area of personal, social and emotional development is now identified as an area of learning, so a broad and balanced curriculum is now acknowledged as including areas of affective development. Children need to be motivated to learn and confident to try, so practitioners need to consider these developmental areas at least as much as the areas of physical, mathematical, creative, knowledge and understanding of the world and communication, language and literacy.

## Legislation and guidance

Within the Code of Practice (DfES, 2001d: s. 7.6) children with behavioural, emotional and social development problems are highlighted as possibly needing additional support: 'Children and young people who demonstrate features of emotional and behavioural difficulties, who are withdrawn or isolated, disruptive and disturbing, hyperactive and lack concentration; those with immature social skills; and those presenting challenging behaviours arising from other complex special needs, may require help or counselling ...'. The Code continues to suggest specific types of support or help that may be needed which would be incorporated within the processes of Early Years Action and Early Years Action Plus as outlined within the Code.

Within the Foundation Stage for three- to five-year-olds all registered settings now have a responsibility to provide for children's personal, social and emotional development. The Early Learning Goals (QCA, 1999) offer ten broad aims to practitioners of which four directly relate to affective development, with the remaining six relating to more 'traditional' curriculum areas such as mathematical development. The key aims include words such as: 'inclusive, valuing children, promoting self-image and self-esteem, enthusiasm for learning, promoting confidence, successful learners, working cooperatively and harmoniously, listening to each other, encouraging attention skills and persistence' (QCA, 1999: 9), clearly indicating the importance and value placed on affective development as a major emphasis within the early years curriculum. Interestingly, when the Early Learning Goals document continues to expand on each of the six learning areas, the goals for personal, social and emotional development come first, giving guidance to practitioners on how they might support development in this area. The document suggests that:

> Successful personal, social and emotional development is critical for very young children in all aspects of their lives. It is also a pre-requisite for their success in all others of learning. It is crucial that settings provide the experiences and support which enable children to develop a positive sense of themselves. (QCA, 1999: 19)

The guidance identifies 'stepping stones' to successful personal, social and emotional development which can be used by practitioners to plan provision in this area and support the breaking down of goals to achievable, small-step targets. So, now we have clear guidance regarding all children within the Foundation Stage documentation and specifically children with special educational needs within the Code of Practice. From an international perspective the United Nations Convention on the Rights of the Child (Internet 10) also reflects the need to respond to children's affective development within its definition of education that should be available to all children. Article 29 highlights that education should:

- Develop the child's personality, talents and mental and physical abilities to their fullest potential;
- Develop respect for the child's parents, his or her own cultural identity, language and values, for the national values of the country in which the child is living, the country from which he or she might originate, and the civilisations different from his or her own;
- Prepare the child for a responsible life in a free society, in the spirit of understanding, peace, tolerance, equality and friendship among all people;
- Develop respect for the natural environment. (Internet 10)

If, as early years practitioners we aim to develop young children to their maximum potential then clearly we have a responsibility to address their affective development as well as the more commonly highlighted areas of physical, creative, communication, mathematical and scientific development. The links between the areas cannot be overlooked and yet training courses, books and journals still tend to separate academic development from affective development highlighting special needs, behavioural difficulties or affective development as separate. It could be argued that sufficient evidence now exists to combine all areas within educational training and provision as inclusive, as supported by the current climate, which would have the benefit of acknowledging the interrelationship between them and thus breaking down the perceived division. This philosophy would add further support to providing for the individual needs of individual children in a holistic manner.

## Personal, social and emotional development

The importance of this area of development has now been established and practitioners need to understand the social and emotional development of young children in order to respond appropriately. Harnett provides a useful summary of research in this area:

> The importance of developing children in this area is well documented from Piaget (1896–1980, quoted in Barnes, 1997) through to writers such as Rogers (1983) and the High Scope Educational Research Foundation (Hohmann and Weikart, 1995). Reports such as Plowden (1967) and Gulbenkian (1982) also highlighted the need for children to have a broad and balanced curriculum that developed the whole child. This has been further refined within the Early Learning Goals by providing explicit guidance on the opportunities that enhance this area of learning. (Harnett, 2002: 62)

To be able to provide for children's needs practitioners need to understand development in each of the specified areas but at the same time acknowledge the interaction across and between them.

## Social development

According to Beaver et al. (1999: 226) the process of socialisation enables children to: 'learn the way of life, the language and behaviour that is acceptable and appropriate to the society in which they live. This is their culture. The process of socialisation involves children learning from the experiences and relationships they have during childhood.'

Beginning with primary socialisation in the child's home environment, this is later extended to secondary socialisation, where children learn that different expectations exist in different situations. As children progress through the stages of social development they learn to adapt behaviour according to the context they are in, being able to change to satisfy the rules of the grouping. A child may behave appropriately at the early years setting but not at home. This is perhaps because the rules and routines in each are different, they become adept at adaptation, as long as they are confident within themselves and clearly understand the rules of each environment. A parallel can be drawn between ourselves discussing our working history and potential at a job interview and the way we may behave when socialising with close friends. We understand the different rules of each situation and adapt accordingly. These skills have been learnt from the experiences and opportunities we had when growing up.

The way these skills are learnt will partly depend on the learning style of the child, partly on his/her situation or culture and how these skills are passed on. Examples of ways in which young children learn social skills would include:

- observing, copying and imitating adults and children around them
- stories and role-play
- being positively rewarded for acceptable and appropriate behaviour within any environment they find themselves in.

Social development will also depend greatly on the family and other outside influences on the child. In the primary socialisation phase the key influencing factors will include the parents, siblings, additional carers (e.g. childminder or daycare worker), neighbours and other close family members. In the secondary socialisation stage influences would extend to include the local community, the television, video and computer, storybooks and peer group. Children clearly need opportunities to develop their social skills within both of these stages to develop appropriately. Any missing elements may have a lasting effect on the child and create difficulties for him/her when entering new and unfamiliar situations.

## Stages of social development

From birth babies tend to demonstrate social development through:

- reactions and reflexes, such as sucking and gripping
- being content cuddled up to a parent or close family member
- indicating distress when hungry or in pain

- an increasing awareness of surroundings.

By the age of six months tremendous progress has already been made demonstrated by:

- laughing, smiling and interacting with their environment
- participating in simple games such as 'peepo'
- amusing themselves for short periods
- appearing eager when a known person approaches them
- showing a preference for certain people
- stopping crying when responded to
- holding and exploring objects (usually by mouthing).

If we now move to a two-year-old toddler we can see further rapid changes demonstrated through:

- being responsive to a wider range of emotions
- acquiring increased language and communication skills
- being very independent and on occasions uncooperative
- finding it difficult to share and wait for a turn
- being able to wait for something but preferring an immediate response
- being able to display love and affection
- playing alongside other children
- joining in with simple repetitive songs and rhymes.

By the grand age of 6 or 7 children demonstrate their social skills through being able to:
- co-operate well with adults and children
- be rebellious and aggressive, miserable and/or sulky
- feel devastated when their best friend deserts them
- be aware of gender differences
- be generally self-confident with people
- persevere with an activity
- be greatly influenced by peers
- be very self-critical.

The rapidity of development indicated in the first seven years of life will hopefully alert practitioners to the importance of supporting development in the early years. In general most of the activities and learning experiences presented within early years settings will naturally enhance children's social development but, rather than allowing this to happen of its own accord, careful planning and individual arrangements should always be considered. This is especially pertinent when supporting children who have difficulties with sharing and/or turn-taking, are shy or withdrawn, are overconfident and may always need to be in control of a situation, have special needs, behavioural difficulties or have simply lacked prior social development opportunities. Any child who has experienced emotional, social and/or behavioural difficulties will probably need additional support in developing additional skills appropriately.

As previously highlighted a child's culture will generally be developed within the home and family where customs, traditions and values will be handed down through generations, but practitioners have a responsibility to be aware of and understand the differences in those cultures. Cultural differences will be tremendously important to children, and within our inclusive, multicultural settings we can inadvertently create significant problems for a child through ignorance of the facts relating to his/her culture and/or religion. Practitioners should be aware of the possibility that the ethos and practices within the setting may not be concordant with the local community as their values may be different. This is not necessarily a problem as both can be proud of their values and customs and the children will all benefit from experiencing equally valid, situational values.

Representational images of a cross-section of children should be displayed within the setting to highlight the sameness as opposed to highlighting the differences between children. Books and resources should also move away from the stereotypical images that were evident only a generation or two ago. This will support positive images of society in general to be generated among the children, staff and all others entering the setting. Similar issues can arise from gender stereotyping which should be avoided in early years settings. Children's awareness of differences, whether regarding gender or any other issue, can be established surprisingly early and we need to be sensitive to this. Often the influences of parents and/or older siblings can have detrimental effects on younger children who are not concerned about any differences between people. Young children play with whomever they choose and are not generally prohibited by any stereotypical images, but other influences can create situations that practitioners should be aware of and ready to respond to. For example, if a young boy is playing hospitals with his peers and wants to take the role of a nurse, he may be inhibited by other children suggesting that this is a girl's role. Lack of awareness that men can and do train as nurses can affect children's play in a negative manner.

The issue of gender is often compounded by the few qualified male early years practitioners and, thus, a lack of positive male role models. Work in the early years and caring for young children is still predominantly viewed as a female domain and recent experiences have indicated that male students following courses in early years or early childhood studies have to be highly committed and motivated as they tend to take some friendly but pointed gender stereotypical comments when socialising with their male peers. However, in a society where there is an increase in the numbers of children being brought up by single mothers and an increase in the number of 'house fathers', perhaps there is a greater need for an increase in numbers of male early years workers to balance out the role models.

It is not always appropriate to treat children as the same due to cultural differences which deserve respect and understanding. It is more important to be aware of multicultural issues in a sensitive manner that is not judgmental, but respectful and valuing. Diversity within our early years settings is positive and, if supported appropriately, will enhance the development of understanding within all the children, and possibly parents and staff as well. Diversity should be celebrated.

## Emotional development

We are all aware of the effects our emotions can have on our ability to perform successfully in our everyday lives, from a short-term panic situation to a longer-term emotional difficulty. The effects can be devastating. If we then consider children's emotional development it should be clear that we should support their gradual development of emotions and emotional understanding while acknowledging that on occasions they, too, will need additional short or longer term help.

Our emotions develop from very basic emotions expressed at a young age (e.g. anger, love, happiness, distress) to much subtler forms of emotion expressed as adults (e.g. pride, jealousy, envy, sympathy, embarrassment). For healthy maturity children need emotional support and understanding throughout childhood.

At birth babies clearly demonstrate very basic emotions in as much as they can be happy and content or fractious and distressed, but from these early days we see continued development in their abilities to demonstrate emotional expression and understanding. Barnes (1995) describes the research of Haviland and Lelwica examining the display of emotions between ten-week-old babies and their mothers expressing facial happiness, sadness and anger concluding that:

> Analysis of video recordings taken of the babies showed that they reacted in distinct ways to each of the displays, but they were not simply copying their mother's expression. They did respond to their mother's happy display with a happy face, but the angry face resulted in either an angry expression or stillness, and the sad display generated an increase in mouthing, chewing and sucking behaviour. (Barnes, 1995: 143)

In the first year of a baby's life the mother will begin to discriminate between a range of emotions expressed by their baby, and the baby, in turn, will become more able to respond to emotional signals from the mother's face and use that information to inform their own emotions. By 18 months, toddlers begin to have an image of their 'self' in relation to others and begin to verbalise their feelings/emotions, but by 3 or 4 years of age children can manipulate their emotions, confident that a desired response will follow, thus they have learnt to use their emotions in a controlling manner. They also have an understanding of the feelings, emotions and desires of others and are beginning to be aware of and understand another person's perspective.

As children mature there is an expectation that they will (or should) be able to control their emotions relating to culturally and socially accepted norms and values. However, this does not mean we should discourage children from acknowledging and expressing their emotions. 'Big boys don't cry' is an out-dated perspective that should not be relevant in today's society. With increased age also comes an ability to experience more complex emotions such as jealousy and embarrassment, and practitioners will be able to identify children who are more sensitive to such emotions. The inability to share as a toddler is more a response to the child's perceived need for an object than a jealous emotive response. Jealousy develops at a later stage.

Young children rely heavily on a firm and secure base in which they develop confidence to build strong emotions. This is further extended by the child's need to form strong attachments with one or more carers. Again practitioners will need to be sensitive to children who do not appear to have experienced this firm foundation and have not developed strong attachments as they may need additional support. Such issues were highlighted in the research of Lafrenière and Sroufe, and Waters, Wippman and Sroufe, summarised by Keenan:

> Further research showed that these same benefits associated with a secure attachment relationship held into the preschool years, with preschool teachers rating securely attached children as less aggressive toward their peers, less dependent on help from the teacher and more competent than insecurely attached children. (Keenan, 2002: 189)

Such research also highlights the importance of acknowledging the relevant areas of development to support later progress and abilities to maximise on the learning experiences offered. Considerable research has been undertaken exploring the qualities of effective schools that support children experiencing difficulties of a social, emotional and/or behavioural nature. Many of these are as relevant to early years settings. Long and Fogell suggest that:

> Schools have a central role to play in supporting all children through adverse and difficult events. Our task in school is to make a difference where we can make a difference. It is not always possible or appropriate for a class teacher to work with children's families. We do not have the power to change their home circumstances but we can ensure that the school environment is emotionally supportive for all children and especially those who are most vulnerable. (Long and Fogell, 1999: 26)

Research such as that of Rutter et al. (1979), Reynolds (1984), Mortimore et al. (1988) and, more recently, Barber (1996) drew similar conclusions regarding effective and supportive school environments. The key features identified in their research include:

- positive leadership and management
- positive and inclusive ethos
- well-developed and regularly monitoring processes of observation, assessment and record-keeping which is manageable and meaningful
- positive reinforcement systems employed
- collaborative parent–school relationships

- pupil participation in school decision-making processes
- high but realistic pupil expectations
- teacher competence at managing the classroom
- teachers as positive role models
- challenging but achievable planning and target setting for children
- limited focus within each lesson to reduce confusion and/or possible failure.

Practitioners should therefore ensure that factors within settings are not compounding the affective development of individual children or groups of children.

## Social, emotional and/or behavioural difficulties

When a child is experiencing difficulties, practitioners should assess whether these are short- or long-term difficulties and plan accordingly. In the case of a child who has rarely left his/her parents from birth and has had limited contact with adults or children from outside his/her home environment, practitioners should rightfully expect some adjustment difficulties on entering the pre-school setting and separating from parents. This may be short-lived or may continue over a period of time and require more thoughtful planning. We cannot expect children to settle quickly, as for some the stages between entering the group and becoming a fully active participant may take time. Planning and support will help this child considerably and, if recorded, may help the child if other difficulties arise later. Each child must be treated as an individual and his/her personality, characteristics and prior experiences fully explored to account for any factors that may be affecting current performance levels. Discussions with parents should help practitioner understanding of the issues. There is much evidence available indicating links between social, emotional and/or behavioural difficulties with learning difficulties and cognitive development and early intervention is necessary to ameliorate later problems. If learning difficulties exist, whether at the pre-school or later stages, then behaviour problems may follow. Repeated failure to achieve success may result in avoidance tactics and may manifest as withdrawal or task avoidance through inappropriate and unacceptable behaviours.

## What can settings and practitioners do?

From the research evidence previously referred to there are key factors indicative of the areas to which settings can respond to address affective development. The following are some practical suggestions for settings to explore:

- awareness and knowledge of the need to address affective development
- caring and sensitive staff who value and respect children and parents
- positive ethos of the setting
- appropriate interactions with children, acknowledging children's likes/dislikes, culture, special needs, gender and identity

- appropriate learning opportunities that offer success and support confidence and self-esteem
- positive reward system
- allowing children to express feelings and emotions
- supporting children to make decisions and gain independence
- planning to include the Early Learning Goals relating to affective development
- individualised planning (IEPs) for children needing specific help
- effective parental partnerships
- the ability to listen to children.

When children are demonstrating distress, perhaps caused by a current issue within the home such as parental separation, practitioners need to be aware in order to support the child. The distress may manifest in a variety of ways but the underlying issues should be examined before any action is taken. It will compound the child's problems if settings deal more firmly with the child to reduce the unwanted behaviours presented, when the child clearly needs support dealing with the distress. We must address the causes not just the symptoms.

Long and Fogell (1999) offer a classroom appraisal questionnaire for consideration by practitioners when reflecting on the supportive elements of their settings. A simple tick sheet, the questionnaire would be a worthwhile exercise for early years settings as it allows practitioners to 'highlight those areas that are going well and maybe some where you would like to make changes' (ibid.: 21).

## Causal factors

Some factors that can positively or negatively impact on children's affective development have already been highlighted but it will be pertinent to present them together to clarify understanding.

### *Within the home*

- Poor parenting skills – too restrictive, protective, lenient, lacking structure and routine, lacking quality family time, lack of or too severe behaviour management.
- Parenting style that lacks love and security.
- Negative parenting that reduces confidence and self-esteem.
- Poor diet and standards of hygiene.
- Child abuse – physical, sexual, emotional or neglectful (all forms of abuse generally have an emotionally abusing effect).
- Poverty and deprivation.
- Alcohol and/or drug abuse of parents.
- Poor attachments.
- Parental separation, bereavement or other loss.
- Unrealistic expectations of parents.

## Within the setting

Many factors within settings have already been discussed in some detail but a few suggestions are offered here that will support children's affective development:

- Effective planning, evaluation and monitoring of curriculum (hidden and pre-scribed).
- High and consistent levels of organisation within classroom/activity room.
- Resources which are readily accessible to the children.
- Effective observation and assessment processes.
- Supportive and positive ethos.
- Structured day and individual lessons/working times.
- Clear guidelines and rules.
- Positive staff attitudes.
- Well-motivated staff.
- Meaningful policies.
- Positive parental partnerships.

## Practitioner

- Good knowledge base of child development.
- Knowledge and understanding of responding to individual needs.
- Familiarity with current legislation and guidance (particularly regarding the foundation stage and special needs).
- Effective planning, record keeping and time management.
- Well organised.
- Appropriate tasks presented for child's current level of performance.
- Not overreliant on standardised worksheets.
- Good classroom management skills.
- High but realistic expectations of him/herself, staff and children.
- Encouraging and motivating qualities.
- Effective management of behaviour.
- Use of positive reinforcement skills for all children.
- Ability to undertake observations that inform planning.
- Ability to plan SMART targets which are appropriate for individual needs.
- Inclusive practices.
- Ability to recognise when additional training is required.
- Awareness of gender and multicultural issues.

## Illustrative example

The ability of practitioners to be critically reflective of their own practices is not always easy but, if confident with colleagues, then peer appraisal or review processes can support this. In my own experience I bravely decided to reflect on the positive verbal feedback I gave children in a reception class. At the time I would have fiercely defended my positive interactions with the children and I thought the exercise would support my views. My nursery nurse noted at random intervals for half an hour at a time, over a month, whether my comments were negative or positive and I confess to being appalled at the outcomes. Despite my positive views the negative statements I uttered totalled 76 per cent and the positive 24 per cent. Interestingly, the observations were classified into academic reinforcement and behaviour reinforcement, and the outcomes indicated that the majority of my positive comments were directed towards academic issues and the negatives towards behaviour issues (see Figure 7.1).

It was evident that a review of my verbal interactions was necessary, and over the next few weeks I focused strongly on positive verbal reinforcement, especially of behaviour, as my negative comments were actually rewarding and encouraging unacceptable behaviours. Through a system of ignoring minor behaviour issues and consistently praising acceptable behaviours the balance of my verbal interactions changed.

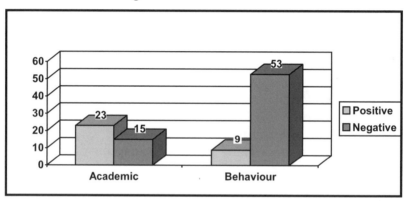

**Figure 7.1**   Positive and negative teacher feedback

Perhaps the most interesting outcome of the exercise was that the children's behaviour, in general, improved considerably, so although this had not been the intention it became a very pleasing outcome. This example highlights three important issues:

- The practitioner (myself) was negatively rewarding unacceptable behaviours.
- The powerful effect of the practitioner's verbal interactions in affecting children's behaviour.
- The value of examining practitioner practices.

# Self-concept

## *Definitions*

Practitioners will be well aware of the importance of enhancing self-esteem but may have limited knowledge of self-concept development and the powerful effects the self-concept can have on very young children. Wall (1996: 82) suggests: 'A child's self-concept is crucial to a positive outlook and progress towards his/her full potential and a range of factors can create a positive or negative self-concept.'

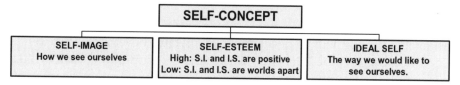

**Figure 7.2**   Dimensions of the self-concept

    The self-concept consists of three interrelated areas and is developed through feedback from significant others in our lives, such as parents, siblings, extended family, teachers/practitioners and peers. The level of self-concept is directly related to both self-image and ideal self in that high self-esteem occurs when self-image and ideal self are both positive and you view yourself as near to your ideal self (see Figure 7.2). Low self-esteem occurs when self-image and ideal self are distanced from each other and your ideal self differs considerably from your self-image. The ideal self is therefore very powerful. It may also be that as adults in a professional capacity we can feel motivated, confident and successful and thus have high levels of self-esteem, while outside work we may feel socially inadequate and therefore have a reduced level of self-esteem. The effects of self-concept cannot be overlooked. Charlton and David offer a helpful summary:

> The self-concept is formed by a process of socialisation by interaction with others and as a result of the feedback of that interaction. 'You are a good boy'; 'You are clever'; 'You are not as good as your sister'. We learn of ourselves by comparison, by competition and by selection processes. The self-concept is related to social skill and like social skill is learned. Failure of social competence leads to rejection, social isolation and subsequently to the formation of poor self-concept. (Charlton and David, 1990: 109)

## Illustrative example

A 3-year-old girl from a deprived household may present at nursery as dirty and unkempt, not wearing fashionable clothes and as hygiene standards at home are poor she has an unpleasant aroma. In my experience, despite many positive characteristics and qualities, she may find it very difficult to make friends and socialise, thus it would be difficult for her to become a full participant of the group. Invitations to play, have tea or attend parties outside the nursery may be limited or non-existent and children may be told by their parents that they are to stay away from her within the nursery. Within the setting children may choose not to sit next to her and, sadly, their naive comments may be very blunt and hurtful. The effects on this little girl could include:

- social difficulties
- emotional difficulties
- poor self-image
- unrealistic ideal self
- low self-esteem
- low self-concept.

Considerable support will be needed for her affective development as well as for any additional difficulties that may arise, such as withdrawal, task avoidance, behaviour difficulties and difficulties accessing the curriculum because of the affective difficulties.

Several writers have summarised the characteristics of children with high and low self-esteem (Mortimer, 2001; Internet 15) but it is pertinent to revisit at this point.

Children with low self-esteem may:

- avoid new tasks
- need reassurance, as they may feel unwanted, unloved or worthless
- feel emotionless or indifferent to emotions
- be quick to respond to frustration and/or failure
- have little faith or belief in themselves
- resist or ignore being corrected or reprimanded
- have a tendency to physical/emotional aggression and/or bullying behaviour
- resist decision-making situations
- have difficulties with learning.

Children with high self-esteem may:

- be confident and independent
- be able to take responsibility
- cope well with frustration and/or failure
- greet new tasks with eagerness and motivation
- acknowledge and understand their own emotions
- help and support others
- accept being corrected or reprimanded
- be aware of their own strengths and weaknesses.

## *Locus of control*

Allied to self-concept theory is locus of control theory, developed from Rotter's (1966) social learning theory. Locus of control relates to the way in which we see success or failure and where the responsibility for that success or failure lies either within our control or from outside our control. If a young boy achieves success and believes this is due to his hard work and effort, then he will have an internal locus of control as he accepts responsibility for the outcomes. However, if he feels his success was due to his brother's help this is an external locus of control as the success is not seen as his own. The same locus of control concept relates equally to failure.

A child's locus of control can therefore affect his/her expectations and future performance either negatively or positively. Some children, usually with internal locus of control, will be able to accept some failures, learn from the experiences and move forwards. Therefore, failure is not necessarily a negative issue; it is the way the child deals with it that is important. Generally speaking very young children begin with an external locus of control but as they mature it is hoped that with appropriate learning experiences and support they will develop an internal locus of control. Lambley (1993: 88) suggests that: 'It has been shown that the self-concept, self-expectation and locus of control beliefs often determine pupils' responses to, and achievements in, the learning situation. The investigation of these factors has highlighted the close relationship between affective and cognitive performance.'

## Factors affecting self-esteem

As mentioned previously, significant others play a vital role in the development of a child's self-esteem and if practitioners are promoting positive self-concept development but the opposite is happening at home then the child's difficulties will be compounded. It will be a constant battle of one step forwards and two steps back, but is nevertheless worth persisting with.

A range of additional factors also affect a child's self-concept including:

- levels of motivation
- positive experiences of learning
- feeling valued and respected
- levels of confidence
- positive feedback for effort as well as achievement
- security and love
- practitioner awareness of affective development
- consistent structure and routine
- clear and realistic expectations of parents, practitioners and the child him/herself
- social and emotional difficulties
- stress.

## Links with other areas

Research continues to highlight links between self-concept and/or self-esteem and other areas of development in children. While some research was conducted focusing on primary and secondary aged children, the important principles are just as relevant to work in the early years. The following indicate a few key links:

- *Academic achievement*: Witter (1988: 94) suggested that 'self-concept and especially academic self-concept have been shown to be related to academic achievement'. He also found that lack of structure within the classroom was a key factor. These findings concur with Coopersmith's (1967) work, Lawrence's (1985; 1987) work and that of James et al. (1991).
- *Pupils' expectations*: Charlton and David (1993) highlighted that expectations are learned and are greatly influenced by significant others affecting our motivation for future learning and performance.
- *Behaviour problems and learning difficulties*: these areas are often interrelated, with self-concept playing a large part within each as children with learning difficulties often exhibit unacceptable behaviours to avoid tasks and/or to gain attention (albeit negative). They also tend to have low self-concept.

## Enhancing the self-concept

Practitioners should remember that the classroom and/or the practitioner can affect children's self-concepts positively or negatively. All interactions and learning opportunities presented to the children will have an effect and it is the practitioner's responsibility to ensure these experiences are positive. A useful resource is the book by Canfield and Wells (1976), offering 100 ways to enhance self-esteem.

*Enhancing the self-concept in the classroom/activity room*:
- Systems of rewarding children for effort as well as achievement.
- Systems of effective target setting.
- Clear rules agreed between practitioners and children.
- Supportive system in which adults accept the blame for children's failures, as the situations may have arisen through inappropriate tasks/mismatch of curriculum.
- Where all individuals are valued and respected.
- Where children's experiences, likes/dislikes, preferred activities, learning styles, background and culture are known and valued.
- Well-organised resources that are accessible to children.
- An ethos that offers security and encourages confidence and independence.

*Practitioner qualities*:
- Having knowledge of children's affective development.
- Being supportive, motivating, encouraging and sensitive.
- Planning for individual needs.
- Setting of challenging but achievable targets.
- Positive classroom management skills.
- Making time to listen to children.
- Valuing and respecting individual children, parents and staff.
- Using positive reinforcement strategies effectively.
- Praising effort as well as achievement.
- Having effective, practical and meaningful recording systems.
- Encouraging peer support and understanding.

## *Self-concept of adults*

Adults within the setting, both staff and parents, should not be overlooked when considering strategies for enhancing self-concept. It is a fact that many of us find it hard to accept praise and will often brush aside comments or devalue the achievement into something less praiseworthy. However, all adults, like children, need support, encouragement, sensitivity and motivation to feel positive about themselves as professionals and from a personal perspective. It is important that we demonstrate the same levels of consideration to all adults we work with, which will help enhance their self-concept as well as support motivation and in turn benefit children.

# Behaviour

Babies are not born behaving inappropriately but as they grow they develop behaviours and strategies as responses to experiences. It therefore follows that the child within an early years setting who displays unacceptable behaviours is not a 'problem child'; it is the learned behaviour that is the problem. These behaviours can be interpreted as appropriate or inappropriate. In a simple, yet quite common example, a toddler wanting a biscuit and wanting it now (as they invariably do) may have learnt the following behaviour pattern:

1 Ask or point, to indicate desire for a biscuit (possibly perceived as a need rather than a desire).
2 If request rejected by adult, persist by repeating request.
3 Continue to persist if unsuccessful, tugging at the adult in the hope they will concede.
4 If this fails, begin whimpering and repeat 'please' constantly.

Possible outcomes: the adult, especially if under pressure, may concede and despite having refused the toddler several times, give the biscuit, or the adult will distract the child or remain firm and no biscuit will be given. Whichever outcome occurs the child will have learnt a useful and valuable lesson for the future. Either, if you persist and whimper you will gain control and win, or it is pointless persisting. The adult's response to this common occurrence may well set the scene for future encounters.

   If we accept that behaviours are learned from significant others, then it follows that behaviour should be defined according to the values and cultures of a child's home environment. Practitioners should reflect on this aspect when responding to behaviours as they may consider a specific behaviour unacceptable by their standards and values that may be highly acceptable within the culture of the home.

## *Learning behaviours*

If behaviours include all our actions, physical, expressive and verbal, then practitioners will need to explore how exhibited behaviours have been learnt and which variables and causal factors are involved.

Young children learn behaviours in much the same way as they develop any other skill, through processes of observing, imitating and experimenting and, as they mature, different variables will emerge that will lead to further changes. Once children enter the pre-school and primary phases of education the importance of the peer group will begin to affect change, while the parents and significant others will still have an important influencing role. When children advance to the secondary phase then the effects of the peer group, combined with the onset of puberty, may well become the stronger forces affecting behaviour.

For the significant others in the lives of very young children the following features would be influential in encouraging positive behaviour:

- consistency of approach
- clear boundaries, rules and expectations
- positive modelling of acceptable behaviours
- strong and positive attachments
- encouraging confidence and independence
- rewarding acceptable behaviours.

## Labelling

In situations where children enter an early years setting and are described by parents and/or other professionals as having behaviour problems, practitioners should be aware of the possible debilitating effects of labelling. Settings should ensure that all adults interacting with the children, whether staff or voluntary helpers, do not allow labels to affect the way they work with the children. Practitioners may inadvertently place unrealistic expectations on the child or simply assume that they will demonstrate unacceptable behaviours and wait for it to happen. If adults expect a child to behave inappropriately then their verbal interactions, gestures and body language may actually encourage such behaviours. If the setting employs positive reinforcement strategies that are different from the child's previous environment(s), then this alone may bring about positive change. Labelling also infers the child is a problem, which we know is not the case. Practitioners should observe, assess and monitor all children and make informed decisions on the basis of the evidence collated, and not make assumptions. In my own experience I had been discussing a child's difficulties with an early years practitioner when a crying child, who claimed a particular boy had smacked him, interrupted us. The adult immediately called out the 'accused' child's name only to discover he was absent that day – an example of assumptions and expectations informing (or misinforming) an adult.

## Causal factors

As with social and emotional difficulties, any child exhibiting unacceptable behaviours should be discussed with parents and staff to agree possible strategies, but before this stage all possible causal factors should be explored. The same range of factors previously explored under social and emotional difficulties should be examined. These can be found in greater detail earlier in this chapter, but cover the areas of:

- the setting
- the home environment
- the practitioner.

If no satisfactory explanations for the current behaviours emerge then observations should take place to establish precisely which behaviours are occurring, how often they occur and how these impact on the child's learning and/or that of other children within the setting.

## *Observations*

Practitioners may find the Pre-School Behaviour Checklist (PBCL) (McGuire and Richman, 1988) helpful in the early stages of assessing the behaviours of an individual child. This short and easy to use checklist helps to focus and clarify thinking about an individual child, but is not a replacement for planned observation and assessment. The authors suggest that: 'The PBCL is designed to help identify children with emotional and behavioural problems by providing a tool for the systematic and objective description of behaviour ... it allows staff to look at the severity as well as the incidence of a particular behaviour' (McGuire and Richman, 1988: 1).

Initially staff should establish the precise behaviours that are causing difficulties and these should be cited in clear and observable terms. 'He/she is aggressive' tells us little about a child's current behaviours, and what is deemed aggressive to one adult may be acceptable to another. 'He/she pushes other children away from desired toys at least six times per three hour session' describes precisely what is happening and how often it occurs, indicating the level of the problem.

The most appropriate observational method must then be selected (see Chapter 5) and several baseline observations completed to indicate the level or frequency of the behaviour. When dealing with unacceptable behaviours it is also beneficial to note the ABC of the behaviour (see Figure 7.3), as it may be the antecedents (A) that are causing the behaviour or the consequence (C) that is rewarding and encouraging the behaviour. For example, if a child receives adult attention each time he/she pushes other children but does not receive adult attention when behaving appropriately, then the adult attention (the consequence) will negatively reward the unwanted behaviour and the child is likely to repeat it. All children (and most adults) like attention and negative attention is better than no attention to young children. On the other hand, if a child snatches a piece of equipment from a second child and the second child reacts negatively creating adult attention, it is the first child's behaviour (antecedent) that needs support not the latter.

**Figure 7.3** The ABC of behaviour

Reverting to the example of the child that pushes others away from a desired toy or piece of equipment, baseline observation (see Figure 7.4) would clarify the extent of the problem and on the basis of this information, combined with knowledge of the child and input from the parents, appropriate strategies can be devised to form an intervention plan. If observations are repeated after a period of time, the results will hopefully show a reduction in the behaviour when compared with the baseline. This evidence will form the basis of any discussions and become a part of the child's records. These would be recorded alongside targets in the form of an IEP or Individual Behaviour Plan (IBP) and would become a working document for future recording. A timescale would be set for the intervention stage and then an evaluation would occur. If successful, the strategies could be gradually withdrawn or if unsuccessful, then revised strategies would need to be prepared.

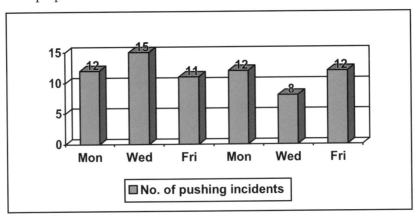

**Figure 7.4** Baseline record of number of times child X pushes another child to gain equipment

Any intervention should be in place for at least three or four weeks before any decisions are made regarding the outcomes, as changes rarely occur overnight. It is also worthy of note that if a child is displaying several or many unacceptable behaviours then these should be prioritised and interventions planned for only one at a time.

If the intervention was unsuccessful and the staff feel that specialist support is needed, the incoming professional will have excellent records through which he/she can identify precisely what the difficulties are and what strategies have been implemented. This will not only save time but will present the staff as competent and thorough in its efforts to support the difficulties.

Monitoring and evaluation will be implicit throughout interventions with recording undertaken throughout the process, guided by the requirements within the Code of Practice (DfES, 2001d).

## *Positive reinforcement*

Intervention strategies will generally include an element of positive reinforcement which requires praise and reward for acceptable behaviours (or the lack of unacceptable behaviours) combined with the avoidance of negative reinforcement. Earlier in this chapter my own experience of verbal interactions in an early years setting was a clear example of inadvertently negatively rewarding undesirable behaviours and not rewarding desirable behaviours enough. In addition there was an imbalance between my reinforcement of academic achievement and behaviour.

Reinforcements do not need to be costly, rather comprising a selection of verbal feedback, use of stickers, drawn pictures or time spent at a favourite activity. It could be that a child always wishes to sit on an adult's lap for circle time activities, so this would be an appropriate reward for that child. Verbal reinforcement should be event specific and child specific to raise its value. To keep repeating 'Well done' throughout the day becomes meaningless whereas 'Well done, XXX, you have tried really hard today', is specific to the child and identifies which behaviour you are rewarding.

When using reinforcement as part of an intervention programme practitioners should be vigilant to catch the child when displaying the desired behaviour, or when not displaying the undesired behaviour. Little and often will reap rewards. With some children it may appear difficult to find an acceptable behaviour to reward, but they can be found. Any reinforcement system should be shared with parents and extended within the home whenever possible to increase the likelihood of success.

## *Summary of behavioural intervention*

The process can be summarised as follows:
1  Identify, discuss and record behaviours causing concerns.
2  Plan and undertake baseline assessments.
3  Examine antecedents, behaviours and consequences.
4  Examine factors within the setting, home and practitioner.
5  Clearly define and record unacceptable behaviours.
6  Discuss with staff and parents, recording outcomes.
7  Prioritise behaviours.
8  Decide on appropriate observational method(s).
9  Implement strategies through IBP, including time limits and SMART targets.
10  Monitor and record progress.
11  Evaluate and record the process.
12  Decide on and record next steps.

Throughout the process discussions with parents and relevant professionals will be ongoing.

## Summary

Throughout this chapter the value and importance of considering the affective development of all children, not just those with special needs, has been emphasised. For children with special needs the fact that they experience difficulties which they may well be aware of makes it all the more important to examine their affective development. Social, emotional and behavioural difficulties are now included within our early years guidance, so practitioners have a responsibility to address this area.

Practitioners should have specific knowledge and skills of average developmental patterns as well as how to provide when difficulties arise, and this may have ramifications for future training needs.

There is an identified need, supported by research, to reflect on a range of possible causal factors including the setting, home and practitioner practices, but at the same time the excellent work already taking place should be acknowledged and celebrated. Issues surrounding personal, social, emotional and behavioural difficulties cannot be overlooked if we aim to provide effectively for the whole child, and practitioners should ensure that provision for these areas of development is included within their planning. Interventions should be planned and evaluated with parental involvement central throughout the process. Self-concept enhancement, of children and adults, should also be an integral part of our work and excellent practices can be seen in evidence nationwide.

This chapter has barely touched on this important area but, hopefully, has given the reader food for thought, reflection and some ideas for future use.

---

### Key issues

- ❖ Practitioner knowledge and skills in the area of affective development are essential.
- ❖ Consideration should be given to personal, social, emotional, behavioural and self-concept development.
- ❖ Factors within the setting, home and practitioner should be examined.
- ❖ Any interventions should be carefully planned, recorded, implemented and evaluated.
- ❖ Parental involvement is essential.

# Suggestions for discussion

## Item 1

Discuss as a staff how your setting addresses the affective development of the children. When providing for the needs of the children do you consider:

- personal development
- social development
- emotional development
- behavioural development
- self-concept development
- the impact of the home, setting and practitioners on young children?

## Item 2

Reflect on one child within your setting whose behaviour is causing concern. Complete the following tasks:

- Define the unacceptable behaviours in precise, observable terms.
- Plan a baseline observation process and consider all possible influencing factors.

If you have not already done so, consider implementing an intervention following the guidelines in this chapter.

## Item 3

As a staff do you feel adequately knowledgeable in the area of affective development? If not, explore possibilities of gaining access to appropriate training.

## Item 4

Think of teachers and colleagues that have inspired and motivated you over the years. List the key characteristics you feel made them so influential in your life. Compare lists as a staff and reflect on which characteristics would best support working in the early years to encourage confidence, motivation and success in young children.

## Item 5

Consider using the MOT questionnaire offered by Long and Fogell (1999: 21–22) within your setting, perhaps as a staff exercise involving discussion of issues raised.

# 📖 Suggested further reading

Barnes, P. (ed.) (1995) *Personal, Social and Emotional Development of Children*. Milton Keynes: Open University Press.

Charlton, T. and David, K. (eds) (1993) *Managing Misbehaviour in Schools*, 2nd edn. London: Routledge.

Long, R. and Fogell, J. (1999) *Supporting Pupils with Emotional Difficulties: Creating a Caring Environment for All*. London: David Fulton.

Mortimer, H. (2000) *Developing Individual Behaviour Plans in Early Years*. Tamworth: NASEN.

# 8

## Inclusive Education for Young Children

### Introduction

Historically early years settings have been accommodating of all children and have sought to provide effectively for each child. In the present climate of increasing inclusion the demands on early years settings are even greater. It could be suggested that early years settings, with reduced adult:child ratios compared with schools, are better placed to provide for individual needs. However, many issues still need addressing and it is these issues that are identified and explored in this chapter using theory and research to support and inform debate. Using poverty as an example, implications for practitioners are raised and practical strategies suggested.

It could be suggested that the inclusive society we strive for, with its inclusive education system, is now becoming a reality. However, others might argue that the reality is still a distance away and that in the fields of early years and special education we have to face considerable challenges to achieve total inclusion. It is these very issues that will be explored. In addition effective provision for all children within all early years settings could be deemed not to be realistic or feasible. Arguments and debate on such views will be raised.

Issues surrounding government legislation and guidance are examined and confusions highlighted. For example, within one of the latest guidance documents for schools, *Inclusive Schooling*, the introduction claims that:

> The Act seeks to enable more pupils who have special educational needs to be included successfully within mainstream education. This clearly signals that where parents want a mainstream education for their child everything possible should be done to provide it. Equally where parents want a special school place their wishes should be listened to and taken into account. (DfES, 2001b: 1)

This clearly indicates a need for special schools, so are we aiming for an inclusive education system or a system with some segregation but mostly inclusion? If the government continues to produce documents on 'Special Educational Needs' such as the *Special Educational Needs Code of Practice* (DfES, 2001d) and *Inclusive Schooling: Children with Special Educational Needs* (DfES, 2001b), then immediately there is a conflict of philosophies. If there is a need to produce such guidance, then the government is highlighting the separate nature of provision for children with special needs. In a truly inclusive system should we not expect guidance purely on early years practice, primary practice and secondary practice, as this should automatically include provision for all children regardless of ethnic background, culture and/or special need?

# Historical development and legislation

While Chapter 1 explored the history of special needs provision, this section will focus on the history and development of inclusion within the field of education. Over the years, but most specifically since the 1970s, the availability of research and literature regarding inclusion has increased tremendously. After the Warnock Report (DES, 1978) integration became a key debating issue which has since progressed to movements towards an inclusive education system for all children.

## *Pre-1970*

The 1913 Mental Deficiency Act placed a requirement on local authorities to identify children between 7 and 16 who were deemed 'ineducable' due to the severity of their difficulties. Many of these children were then placed in institutions and lived out their lives there. At this stage segregation was clearly evident and reflected the philosophies of the time.

Following the 1944 Education Act (Ministry of Education, 1944) more teachers were trained to teach children with learning difficulties but some children were still deemed ineducable and were classified as mentally handicapped, having their needs addressed by the health authorities. The segregated approach therefore continued.

## *1970–85*

Perhaps the greatest changes came after the 1970 Education Act when LEAs took responsibility for all children of statutory school age, removing thousands of children from institutions as they were no longer classified as ineducable. An increased range of segregated provision arose in the UK to address the needs of all children classified as incapable of coping with mainstream schooling. At this time medical input was still a key influence. The special school system gave teachers opportunities to train in the field of special educational needs, giving them specialised knowledge and skills which are still perceived by many today as 'expert' knowledge beyond that of mainstream teachers.

Following the Act an increased range of special schools emerged and debate began regarding the most appropriate ways of educating children who were not able to be catered for in mainstream schools. This debate continued until the establishment of a Committee of Enquiry to examine the education of children and young people with learning difficulties. This committee, chaired by Mary

Warnock, produced its report known as the 'Warnock Report', in 1978, which was seen by many as an influential turning point for special education and special educational provision. The report offered a continuum of special educational needs as opposed to specific categories such as educationally subnormal (ESN) and moderate learning difficulties (MLD). A shift of emphasis was suggested offering three forms of integration for consideration by LEAs:

1 Locational: special provision on a mainstream site but with no interaction between the two groups of children.
2 Social: special provision on a mainstream site with children from both settings meeting for non-academic times such as play times and assemblies.
3 Functional: all children share the school day and all activities within it. This is the closest form of integration to today's inclusive philosophy, but required greater understanding and changes from national level to teachers, non-teaching staff and parents.

The ensuing Education Act (1981) adopted many of the recommendations contained within the Warnock Report for special education, however, there were many critics. Parents as well as researchers such as Hornby, Atkinson and Howard identified the conditions for integrating an individual child as a major loophole through which many children were excluded from their local schools by the LEA:

> The four criteria were:
> • that this was in accordance with the parental wishes;
> • that the child's educational needs could be met in the ordinary school;
> • that it would be consistent with efficient use of resources;
> • that it would not detract from the education of the SEN child's classmates.
> (Hornby, Atkinson and Howard, 1997: 70)

The 1981 Education Act also introduced the statementing process through which children with special educational needs were assessed by the LEA and a statement of their needs produced, indicating the provision required to meet their needs. Following this, and the fact that parents had no means of appealing against LEA decisions, parents' groups such as Network 81 (named after the Act) were established to lobby government, support other parents and to address the many issues that emerged in subsequent years regarding the legislation.

Another issue raised at the time was that of training. Many writers, such as Gulliford (1981), felt it was important that all teachers should receive considerable input regarding provision for children with special needs in their initial training and that specialist courses should be available to existing teachers extending their knowledge and expertise to provide for children with special educational needs. At the same time however, it was generally felt that the Warnock Report raised awareness of key issues and the beginnings of inclusion and was therefore very positive. Today, in the new millennium and over 25 years later, we are still striving to achieve full inclusion for all our children in an educational sense.

## *1985 to date*

As the 1981 Education Act began to change the face of special education, concerns and further issues arose as time progressed. To address some of these, the 1993 Education Act came into force followed by the Code of Practice (DfEE, 1994). While not moving inclusion any further forwards, the continuum of provision from segregated provision to integration was again emphasised but critics again voiced concerns. Booth (1994) expressed concerns as he saw that inclusion was yet again overlooked in favour of integration.

The Code of Practice (DfEE, 1994) also introduced the five-staged approach to the identification and assessment of special educational needs culminating, if appropriate, in a statement of special educational needs produced by the LEA. In the revised Code of Practice (DfES, 2001d) this has been updated to a graduated approach which in the early years equates to Early Years Action and Early Years Action Plus.

In the same year, the international *Salamanca Statement on Principles, Policy and Practice in Special Needs Education* (UNESCO, 1994) was produced, supported by over 90 governments, including the UK, and indicating total commitment to inclusive education. Within the UK this was closely followed by a government Green Paper *Excellence for All: Meeting Special Educational Needs* clearly indicating an intention to move towards greater inclusion, with fewer children in segregated, special school provision:

> The ultimate purpose of SEN provision is to enable young people to flourish in adult life. There are therefore strong educational, as well as social and moral, grounds for educating children with SEN with their peers. We aim to increase the level and quality of inclusion within mainstream schools, while protecting and enhancing specialist provision for those who need it. (DfEE, 1997: 43)

At the end of the same chapter targets for 2002 were produced including:

- more mainstream schools accommodating children with SEN
- national and local programmes to support increased inclusion
- mainstream schools utilising the resources (human and material) from special schools to develop and support inclusive practices.

Since this time, government funding initiatives have been developed to support LEA inclusion developments as it is acknowledged that planning and financial support will be necessary. Currently, schools can work with the LEA to vie for funding allocations or in some cases, can apply directly to the government. The Standards Fund offers grants to support the improvement of a range of educational standards including inclusion. The SEN Standards Fund Grant aims to support schools in the development of their inclusive policies, particularly in light of the new legislation and guidance in 2001. In total, £82 million was available during 2001–02. However, some LEAs have spent considerable amounts on audits of existing provision, thus reducing the amounts directly available to schools. While the benefits of audits cannot be overlooked, the resulting effect is still reduced funding to the education providers, the schools. The Schools Access Initiative, which is also available to pre-school providers, aims to support the improvement of the physical nature of the building to increase access potential. Over the period 2001–04 it is expected that £220 million will be made available.

The Special Education Needs and Disability Discrimination Act (SENDA) (DfES, 2001c) has an underlying philosophy based on a belief in inclusion for all children. The supporting guidance document, *Inclusive Schooling: Children with Special Educational Needs* (DfES, 2001b: 1) details the current situation: 'The Special Educational Needs and Disability Act 2001 delivers a strengthened right to a mainstream education for children with special educational needs. The Act seeks to enable more pupils who have special educational needs to be included successfully within mainstream education.'

# Definitions and models

## Models

Models of disability have changed over the years to accommodate increased knowledge and beliefs informed by research. To appreciate and understand inclusion, practitioners need to be aware of two key models: the medical model and the social model. These have been selected as there is evidence from people with disabilities indicating these models were most commonly used in their experience (Internet 16). Awareness is also needed of a variety of models suggested by researchers over the years, such as Sandow's (1994) models for special needs:

- the magical model
- the moral model
- the medical model
- the intellectual model
- the social competence model
- the disadvantage model
- the social conspiracy model.

### The medical model
This model is based on making a diagnosis of a condition and then recommending the cure or treatment. It does not reflect on the individual under diagnosis and assumes that treatment or special school provision will enable the individual to become more 'normal', which in turn will improve his/her life and prospects. The child is seen as having a problem and the outcome is often removal from the family and community to special provision, and in some cases in another county. This model clearly labels and segregates.

*The social model*

In contrast, the social model perceives every individual as a part of the social community and therefore is more inclusive. As a society we have created considerable physical barriers such as steps, escalators and lack of hearing/visual facilities and, therefore, have segregated by the design and layout of our lifestyles. The social model acknowledges that barriers should be removed to enable access for all members of the community in all aspects of their chosen life.

Over the last 100 years we have slowly progressed from the medical model of identifying and supporting special needs to a more inclusive system, which is perhaps aiming for the social model of total inclusion for individuals within our society.

## Definitions of inclusion

We have already discussed the move from integration policies to inclusive education policies, but often the term 'inclusion' is used alone. Perhaps the most helpful source of information is the Centre for Studies on Inclusive Education (CSIE) (Internet 15, 2002: 1) that defines inclusion as: 'The processes of increasing the participation of students in, and reducing their exclusion from, the cultures, curricula and communities of local schools.'

Within this definition inclusion is seen as a gradual and developing process working towards inclusion for all pupils so individual settings, schools and LEAs will be at different stages of the process but striving toward the same end. The CSIE highlights the difference between integration and inclusion, which supports our understanding. Integration is viewed as moving a child into a different environment and then adapting to accommodate his/her needs, while inclusion exists where all children have a right to be able to access all facilities offered and are therefore a part of that community. The CSIE position for the future (Internet 15, 2001: 2) is 'full inclusion means the deconstruction and eventual closure of separate special schools, the transfer of resources to the mainstream and the restructuring of ordinary schools'.

An alternative definition of inclusion is offered by Farrell (2001: 7): 'For inclusion to be effective pupils must actively belong to, be welcomed by and participate in a school and community – that is they should be fully included.'

In summary inclusion within early years settings is a process by which *all* children can access, at all times, all aspects of the provision. It is not a process in which practitioners welcome a child and adapt the curriculum and/or resources to provide for that child, rather that the inclusive setting will automatically be catering for individual needs and will therefore offer effective provision to every child. Provision will not offer deficit services that adapt to meet perceived or identified deficits within children but will offer entitlement to all children.

Common principles of early years practice, as identified by Blenkin (1994) and Bruce (1987) among others, have now been likened to the principles suggested for inclusion in educational settings. Lloyd concludes that:

High-quality, effective early years education can clearly be seen, then to provide a vitally important foundation stone for the whole of education, for all children. An education system which built upon this firm foundation and used its principles as a model to underpin the policy, provision and organisation of further levels to develop a genuinely inclusive education for all, clearly would offer real access to educational opportunity to all as an entitlement. (Lloyd, 1997: 178)

Therefore for early years settings the gap between existing and inclusive practices should not be too great. With increased knowledge and funding, effective inclusion for all children should be feasible. These and other relevant issues will be discussed further later.

## *Principles*

If practitioners are required to work towards an inclusive system, then we need to be clear on the underlying principles that inform such work. The definitions of inclusion give us an indication of some of the key principles:

- access for all children in their local settings
- full participation for all children in all aspects of the provision
- appropriate opportunities for individual children to work towards their full potential
- the breaking down of barriers to access and participation
- the right to belong to the local community
- respect for all individuals.

The *Index for Inclusion* (Booth et al., 2000) was produced by the CSIE and circulated to all schools. Offering guidance for schools to offer greater inclusion, the publication is currently recommended in many legislative and guidance documents and is now being used in many countries including Norway, Spain and Brazil. The Index offers five progressive stages to settings to work through as a collaborative process that will lead to increased inclusive working practices:

- Stage 1: Starting the process
- Stage 2: Finding out about the school (setting)
- Stage 3: Producing a development plan for future work
- Stage 4: Implementing developments
- Stage 5: Reviewing the process.

The Index offers the Inclusion Charter which was first produced in 1989 and contains the fundamental principles on which the Index was based. In summary they are:

- an end to segregated education
- all children share equal value and status
- the transfer of resources from special to mainstream provision

- segregated education supports society's segregated approach when children with disabilities complete their education and move into adulthood
- increased community opportunities for children with disabilities will be jeopardised unless segregated educational provision is reduced
- local and central governments should support the reduction and eventual removal of all special schools (adapted from Internet 15).

On the other hand the Inclusive Schooling guidance document suggests that practitioners should use the following as 'key principles':

- Inclusion is a process by which settings and authorities develop their cultures, policies and practices to include pupils.
- With the right training, strategies and support nearly all children with special educational needs can be successfully included in mainstream education.
- An inclusive education service offers excellence and choice and incorporates the views of parents and children.
- The interests of all pupils must be safeguarded.
- All involved should actively seek to remove barriers to learning and participation.
- All children should have access to an appropriate education.
- Mainstream education will not always be right for every child all of the time. (DfES, 2001b: 2)

It is interesting to note that the principles from the Index focus greatly on the reduction and final elimination of all segregated forms of provision, while the DfES guidance focuses more on the features of an inclusive education service and the rights of parents and children alike yet still segregates some children. Clearly the emphases differ, which creates an uncertainty as to the underlying philosophy of inclusion.

## Reasons for inclusion

Many of the reasons for moving towards inclusion will be known to practitioners but are worth revisiting. If we include young children within our early years settings and they are able to progress with their neighbourhood peers to primary and secondary schools then we will be offering them a more inclusive future. Their perceptions of each other will be influenced by individual characteristics and personalities rather than abilities, disabilities, culture or race and they will all be members of society who have shared equal opportunities throughout childhood and will therefore expect the same in adulthood. This should ultimately lead to considerable and positive societal changes of attitudes and values. If we segregate young children with special needs from their local friends we are encouraging a segregated existence from a very early age. All children have rights to be treated equally, valued and respected and it is difficult to satisfy these requirements in a segregated society. The benefits to individuals and wider society will be wide-ranging but should help to break down barriers and encourage greater tolerance and understanding, thus valuing diversity. As Chizea, Henderson and Jones suggest:

> pre-schools are part of their local community, the focus very often of community involvement and support. The pre-school model of society, in which all members have something to offer and in which all members can find the level of support they need, can provide an inclusive approach to the needs of all children. (Chizea, Henderson and Jones, 1999: 5)

In an inclusive early years setting, all children, including those with special needs, should therefore be able to develop positive attitudes between children and to their learning environment, encourage confidence, motivation to learn and enhance self-concepts. Each child will be valued and acknowledged as a unique individual and his/her needs (special or otherwise) will be addressed appropriately through careful planning and the introduction of relevant, meaningful and individualised tasks and experiences. However, it should be recognised that a learning opportunity for one child will not necessarily be appropriate or relevant to other children, so differentiation of tasks is an important consideration for all young children. For those children experiencing difficulties every causal factor and variable must be reflected upon before targets can be set and opportunities presented; this includes consideration of the affective as well as curricular needs of individual children.

The CSIE again offer their own suggestions as to why practitioners should support inclusive practices:

> Ten reasons for Inclusion:
> - All children have the right to learn together.
> - Children should not be devalued or discriminated against.
> - Disabled adults, describing themselves as special school survivors, are demanding an end to segregation.
> - There are no legitimate reasons to separate children for their education. Children belong together, with advantages and benefits for everyone. They do not need to be protected from each other.
> - Research shows children do better, academically and socially, in integrated settings.
> - There is no teaching or care that cannot take place in an ordinary school.
> - Given commitment and support, inclusive education is a more efficient use of educational resources.
> - Segregation teaches children to be fearful, ignorant and breeds injustice.
> - All children need an education that will help them develop relationships and prepare them for life in the mainstream.
> - Only inclusion has the potential to reduce fear and to build friendship, respect and understanding. (Internet 15)

## Enabling inclusion in early years settings

Perhaps the most obvious requirement enabling inclusive education in our early years settings is that of the commitment and support of staff and parents. All involved must be aware of the changes that will be required which will be informed by the acknowledgement of the benefits of real inclusion for all. The principles of inclusion and the Index for Inclusion would prove useful starting points for settings considering a move towards inclusion as they both offer clear guidance backed up by research. Although the process may seem daunting many early years settings already incorporate many features of inclusion, so when further explored the changes required may not be as great as originally thought. If we consider some key features of inclusive practice the existing similarities with good early years practice should emerge:

1  Awareness and understanding of inclusive practices, including legislation and guidance.
2  Commitment and support of parents and staff.
3  Effective inclusive education policy.
4  Respect of each individual involved with the setting (children and adults).
5  Physical access for all children and adults.
6  Access to all learning opportunities and resources.
7  An appropriate curriculum to support individual learning.
8  The use of teaching strategies to enable all children access to learning opportunities.
9  The effective use of support staff and SENCO to enhance inclusion and reduce withdrawal and thus segregation.
10  Effective planning and monitoring of progress.
11  Effective policies for responding to special educational needs and affective developmental needs.
12  Removing the use of labels.
13  Positive parental partnerships.
14  Positive interagency working practices.
15  Positive adult role models.

To achieve these aims practitioners will need to reflect on the planning, monitoring and recording systems, the curriculum, the use of teaching support and physical access issues. This may result in the emergence of issues regarding training and/or funding which the setting will clearly need to address.

The Organisation for Economic Cooperation and Development (OECD) continues to instigate research into making inclusion work in mainstream settings in eight countries: Australia, Canada, Germany, the UK, the USA, Italy, Denmark and Iceland. The findings of these studies have resulted in ten key points deemed central to the inclusion process, which can be summarised:

• All involved with education to accept responsibility to educate all children.
• Schools should be set up to be learning environments, to include flexibility, ability to adapt, develop inclusion, funding and training.
• Teachers' abilities to adapt learning situations to accommodate the needs of all children.

- Recognition of need for initial and ongoing training.
- Teacher recognition of the limitations of their own knowledge and skills and readiness to call in specialist support.
- Need for specialists to be prepared to support teachers.
- Involvement of the whole community.
- Need for public accountability.
- Funding issues to be addressed.
- Leadership at government level for the development of effective policies. (adapted from Evans, 2000: 37–8).

However settings approach the process of increasing inclusion, all staff need to plan ways forwards. Change does not just happen; an action plan and/or development plan should be drawn up with target dates. The process will be ongoing and depend at times on outside agencies, for example for the resolution of training and funding issues. However, settings should begin the process to follow current legislation and ensure children their right to belong and be equal.

# Issues and barriers

An inclusive education that provides effectively for all children is still a way off in the UK but in our attempts to progress in this area we uncover many issues that need addressing and barriers to be overcome. Early years practitioners need to be aware of these issues and potential barriers in order to succeed.

## *Speed of change and practitioner concerns*

If one of the key principles for effective inclusion is that of support of all staff involved, then clearly teacher commitment is essential. It could be suggested, however, that some teachers may be concerned about the speed of recent educational changes that have been implemented, as well as raising concerns about realistically being able to provide for the needs of all the children all the time while still delivering the curriculum and completing planning and recording documentation. This view is supported by Scruggs and Mastropieri's (1996) review of research on teachers' views undertaken between 1958 and 1995. Hornby, Atkinson and Howard discuss the findings and suggest that:

> The major finding was that, although on average 65% of teachers supported the general concept of inclusion, only 40% believed that this is a realistic goal for most children. Fifty-three per cent of teachers reported that they were willing to teach students with disabilities and 54% considered that such students could benefit from inclusion. However, only 33% of teachers believed that the mainstream classroom was the best place for students with disabilities and 30% suggested that they could have a negative affect on the classroom environment. (Hornby, Atkinson and Howard, 1997: 79)

Another factor within this research highlighted that less than a third of teachers felt they had the necessary knowledge and skills to provide appropriately for children with disabilities. If this review of research was updated then clearly a more recent picture would emerge which could indicate a change in teacher perspectives. However, if the changes are not considerable then there are some significant issues to be addressed.

In my own very recent experience I encountered a young teacher who admitted she was struggling to cope with a class of 30 5-year-olds, including two autistic children, one with Down syndrome and three with Attention Deficit Hyperactivity Disorder. She felt demoralised and that she was failing herself and the children. The National Curriculum, Literacy and Numeracy Strategies and planning and recording were commanding a great deal of her time and her lack of knowledge regarding providing for children with special needs was compounding her difficulties. Thankfully at the time of meeting her she was attending a relevant course that would hopefully extend her knowledge and skills.

Without sufficient training, knowledge, skills and support practitioners will not necessarily be able to provide the inclusive education system that the UK is currently striving for. These in turn raise issues regarding funding, support and the availability of relevant training for practitioners.

## *Parental perspectives*

Current legislation rightly offers parents a voice in the choice of school for their child, however there are many instances where it has been suggested that this choice is diminished. Perhaps sensationalised by media, there are suggestions that children are being refused places at their chosen schools for a range of reasons. Some would suggest that the effects of the league tables and schools' accountability force some schools to be somewhat selective about their intake. For children with special educational needs it may be that the league table results would be lower due to results of statutory testing or that other parents are concerned about the effects on their own child. For children with specific difficulties such as autism it may be that the parents would prefer the child to be educated away from home at a specialist school in another county and are asking their own county to fund this. Practitioners need to be aware of such issues but without significant research the issues cannot be addressed in a professional manner.

Existing research on parental perceptions of segregated versus integrated provision for their children tends to be quite dated now, but as an indicator Hornby, Atkinson and Howard (1997: 79) summarise the findings of research undertaking during the 1980s and early 1990s: 'the findings of research on parent perceptions of segregated and integrated placements suggest that parents are neither overwhelmingly for or against the practice of integration'.

The current situation remains that there are systems in place to support parents of children with special educational needs who are unhappy about the selected school for their child, including the Parents in Partnerships schemes and the SEN tribunal. In addition organisations such as the Advisory Centre for Education would be a useful source of support and information. The SENDA (DfES, 2001c) also supports parental choice.

## Funding and training

Funding appears to be a recurring issue within early years, and funding to support required inclusion is no exception. Areas for consideration and issues of concern have been raised throughout the chapters of this book and funding is often present as an influential factor. One of the problems within early years is the diversity of provision and if we take the two examples of a nursery class attached to, and partly funded by, a mainstream school and a self-funding pre-school then differences will become clear. Staff working under the school management will be able to access a range of training that will invariably be funded by the school if the relevance and appropriateness of the course is apparent. However, for pre-schools, funds for training may be limited or even non-existent. The fact that pre-schools have experienced periods of closure through lack of financial viability indicates the level of this problem. This clearly represents an inequality. In addition many relevant training courses are offered by local colleges and universities but the costs are prohibitive to many pre-school practitioners. The usual process of advertising college training courses is through the schools' mail service so mail shots and newsletters will be sent out in this way. They do not, therefore, arrive at private nurseries, childminders, day nurseries and pre-schools so these practitioners are not necessarily aware of the availability of the training. In addition, the costs of such courses are often prohibitive to pre-schools, day nurseries and childminders. This issue needs addressing.

As we have already identified that early years practitioners need the knowledge, skills and expertise to provide for the individual needs of a range of children with special needs, then training should be accessible to all early years practitioners if inclusion is to succeed.

## Use of learning support workers

The way in which learning support workers are used and funded will greatly influence the success of inclusive practices. Many learning support workers are not qualified teachers, but in many instances the expectations that are placed on them are considerable. It could be suggested that, if a support worker is working with an autistic child, he/she should have as a minimum, knowledge of child development, special educational needs and autism. In my experience this is not always the case. Again training, and thus funding, may be issues to be addressed.

As inclusive education becomes more widespread the skills and expertise within existing special facilities could be accessed and used effectively via a range of training and support work to ensure that support workers have the necessary skills to provide for the needs of all children and support the practitioners. It is essential that existing skills and expertise should be shared with non-statutory providers.

To support full inclusion, settings also need to reflect on the use of support workers, as it is important that support workers and practitioners work together to plan in a coordinated manner to ensure consistency for the child. It could be suggested that there is no longer a place for withdrawing a child into a separate area for individual work with a support worker, but there are occasions when withdrawal may be appropriate. However, there would need to be joint planning to ensure transference of skills and cohesion.

## Issues of access

Issues of access relate to both physical access to the building and access to the curriculum. With the SENDA (DfES, 2001c) schools must adhere to new regulations on access to buildings. Schools may not refuse a disabled child without 'lawful justification' and they must show that they are making every effort to accommodate the child and are working to improve access for all (adults and children).

Clearly, this will have a huge impact on the majority of schools and early years settings around the UK and development plans are being drawn up to improve access and any new schools being built will have to address the new legislation. As previously mentioned the Schools Access Initiative is making money available to support access initiatives.

As regards access to the curriculum (explicit and hidden) the responsibility will lie with the practitioners to ensure that the provision offered enables equal opportunities and access to all children within the setting. This may again indicate within some or many settings that training is needed to support and develop these skills and, in turn, this impacts on funding.

## Positive outlook for early years

It can be seen that a range of issues may emerge when practitioners address the new guidance and work towards greater inclusion within their settings. These issues will all need addressing, whether at local or national level. I do not want to infer that inclusion is therefore not feasible because there are too many barriers to be overcome. I consider inclusion is feasible and achievable and that early years practitioners are more than capable of offering inclusion, acknowledging that successful inclusion already occurs in many settings. However, this will not be the case for all settings and will therefore depend on, first, the acknowledgement of potential barriers and, secondly, the motivation and support (practical and financial) to address those issues for those settings.

Lewis (2000) highlighted some important concerns with regard to inclusion which may offer some food for thought for many practitioners. He suggests that terminology has moved from 'inclusive education' to 'inclusion', which I am guilty of within this chapter, and his concern is that we are forgetting the 'education' element of inclusion. He contends that if we are aiming to include all children within our current education system then there is an assumption that the current education system is successful and positive, provides for all children and therefore should be available to more children. Lewis questions this assumption by asking if the existing system is successful then why are so many children being excluded from primary and secondary schools? If it is suggested that the existing system is not necessarily appropriate for all, then should we not be focusing on improving that system before opening it up to possibly more vulnerable children? While this may not seem appropriate within an early years book it could be suggested that as early years build the foundations for that later learning then the issues are relevant. I offer this as food for thought.

## Including disadvantaged children

As with any other individual need, practitioners need to be aware of the specific implications of disadvantage within an early years setting but at the same time focus on the needs of the individual child as opposed to the label of disadvantage. As discussed throughout this book, the most important practitioner attributes will be to reflect on a child's individual needs within the context of the setting and identify the most appropriate approaches to respond to the child. These would be developed through a process of spending time getting to know the child, reviewing previous assessments and reports, and talking to his/her parents. These would be supplemented by clear and purposeful observations to identify the child's strengths and any weaker areas. From this point the staff and parents can discuss possible strategies, outline SMART targets for future intervention and agree a review date. Then the work will start.

However, it would be preferable for the practitioners involved to be aware of the effects of disadvantage on young children to inform their understanding of the child and the family. This should enable reflection on the child's affective development as well as general and academic development.

The limitations of the context of this chapter mean that only a snapshot of disadvantage can be presented, so I recommend that readers further their knowledge through the suggested further reading and the bibliography.

### Background information on disadvantage

As a starting point it is worth highlighting that in 1994 the UK had the highest child poverty rates of all the European Union countries. In addition the Department of Social Security statistics (2000) revealed that between 1994 and

1998–99 the number of children being brought up in homes where the income was below half the national average increased over threefold, rising from 10 per cent to 35 per cent. If the implications of this are translated into early years provision then clearly they are far reaching. Bradshaw suggests reasons for this increase:

> The reasons for this record are fairly clear. Our family demography does not help; a comparatively high fertility rate, low age of first marriage, high divorce rate, low mean age of child-bearing, high birth-rate outside marriage, high proportion of lone parents, high proportion of cohabiting couples, high proportion of families with three or more children (Ditch et al, 1998). All these factors are likely to be associated with high rates of child poverty. (Bradshaw, 2001: 15)

However, Bradshaw contends that as the demography of the UK is similar to that of France, which is perhaps questionable, why does the UK have by far the highest rate of child poverty? This is an issue that he continues to explore and debate in his work.

Generally speaking children classified as living in poverty would live in temporary or council-owned properties which tend to be concentrated in large estates. Thus the effects of poverty will affect early years settings in such areas far more than other areas of the UK. However, in my experience there are many local authorities that own rural properties and the children will feed into their local provision, such as pre-schools. In these instances practitioners will need to be aware of the individual needs of the child and his/her family to be able to respond appropriately.

The current Labour government has declared it will fund a range of initiatives such as SureStart, improve the welfare benefits system and encourage mothers to return to work in an attempt to remove a million children from deprived situations, meanwhile practitioners will need to support these vulnerable children.

## Outcomes of poverty

The outcomes of poverty can be devastating, long term and part of an ongoing cyclical process. Research has highlighted key links between poverty and child mortality rates, child abuse, child homelessness, teenage pregnancies, teenage drug and alcohol abuse, crime and violence, child mental health, suicide, anti-social behaviour and poor educational achievement (see Bradshaw, 2001). While schools cannot and should not resolve all these issues, practitioners can certainly work to improve the educational achievements of disadvantaged children.

## Education and poverty

Having established the levels of child poverty and thus identified the magnitude of the issue we need to highlight the importance of effective educational opportunities to support children living in poverty and increase their chances of climbing out of poverty in the future.

The current cycle of many deprived children involves the links between academic performance and future career prospects. Clearly, if a young person leaves school with few or no qualifications (academic or vocational) then the opportunities for gaining employment will be limited. Thus the cycle of poverty continues. This complex issue is also compounded by the fact that many children from disadvantaged backgrounds become disillusioned with schools, often due to repeated failures, and are excluded for a variety of reasons. Conversely, they may remove themselves from the school situation. Either of these actions will reduce their chances for employment further.

There are schools that have effective pastoral care programmes that have been proven to support the needs of disadvantaged children extremely well, thus reducing the disabling effects of poverty. Many of the issues highlighted in the previous chapter, relating to children's affective development, will be features of the systems evident in such schools. The foundations for such effective practice should be evident in all our early years settings and continued throughout the statutory school system to offer children opportunities to support their needs and increase future potential.

Research has historically focused on the links between poverty and academic achievement within the statutory school age range. As the early years continue to become more established future research will hopefully include more data relating to this crucial period to directly inform our future planning. However, Quilgars offers a helpful summary of research evidence relating to primary aged children:

> Other studies, including Bondi (1991) and Hutchinson (1993), also report that pupils from disadvantaged backgrounds remain behind their peers or fall further behind their peers over the primary school years. Overall, the available research consistently reveals a clear link between a range of poverty indicators and educational achievement and progress in primary school. (Quilgars, 2001: 126)

In summary, this relevant background knowledge informs early years practitioners as to the potentially damaging effects that poverty can have on children and young people. If we can provide effectively for the needs of children from disadvantaged backgrounds in the early years, followed by continued progress throughout statutory schooling then, hopefully, we will enable more children to escape the poverty trap as adults. By considering a case study, appropriate strategies for supporting children in the early years will be highlighted along with key issues raised.

## Case study

A 3-year-old girl, Debbie, is referred to a pre-school group by the family's health visitor. The accompanying report suggests that Debbie's difficulties lie in the areas of social and emotional development and general developmental delay, and that the family comprises a lone parent mother and three siblings, aged 6, 4, and 18 months living in a council flat. The family is described as living in squalid and impoverished conditions. Debbie's father is also the father of her younger sibling but the older siblings have a different father. Debbie's father is currently serving a two-year prison sentence.

A member of staff undertakes a home visit to discuss the placement with Debbie's mother who is keen for her to attend. It is agreed that Debbie will initially be observed and then staff will again meet with her mother to discuss any interventions considered appropriate.

A key worker for Debbie is agreed who then undertakes a range of initial observations to inform future planning. These highlight the following:

- Debbie loves books, stories and rhymes.
- Debbie initially found adult attention difficult to deal with but has adapted quickly and now seeks adult attention.
- Debbie is very keen to please adults.
- Debbie has a good attention span.
- Debbie's cognitive development appears to have improved considerably in the short time she has been attending.
- Debbie now shows age appropriate skills with regard to fine motor, gross motor, hearing and speech and cognitive skills.
- Debbie finds it difficult to interact appropriately with peers as she withdraws when other children approach her or speak to her.
- Some children react negatively to Debbie.

The outcomes were discussed by the staff and the following strategies were agreed with parents:

*Specific:*
Debbie will work initially in a one-to-one situation with her key worker for 5–10 minute periods at least three times in each session she attends. This will later be extended to include another child. In time this will be extended to three and four children working together with the key worker taking less of an active role.

*General:*
- Debbie's love of books, stories and rhymes will be encouraged through the usual planned activities within the group.
- Staff will ensure consistent positive praise and positive reinforcement to support Debbie's social and emotional development and enhance her self-concept.

- As a whole group the topic of friends will be developed for the next half term to help improve the skills of all children within the group.

Before the review meeting Debbie's key worker had liaised constantly with the health visitor and the need for support regarding basic hygiene was highlighted. Within the setting a few children had made negative comments regarding Debbie's attire and an unpleasant aroma. This was to be addressed within the setting through a group topic, but it was felt that some support and advice from the health visitor to the mother could also help to alleviate the difficulty.

At the review meeting six weeks later it was reported that Debbie had settled very well and was improving in all developmental areas. In the areas of fine motor and cognitive skills she was demonstrating skills above expectations for children of her age. She was beginning to interact more with her peers but this was still at an early stage of development and would be continuing. The 'Friends' topic had commenced and it was hoped that all children in the group would benefit. Staff were delighted to see that Debbie was now less withdrawn and was delighted with her 'new' clothes. She had also been very proud to share her 'new' clothes with the group at news time, supported by her key worker.

## Issues arising

From the case study the following issues can be highlighted:

- The practitioner's home visit and initial observation informed planning positively.
- Liaison with the health visitor regarding Debbie's dress supported the work that was undertaken within the group regarding developing Debbie's social skills.
- The mother was praised at the review meeting for the improvements in Debbie's appearance to help support the mother's low self-concept. This could indirectly enhance her parenting skills and interactions with her children.
- Debbie's individual needs were identified and provided for appropriately with positive outcomes. Although the topic was for the benefit of all the children the intentions were clearly to support the reactions of some of the other children, which would in turn support Debbie.
- The strategies identified to support Debbie acknowledged and supported her affective development as well as her academic development.
- The setting acknowledged that they could not remove the poverty issues but responded to those issues that were within their control.

This setting addressed Debbie's individual needs effectively and with few real changes to existing planning and provision systems. The processes of home visiting, observation, identifying strengths and weaknesses/likes and dislikes, planning interventions and evaluating progress combined with parental involvement and liaison with outside professionals have all been seen to support a child's needs. Viewing Debbie as an individual and taking into account her family and their needs, her background and the effects of that background combined with an understanding of the effects of poverty and deprivation have all helped to present an holistic understanding of Debbie. Once that stage has been reached then informed and effective decisions can be made.

This case study highlights the effects of a deprived background on a little girl and ways to individualise planning to accommodate her needs. Debbie's individual needs were addressed, not the poverty. Many early years settings would already support a child in such a manner that again identifies the commonalities between early years practice and inclusive practices.

## Summary

Throughout this chapter we have explored inclusion within current legislation and guidance as well as ways in which early years settings could begin moving towards increased inclusion. As with any changes, concerns and issues will arise, but with commitment and appropriate support these can be resolved.

The young teacher I recalled in this chapter was attending an in-service training course on special needs in the early years which led to a further qualification and was funded by her school. This is the type of training that should be accessible to all those working within the early years. Noticeably the majority of course participants were teachers, funded by their schools. Those from pre-school settings were funded by European Union grants or worked within private nurseries that funded them. Although there is a range of highly appropriate courses available to pre-school practitioners, the issue of equity for all early years practitioners must be addressed. The speed at which new initiatives are implemented is often greater than the speed at which appropriate training can be organised, accessed and undertaken.

Inclusion is, hopefully, not too far in the distance but in the meantime we all need to address the key issues to ensure that in the early years, all practitioners and settings are equipped to offer effective inclusion.

---

### *Key issues*

- ❖ Inclusion is now a requirement.
- ❖ Inclusion supports the individual needs of all children at all times and breaks down barriers to segregation.
- ❖ There are issues to be addressed before full inclusion becomes a reality.
- ❖ Inclusion is the right of all individuals.

## Suggestions for discussion

### *Item 1*

Reflect on the provision within your setting. As a staff discuss whether your provision for children with SEN is:

- separate and additional to other provision
- inclusive.

### *Item 2*

Using the section on 'Enabling inclusion in early years settings' work through the 15 points indicative of inclusive practices and assess how well advanced your setting is regarding these practices. Suggest possible ways forward.

### *Item 3*

Identify any potential barriers or issues regarding inclusion within your setting. Suggest ways in which these could be addressed.

### *Item 4*

Consider one child within your setting who needs additional support. Discuss and plan an intervention for that child which would support inclusive practices.

## Suggested further reading

Cox, T. (2000) *Combating Educational Disadvantage: Meeting the Needs of Vulnerable Children*. London: Falmer Press.

Hornby, G., Atkinson, M. and Howard, J. (1997) *Controversial Issues in Special Education*. London: David Fulton. (Chapter 5.)

Centre for Studies in Inclusive Education website: www.inclusion.uwe.ac.uk

# 9

## Issues for Consideration

As I have worked through the chapters of this book I have discovered the journey to be a reflection of my own developing philosophies of special needs. Theory and research have been accessed to support my discussions and debates, along with the use of personal experiences to highlight key issues. Progress to date in the field of supporting young children with special needs has been explored with the allied and ever-changing legislation and guidance. Four key issues immediately spring to mind.

First, it could be suggested that it is time to move away from the terms 'special needs' and 'special educational needs' as they are indicative of segregation. If we are truly working towards an inclusive education system, then provision for any child with special needs will be implicit within those systems. Within inclusive education all children will be appropriately provided for within all settings and schools. As long as the government continues to produce separate documents regarding special educational needs then special needs provision will continue to be perceived as something separate and different from mainstream provision. *Clarification is therefore needed on the continued use of the terms 'special needs' and 'special educational needs' within a system that is advocating inclusive practices.*

Secondly, extending this issue further, the fact that young children are sometimes labelled with terms such as autistic, ADHD and behavioural difficulties can affect practitioner and parental expectations and inadvertently be reflected within provision, thus compounding the child's difficulties. If we perceive all children in a holistic manner, addressing all possible causal factors for any difficulty they may be experiencing and then responding appropriately, we will be more likely to address their needs effectively. Practitioners would then be addressing the difficulties being experienced at that particular time, which may be short or long term. At that point in time the child would be perceived as having individual needs, in the same way that we all need different support at different times. *My philosophy is based on a process that identifies and supports individual needs and therefore should not use terms such as special needs or special educational needs. This is in line with a fully inclusive early years system.* As long as the documentation and legislation continue to use such terminology practitioners will remain unclear and, to a degree, be encouraged to use the terminology.

Thirdly, if the government is advocating inclusive education then special school provision should no longer be viable. At the current time within the inclusive education guidance there is a clear indication of the continued need for special provision and such thinking continues to confuse the issue. *The term 'inclusion' should therefore be further clarified to indicate whether a fully inclusive system is advocated or a partially inclusive system.*

Fourthly, the general diversity of pre-school provision across the UK means that for many families the options and choices of settings available to them may be limited. Similarly, the costs of places within these settings will vary and may exclude some children from entry. If the range of settings accessible to children with special needs is then explored, another diversity appears. For example, specialist provision for children with autistic spectrum disorders will vary across the UK with some counties offering autism specific schools with highly trained autism specialist teachers, while in other counties children with autism may be placed in pre-schools. *Equity of provision for all children and their families is an issue that should be acknowledged and addressed.*

Continuing from these fundamental issues each chapter raised its own issues, some of which practitioners will already be aware, while others may have given cause for reflection. Along with the discussion points and key readings, these issues can be further explored and debated.

Chapter 1 set the rest of the book within its historical context as it unravelled the development of early years provision since the late 1800s, taking us through a journey of pioneers such as Robert Owen and Rachel and Margaret McMillan. Each development and legislative document should be considered within its time and place in history to understand the political and social agendas of the time that would have informed those changes. After considering the typical range of early years providers in today's society the historical development of special needs provision was explored from the early 1800s to the present time, beginning with the development of asylums for 'idiots' through key legislative changes until the present day, with the SENDA (DfES, 2001c), Inclusive Schooling guidance (DfES, 2001b), Code of Practice (DfES, 2001d)) and the introduction of the Foundation Stage (QCA, 2000). For purposes of clarity, some definitions were offered. Perhaps the most important issue to acknowledge from this chapter is that *legislation, guidance and provision for young children experiencing difficulties have advanced tremendously but there are still major issues to be addressed to ensure continued and appropriate progression.*

In Chapter 2 the perspectives of the parents and other family members of children with special needs were examined. This is an area that many practitioners may not have reflected on in depth, unless familiar with the works of researchers such as Carpenter (1997; 2000), Dale (1996) and Herbert (1994). While practitioners are working with parents all the time, it could be suggested that, with other professional pressures, the family and parental perspectives would not necessarily take priority. However, research evidence highlights the importance of considering all involved perspectives if we are to consider the child holistically. Each child should be viewed within the context of his/her home, family and community to ensure consideration of all areas impacting on their lives in a variety of ways. To consider a child without such broad reflection could be viewed as offering only a narrow perspective. In practice this relates to practitioners critically examining factors within the home, within the setting and within themselves in an attempt to identify which factors may be compounding the child's difficulties. Those within practitioner control can then be addressed. *Practitioners should therefore acknowledge the impact that family members have on young children and consider the needs of each family member as an integral part of their support of the child.*

The perspectives of mothers and fathers were explored separately as, while they may share some experiences and feelings, their perspectives and needs will differ at times. The somewhat outdated notion that the father should be the strong supportive partner should now be replaced with an understanding of mutual support and fathers should not be marginalised from events. *Any interactions with parents should be carefully considered and planned, whether pre- or post-diagnosis, and our policies and practices should reflect this.*

Andrew's case study highlighted issues for practitioners and parents alike but, hopefully, offered the reader the opportunity to consider the extensive range of professionals involved with just one child. This then extended to a consideration of the individual impact on the child, his parents, grandparents and extended family, and friends, when coping with diagnoses, appointments, disappointments, successes, as well as regular journeys to and from the early years setting.

Chapter 3 continued to explore parental partnerships within special education and early years, yet acknowledging that parents tend to be more actively involved in settings during the pre-school phase. As the child progresses throughout the statutory education system that involvement changes in many ways. The balance of power within any partnership should be equal with mutual respect central. Clearly, it should not be assumed that as practitioners are the so-called 'experts' they should control the partnership, as this will immediately create an imbalance and affect interactions between the two parties. Successful partnerships will be based on trust and approachability with an acknowledgement that we each have our own knowledge and expertise concerning the child that would be enhanced by collaboration. *Partnerships with parents can only succeed if both parties respect and value each other's contributions. The balance of power and quality of partnerships will be influential, as will the equalities within the relationship.*

The balance between encouraging positive changes and enforcing changes to existing parenting skills and styles was debated, as practitioners should acknowledge that parenting styles often reflect the family's cultural background. Practitioners should thus be cautious and sensitive when responding to such personal issues with parents.

The range of positive outcomes from effective partnerships for parents, children and practitioners was highlighted using research evidence to support discussions along with the expectations contained within the Early Learning Goals

(QCA, 1999), indicating the current philosophy based on the understanding that parents are a child's 'first and most enduring educators'. The benefits for all parties would include raising confidence, raising awareness of other perspectives and increased knowledge and skill base. It was suggested that some settings might wish to review existing partnership policies and areas to stimulate appropriate discussions were indicated as:

- the sharing of information between parents and staff
- mutual support
- participation outcomes and benefits
- skill-sharing
- teaching.

Issues and questions for consideration were also offered to support practitioner development of existing partnership practices relating to special needs provision. This would ensure that parents who need access to information and support know who to contact initially and/or how to find the relevant information. The difficult issue of raising concerns with parents was also highlighted as the quality of interaction at this time would set the scene for future encounters. *Practitioners should reflect on existing partnership policies and practices to ensure that maximum benefit is gained by all parties within a framework based on a desire to empower parents.*

Interagency working was unravelled in Chapter 4 which began by offering a range of terminology currently used to describe agencies working together. The term 'interagency working' was used for the purposes of later discussion, as this is the term used within current legislation. The legislation suggests that early years work should be progressing towards a 'seamless' service with effective communication between professionals combined with shared policies and protocols (DfES, 2001d). The nature of working with young children with special needs implies that we work alongside professionals from a range of disciplines, and a spectrum of working practices could be suggested. This would extend from practitioners working separately with a child and his/her family with no joint planning or reviewing of progress. At the opposite end of the spectrum we would see practitioners who acknowledge and respect each other's roles, do not erect professional barriers and plan each step of provision in a collaborative manner along with parents.

Jodie's case study helped to identify fundamental issues and was selected as it represented a young girl who was clearly affected by her environment and was assessed as being generally delayed in her development. Through effective interagency working and the provision offered by the setting her needs were met, her parents supported and Jodie's progress was very rewarding. Involvement of the drug and alcohol abuse team would not be a situation met by many practitioners but highlighted again the need for knowledge of all local supporting agencies and the work they undertake. *Practitioners need to ensure all members of staff are aware of the diverse range of supporting agencies that can be accessed to support their work with young children and their families. All those working in the early years should acknowledge the importance of effective collaboration.*

Highlighting the key professionals involved with young children with special needs gave us an overview of their key roles and responsibilities, but practitioners would be advised to clarify their own local knowledge. In my own experience, spending two days shadowing a local social worker gave me a practical and realistic understanding of her work that greatly enhanced our working relationship and working practices. It was not an easy event to organise but the benefits far outweighed the obstacles. *Practitioners should overcome barriers to enhancing collaborative working with colleagues from other professional disciplines.*

While barriers to interagency working may exist practitioners should reflect on ways forward to enhance existing practices. *The following issues are suggested to support interagency working:*

- *joint funding initiatives*
- *appropriate training and resources (human and material)*
- *greater unification of services*
- *joint planning to support the needs of individual children*
- *training for effective interagency work*
- *the sharing of professional cultures.*

Expectations of early years providers continue to change and training courses are adapting to provide the UK with highly qualified and skilled early years practitioners who the report of Atkinson et al. (2002) identified as a 'new and hybrid professional'. *Initial and ongoing training, which is accessible to all early years practitioners, is essential. In addition, local and national policies should indicate a commitment to supporting and enhancing interagency working and time should be made available for practitioners to develop their skills in this area.*

In Chapter 5 the need for regular observations and assessments was examined in order to inform our planning, our understanding of current situations and for information sharing with parents and other professionals. All practitioners will be familiar with regular, less formal observations of children but the benefits of planned and documented observations, as part of a cyclical process of provision, cannot be overemphasised. In addition to informing decisions about individual children the benefits of observing areas of the room and/or the practitioner were also offered. *Current legislation and guidance clearly supports the need for observation and assessment to be a regular aspect of early years practice.*

From my own experience I have undertaken many observations that have revealed significant issues that I was previously unaware of, so *it is highly recommend that practitioners use observations consistently and regularly.* At times it may appear difficult to organise the required time to undertake observations, but the benefits should encourage every effort to be made to enable regular observations within early years settings. As with most situations in life, if we can see the advantages, then we will generally overcome obstacles to achieve them.

Having outlined the principles of observing, a range of observational methods was explored in some detail to guide practitioners through the processes of planning, observing, intervention and evaluating outcomes in such a way that the benefits could be appreciated. Short illustrative examples throughout clarified understanding. *Practitioner knowledge of child development and the range of observational methods available are essential for undertaking and evaluating observations.*

In Chapter 6 the value of early intervention for young children with special needs was reinforced and interventions placed within a cyclical approach to supporting individual needs. Additional features of effective intervention programmes were suggested as:

- responding to legislation and guidance
- responding appropriately to individual needs
- having measurable outcomes
- involving and informing professionals and parents.

When planning any intervention, practitioners should use information gained from previous reports and parents, combined with observational findings to support the development of short- and long-term targets for the future. This was further explored by considering the use of SMART targets which are specific, measurable, achievable, relevant and time bound.

These SMART targets ensure clarity for all who read them, so parents, staff members and other professionals are able to see what the specific intended outcomes are and the time to elapse before the evaluation of outcomes and review of progress. These targets are included in the IEP prepared for the child, which is an ongoing working document and becomes part of the child's records. The IEP is formulated after discussions with staff and parents, as they are able to contribute to the process and may be able to support strategies within the home environment. An illustrative example of an IEP was offered to clarify understanding. *Practitioners should be familiar with producing positive and meaningful IEPs that are agreed with and supported by parents and professionals.*

Providing for young children with speech and language difficulties was explored, offering some basic information to inform practitioners. Key terminology that would appear in speech and language reports was explained and the possible effects of speech and language difficulties highlighted. Without such basic information practitioners might unintentionally compound a child's difficulties, so background knowledge is essential for increased understanding and awareness of the subject and to ensure appropriate provision for young children and their families. As with many issues raised in this book *knowledge and thus training are again identified as central to support provision for children with special needs.*

Practical suggestions for use in early years settings were highlighted but it should be noted that these offer only a brief introduction and practitioners are recommended to explore the suggested further reading or take up specific training to gain more detailed knowledge and skills.

The numbers of children with speech and language difficulties attending mainstream settings appear to have increased in my experience. Practitioners have become extremely competent at supporting children effectively and working collaboratively with speech and language therapists. An ongoing concern is that of continued speech and language therapy support on transfer to primary education for those children who need it. *Issues surrounding the availability of qualified speech and language therapists and joint funding continue to be debated but resolution at national and local levels is necessary to ensure children's needs in this area are met.*

Our attention was then drawn to consider providing for children with autistic spectrum disorders. In my own experience such children were not generally included in mainstream settings until relatively recently. When working in an early years special needs unit I soon became aware of my lack of basic knowledge of autism and felt frustrated attempting to provide for autistic children, as I felt unable to communicate or interact with them and, equally, they appeared to have little interest or reason for interacting with me. I realised that I should extend my knowledge considerably and rapidly if I did not want to fail these children and their families. Many of the families were still struggling to come to terms with the diagnosis or were at a loss themselves as to how to support their child and were looking to staff to advise and support them. Having accessed information and training at both local and national levels, I began to understand the autistic world and to support the children with varying degrees of success. I also realised that some of my prior attempts to interact were probably compounding the children's difficulties.

This leads to my concern regarding whether all early years settings can provide for children with autistic spectrum disorders without considerable knowledge and training. Such training could include introductory knowledge of special needs provision but would also need to be extended to cover specific areas and issues such as providing for autistic spectrum disorders. *If we are working towards inclusive provision then a coordinated and extensive training programme needs to be available to all early years practitioners to ensure the effectiveness of provision.*

Within the limitations of this book a basic overview of autism, the impact of autism, diagnosis and intervention approaches were outlined to inform the reader. The case study highlighted some of the key points and issues raised, and again it is recommended that practitioners extend their knowledge through further reading and accessing appropriate training.

Chapter 7 led us to consider the affective development of young children and how practitioners can support this. Again this is an area where, in my experience, lack of knowledge and information in early years is evident. As practitioners we have been aware of the need to provide for children's personal, social and emotional development for some years but an extension of existing knowledge was deemed pertinent. For the purposes of the chapter, social, emotional and behavioural development were separated to a degree, but in reality they are so interrelated that to separate them may not be helpful.

Background information was offered along with some practical strategies for working practice, before extending our reflection to consider the range of possible causal factors that can influence a child's development in these areas. The setting, home and practitioner were identified as significant factors, and positive features were highlighted to support practitioner and setting development. *The importance of considering the affective needs of children and exploring all the possible causal factors when difficulties occur, should not be overlooked by early years practitioners.*

The illustrative example of critical reflection by a practitioner was indicative of just how significant practitioner behaviour is. This personal reflection highlighted the need to reflect on ourselves in an attempt to support the child. *Critical, personal reflection is not always easy to undertake but is highly recommended to early years practitioners, as is critical reflection of other factors within the home and the setting.*

The development of the self-concept and locus of control were explored in some depth, offering background knowledge, as the relationship between self-concept and academic achievement and/or behavioural difficulties has been highlighted in research (Charlton and David, 1993). Strategies to enhance self-concept were offered for use in early years settings. *Early years practitioners should consider the impact of self-concept on other developmental areas. They should also be aware of the importance of enhancing the self-concept of all children and adults within the setting.*

Consideration then moved to explore children's behaviour and how to support those children demonstrating undesirable behaviours, with the influences of the home, setting and practitioner again featuring prominently. Purposeful observations will ensure greater understanding of current levels of difficulty and should inform future planning. If a behavioural intervention is deemed appropriate, then baseline observations would enable the success (or otherwise) of the intervention to be visible. The stages within a behavioural intervention were listed and the use of positive reinforcement identified as a useful and practical method of supporting an intervention programme. The cyclical process of identifying a behavioural difficulty, undertaking observations, planning an intervention and evaluation were emphasised, as was the use of an IBP for clarity of understanding and for recording purposes. *Early years practitioners should acknowledge all possible causal factors and implement planned strategies to encourage and support changes in undesirable behaviours. Parental involvement will be essential throughout.*

In Chapter 8 the current moves towards an inclusive education system were debated, with legislation, both general and within the field of special needs, encouraging inclusive practices. *The move towards an inclusive education system has a significant impact on early years practitioners and teachers within mainstream and special settings.*

Currently many special schools are closing down, with the children being transferred to their local mainstream schools. The increase in numbers of children with special needs within mainstream settings has been accompanied with guidance such as Inclusive Schooling (DfES, 2001b), the Code of Practice (DfES, 2001d), the SEN Toolkit (DfES, 2001e) and the Index for Inclusion (Booth et al., 2000). However, this increase in guidance documents, each of them fairly lengthy, is additional work for already overstretched practitioners. The Foundation Stage and National Curriculum have already changed working practices and introduced amended or additional planning and recording demands. Any new initiative will bring with it more information that needs to be accessed and absorbed before practice can be brought into line. Issues surrounding the availability and cost of appropriate training emerge yet again. In my experience there have been many instances when new legislation and guidance have been introduced and practitioners have not had sufficient time to access all the relevant information, secure training if needed and plan and instigate any changes to working practices or settings. *Without the expertise and skills to provide effectively for all children it should not be assumed that all practitioners will be able to do so. If training is not available then practitioners may inadvertently be compounding children's difficulties.*

Models and definitions of inclusion were explored along with the key principles of effective inclusive practices, with the rights of all children (and adults) being of paramount importance. We all have a right to be included within a society that respects us as individuals and allows us equal access to all services. This philosophy applies to education and to all children. Issues of special needs, race and culture would no longer be separate or significant within such an inclusive education system. *Practitioners should therefore be committed to the principles of inclusion in order to implement appropriate changes to policies and practices.* Practitioners' beliefs in implementing inclusive changes to provision can, however, change in the light of sufficient evidence. Thomas, Walker and Webb (1998: 198) concluded that: 'One of our clearest findings has been that while many mainstream staff were highly sceptical about the inclusion project before it started, they had changed their views entirely after several months of seeing it in practice and were fulsome in their support for inclusion.'

Suggestions for supporting inclusive practices within early years settings were offered, which should be carefully considered and planned prior to implementation. Issues and potential barriers that could arise during such discussion and planning were suggested, including:

- speed of change and practitioner awareness
- parental perspectives
- funding and training
- use of learning support workers
- access.

Each of these would need consideration and resolution to support moves towards inclusion, with support, at local and/or national levels, in place and accessible.

The issue of providing for children living in poverty was then explored within the context of inclusive practices and, again, basic information was offered to inform practitioners. The links between poverty and education were identified to enable understanding of the impact on children's academic achievement and this was supported by an illustrative case study to convert theory into inclusive practice.

## *Concluding comments*

Many of the chapters within this book are interrelated, as providing for all children is a complex process which is informed by extensive knowledge, expertise and skills. This should be embedded within a thorough working knowledge of child development and mainstream education and care. The fact that many practitioners in the past progressed through mainstream settings into special units or schools ensured they had mainstream skills before extending those skills further. In this climate of inclusion we are expecting practitioners to provide for all children at all times, and this is a considerable task. *Support, guidance, funding and training will continue to be crucial issues for success.*

*All children have the right to be respected, valued and included, so locally and nationally we must ensure that all practitioners have the knowledge and skills to offer that respect within an inclusive system and, hopefully, within a more inclusive society. Young children would no longer be classified as having 'special needs' and their families would no longer be 'different', but they would be mainstream children and families, as long as potential barriers to inclusion are confronted, debated and resolved.*

# Bibliography

Advisory Centre for Education (ACE) (2002) *Special Education Handbook: The Law on Children with Special Educational Needs.* London: ACE.

American Psychiatric Association (1994) *Diagnostic and Statistical Manual of Mental Disorders,* 4th edn (DSM-lV). Washington: American Psychiatric Association.

Anderson-Ford, D. (1994) 'Legal aid: how special education is defined in law', in S. Sandow (ed.),*Whose Special Need?* London: Paul Chapman Publishing.

Atkinson, M., Wilkin, A., Stott, A., Doherty, P. and Kinder, K. (2002) *Multi-Agency Working: A Detailed Study.* Slough: NFER.

Attwood, R. and Thomson, D. (1997) 'Parental values and care for the child with special needs', in G. Lindsay and D. Thomson, *Values into Practice in Special Education.* London: David Fulton.

Barber, M. (1996) 'Creating a framework for success in urban areas', in M. Barber, and R. Dann, *Raising Educational Standards in The Inner Cities: Practical Initiatives in Action.* London: Cassell.

Barnes, P. (ed.) (1995) *Personal, Social and Emotional Development* of *Children.* Milton Keynes: Open University Press.

Baron-Cohen, S., Allen, J. and Gillberg, C. (1992) 'Can autism be detected at 18 months? The needle, the haystack and the CHAT', *British Journal of Psychiatry,* 168: 158–63.

Beaver, M., Brewster, J., Jones, P., Keene, A., Neaum, S. and Tallack, J. (1999) *Babies and Young Children. Book 1: Early Years Development.* Cheltenham: Stanley Thornes.

Beaver, M., Brewster, J., Jones, P., Keene, A., Neaum, S. and Tallack, J. (2000) *Babies and Young Children. Book 2: Early Years Care and Education.* Cheltenham: Stanley Thornes.

Beveridge, S. (1997) 'Implementing partnership with parents in schools', in S. Wolfendale (ed.), *Working with Parents of SEN Children after the Code of Practice.* London: David Fulton.

Birrell, I. (1995) 'The invisible children: a story of heartbreak and hope', *Sunday Times News Review,* 3 December, 1–2.

Blamires, M., Robertson, C. and Blamires, J. (1997) *Parent–Teacher Partnership. Practical Approaches to Meet Special Educational Needs.* London: David Fulton.

Blenkin, G. (1994) 'Early learning and a developmentally appropriate curriculum: some lessons from research', in G. Blenkin and G. Kelly (eds), *The National Curriculum and Early Learning: An Evaluation.* London: Paul Chapman Publishing.

Bluma, S., Shearer, A., Frohman, A. and Hillard, J. (1976) *Portage Guide to Education Checklist.* Windsor: NFER-Nelson.

Booth, T. (1994) 'Continuum or chimera?', *British Journal of Special Education,* 21 (1): 21–4.

Booth, T., Ainscow, M., Black-Hawkins, K., Vaughan, M. and Shaw, L. (2000) *Index for Inclusion.* Bristol: CSIE.

Bradburn, E. (1976) *Margaret McMillan: Framework and Expansion of Nursery Education.* Redhill: Denholm Press.

Bradshaw, J. (ed.) (2001) *Poverty: The Outcomes for Children.* London: Family Policy Studies Centre.

Bronfenbrenner, U. (1979) *The Ecology of Human Development: Experiments by Nature and Design.* London: Harvard University Press.

Bruce, T. (1987) *Early Childhood Education.* London: Hodder and Stoughton.

CACE (1967) *Children and their Primary Schools* (Plowden Report). London: HMSO.

Canfield, J. and Wells, H.C. (1976) *100 Ways to Enhance the Self-Concept in the Classroom: A Handbook for Teachers and Parents.* Englewood Cliffs, NJ: Prentice Hall.

Carpenter, B. (ed.) (1997) *Families in Context: Emerging Trends in Family Support and Early Intervention.* London: David Fulton.

Carpenter, B. (2000) 'Sustaining the family: meeting the needs of families of children with disabilities', *British Journal of Special Education*, 27 (3): 135–43.

Charlton, T. and David, K. (eds) (1990) *Supportive Schools.* Basingstoke: Macmillan.

Charlton, T. and David, K. (eds) (1993) *Managing Misbehaviour in Schools*, 2nd edn. London: Routledge.

Charlton, T. and Jones, K. (1990) *Working on the Self.* Cheltenham: College of St Paul and St Mary Press.

Chizea, C., Henderson, A. and Jones, G. (1999) *Inclusion in Pre-School Settings – Support for Children with Special Needs and their Families.* London: Pre-School Learning Alliance.

Coopersmith, S. (1967) *The Antecedents of Self Esteem.* London: Freeman.

Court, S.D.M. (1976) *Fit for the Future: The Report of the Committee on Child Health Services. Volume 1* (Court Report). London: HMSO.

Cox, T. (2000) *Combating Educational Disadvantage: Meeting the Needs of Vulnerable Children.* London: Falmer Press.

Cumine, V., Leach, J. and Stevenson, G. (2000) *Autism in the Early Years: A Practical Guide.* London: David Fulton.

Dale, N. (1996) *Working with Families of Children with Special Needs.* London: Routledge.

David, T. (1990) *Under Five – Under-Educated?* Buckingham: Open University Press.

David, T. (ed.) (1994) *Working Together for Young Children: Multi-professionalism in Action.* London: Routledge.

Department for Education and Employment (DfEE) (1988) *Education Reform Act.* London: HMSO.

Department for Education and Employment (DfEE) (1993) *Education Act.* London: HMSO.

Department for Education and Employment (DfEE) (1994) *Code of Practice on the Identification and Assessment of Special Educational Needs.* London: HMSO.

Department for Education and Employment (DfEE) (1996) *Nursery Education and Grant Maintained Schools Act.* London: HMSO.

Department for Education and Employment (DfEE) (1997) *Excellence for All: Meeting Special Educational Needs.* London: The Stationery Office.

Department for Education and Employment (DfEE) (1998) *Schools Standards and Frameworks Act.* London: HMSO.

Department for Education and Skills (DfES) (2001a) *Access to Education for Children and Young People with Medical Needs.* London: HMSO.

Department for Education and Skills (DfES) (2001b) *Inclusive Schooling: Children with Special Educational Needs.* Nottingham: DfES.

Department for Education and Skills (DfES) (2001c) *Special Educational Needs and Disability Discrimination Act 2001.* London: HMSO.

Department for Education and Skills (DfES) (2001d) *Special Educational Needs Code of Practice.* Nottingham: DfES.

Department for Education and Skills (DfES) (2001e) *Special Educational Needs Toolkit.* Nottingham: DfES.

Department of Education and Science (DES) (1970) *Education (Handicapped Children) Act*. London: HMSO.

Department of Education and Science (DES) (1978) *The Report of the Committee of Enquiry into the Education of Handicapped Children and Young People* (Warnock Report). London: HMSO.

Department of Education and Science (DES) (1981) *Education Act*. London: HMSO.

Department of Health (DoH) (1991) *The Children Act Guidance and Regulations. Volume 2: Family Support, Daycare and Educational Provision for Young Children*. London: HMSO.

Department of Social Security (2000) *Households Below Average Income. 1994–1998/9*. London: The Stationery Office.

Devereux, J. (1996) 'What we see depends on what we look for: observation as a part of teaching and learning in the early years', in S. Robson and S. Smedley (eds), *Education in Early Childhood: First Things First*. London: David Fulton.

Di Lavore, P.C., Lord, C. and Rutter, M. (1995) 'The pre-linguistic autism diagnostic observation schedule', *Journal of Autism and Developmental Disorders*, 25: 355–79.

Disability Rights Commission (2001) *Draft Code of Practice (Schools)*. London: Disability Rights Commission.

Draper, L. and Duffy, B. (2001) 'Working with parents', in G. Pugh (ed.), *Contemporary Issues in the Early Years*, 3rd edn. London: Paul Chapman Publishing.

Drifte, C. (2001). *Special Needs in Early Years Settings: A Guide for Practitioners*. London: David Fulton.

Edwards, A. and Knight, P. (1994) *Effective Early Years Education: Teaching Young Children*. Buckingham: Open University Press.

Emad, H. (2000) 'The vital link between home and school', *Early Years Educator*, 2 (7): 48–9.

Evans, P. (2000) 'Including students with disabilities in mainstream schools', in H. Savolainen, H. Kokkala and H. Alasuutari (eds), *Meeting Special and Diverse Educational Needs: Making Inclusive Education a Reality*. Helsinki: Ministry for Foreign Affairs of Finland.

Farrell, P. (2001) 'Special education in the last twenty years: have things really got better?', *British Journal of Special Education*, 28 (1): 3–9.

Goldenberg, I. and Goldenberg, H. (1985) 'Family therapy: an overview', in B. Carpenter (2000) 'Sustaining the family: meeting the needs of families of children with disabilities', *British Journal of Special Education*, 27 (3): 135–43.

Goodall, J. (1997) 'All young children have needs', in S. Wolfendale (ed.), *Meeting Special Needs in the Early Years. Directions in Policy and Practice*. London: David Fulton.

Gorrod, L. (1997) *My Brother Is Different*. London: NAS.

Griffiths, R. (1970) *The Abilities of Young Children*. London: Child Development Research Centre.

Gulliford, R. (1981) 'Teacher training and Warnock', *Special Education Forward Trends*, 8 (2): 13–15.

Harnett, A. (2002) 'Developing children as independent and confident learners: personal, social and emotional development', in I. Keating (ed.), *Achieving QTS: Teaching the Foundation Stage*. Exeter: Learning Matters.

Hayman, S. (1999) *The Relate Guide to Second Families: Living Successfully with Other People's Children*. London: Vermillion.

Herbert, E. (1994) 'Becoming a special family', in T. David (ed.), *Working Together for Young Children: Multi-professionalism in Action*. London: Routledge.

Herbert, E. and Carpenter, B. (1994) 'Fathers – the secondary partners: professional perceptions and a father's reflections', *Children and Society*, 8 (1): 31–41.

Hobart, C. and Frankel, J. (1994) *A Practical Guide to Child Observation and Assessment*, 2nd edn. Cheltenham: Stanley Thornes.

Hohmann, M. and Weikart, D.P. (1995) *Educating Young Children*. Ypsolanti, MI: HighScope.

Home Office, Department of Health, Department of Education and Science and the Welsh Office (1991) *Working Together under the Children Act 1989: A Guide to Arrangements for Inter-agency Co-operation for the Protection of Children from Abuse*. London: HMSO.

Hornby, G. (1995) *Working with Parents of Children with Special Needs*. London: Cassell.

Hornby, G., Atkinson, M. and Howard, J. (1997) *Controversial Issues in Special Education*. London: David Fulton.

Hurst, V. (1997) *Planning for Early Learning: Educating Young Children*. London: Paul Chapman Publishing.

James, J., Charlton, T., Leo, E. and Indoe, D. (1991) 'Using peer counsellors to improve secondary pupils' spelling and reading performance', *Maladjustment and Therapeutic Education*, 9 (1): 33–40.

Keenan, T. (2002) *An Introduction to Child Development*. London: Sage.

Knowles, W. and Masidlover, M. (1982) *Derbyshire Language Scheme*. Derby: Derbyshire County Council.

Lambley, H. (1993) 'Learning and behaviour problems', in T. Charlton and K. David (eds), *Managing Misbehaviour in Schools*, 2nd edn. London: Routledge.

Lawrence, D. (1985) 'Improving self-esteem and reading', *Educational Research*, 27 (3): 119–24.

Lawrence, D. (1987) *Enhancing Self-esteem in the Classroom*. London: Paul Chapman Publishing.

Lewis, J. (2000) 'Let's remember the "education" in inclusive education', *British Journal of Special Education*, 27 (4): 202.

Lindsay, G. (1997) 'Values and legislation', in G. Lindsay and D. Thompson (eds), *Values into Practice in Special Education*. London: David Fulton.

Lloyd, C. (1997) 'Inclusive education for children with SEN in the early years', in S. Wolfendale (ed.), *Meeting Special Needs in the Early Years. Directions in Policy and Practice*. London: David Fulton.

Long, R. and Fogell, J. (1999) *Supporting Pupils with Emotional Difficulties: Creating a Caring Environment for All*. London: David Fulton.

Mallet, R. (1997) 'A parental perspective on partnership', in S. Wolfendale (ed.), *Working with Parents of SEN Children after the Code of Practice*. London: David Fulton.

McConkey, R. (2002) 'Reciprocal working by education, health and social services: lessons for a less-travelled road', *British Journal of Special Education*, 29 (1): 3–8.

McFarlane, T. (1993) 'Promoting inter-professional understanding and collaboration', in H. Owen and J. Pritchard (eds), *Good Practice in Child Protection*. London: Jessica Kingsley.

McGuire, J. and Richman, N. (1988) *Pre-School Behaviour Checklist*. Windsor: NFER-Nelson.

McKenna, K. (1999) 'What does the National Childcare Strategy mean for you?', *Practical Pre-School* (16).

Ministry of Education (1944) *Education Act*. London: HMSO.

Mortimer, H. (2000) *Playladders*. Lichfield: Q.Ed.

Mortimer, H. (2001) *Special Needs and Early Years Provision*. London: Continuum.

Mortimore, P., Sammons, P., Stoll, L., Lewis, D. and Ecob, R. 1988. *School Matters*. Wells: Open Books.

Moyles, J. (1989) *Just Playing? The Role and Status of Play in Early Childhood Education*. Milton Keynes: Open University Press.

National Association for Special Educational Needs (2000) *Membership Response to Proposed Revision of the Code of Practice and Accompanying Guidance on SEN Thresholds*. Tamworth: NASEN.

Oberhuemer, P., and Ulich, M. (1997) *Working with Young Children in Europe. Provision and Staff Training*. London: Paul Chapman Publishing.

Owen, G. (1928) Cited in S. Northen 'Recognition of early years takes its time', *Times Educational Supplement*. December 1999: 15.

Paige-Smith, A. (1997) 'The rise and impact of the parental lobby: including voluntary groups and the education of children with learning difficulties or disabilities', in S. Wolfendale (ed.), *Meeting Special Needs in the Early Years. Directions in Policy and Practice*. London: David Fulton.

Policy Analysis Unit (1986) *Voluntary Organisations and Childcare: Issues and Challenges*. London: NCVO.

Pugh, G. (1988) *Services for Under Fives: Developing a Co-ordinated Approach*. London: NCB.

Pugh, G. (ed.) (1996) *Contemporary Issues in the Early Years*, 2nd edn. London: Paul Chapman Publishing.

Pugh, G. (ed.) (2001) *Contemporary Issues in the Early Years*, 3rd edn. London: Paul Chapman Publishing.

QCA (1999) *The Early Learning Goals*. London: QCA/DfEE.

QCA (2000) *Curriculum Guidance for the Foundation Stage*. London: QCA/DfEE.

Quilgars, D. (2001) 'Educational attainment', in J. Bradshaw (ed.), *Poverty: The Outcomes for Children*. London: Family Policy Studies Centre.

Read, M. and Rees, M. (2000) 'Working in teams in early years settings', in R. Drury, L. Miller and R. Campbell (eds), *Looking at Early Years Education and Care*. London: David Fulton.

Rennie, J. (1996) 'Working with parents', in G. Pugh (ed.), *Contemporary Issues in the Early Years: Working Collaboratively for Children*. London: Paul Chapman Publishing.

Reynolds, D. (1984) 'Creative conflict: the implications of recent educational research for those concerned with children', *Maladjustment and Therapeutic Education*, 2 (2): 14–23.

Robson, B. (1989) *Special Needs in Ordinary Schools: Pre-School Provision for Children with Special Needs*. London: Cassell.

Roffey, S. (1999) *Special Needs in the Early Years: Collaboration, Communication and Co-ordination*, London: David Fulton.

Roffey, S. (2001) *Special Needs in the Early Years: Collaboration, Communication and Co-ordination*, 2nd edn. London: David Fulton.

Rogers, C.R. (1983) *The Freedom to Learn in the 80's*. Columbus, OH: Merrill.

Rotter, J. (1966) 'Generalised expectancies for internal versus external control of reinforcement', *Psychological Monograph*, 80: 609.

Rutter, M., Maughan, B., Mortimore, P. and Ouston, J. (1979) *Fifteen Thousand Hours: Secondary Schools and their Effects on Children*. London: Open Books.

Sandow, S. (ed.) (1994) *Whose Special Need? Some Perceptions of Special Educational Needs*. London: Paul Chapman Publishing.

SCAA (1996) *Desirable Outcomes of Children's Learning on Entering Compulsory Education*. London: SCAA.

Schopler, E., Reichler, R. and Rochen-Renner, B. (1988) *Childhood Autism Rating Scale (CARS)*. Los Angeles, CA: Western Psychological Services.

Scruggs, T.E. and Mastropieri, (1996) 'Teacher Perceptions of Mainstream Inclusion, 1958-1995: A research synthesis', *Exceptional Children*, 63 (1): 59–74.

Smith, H. (1996) *Procedures, Practice and Guidance for SENCO's*. Tamworth: NASEN.

Spenceley, L. (2000). 'Communicate if you want to educate', *Early Years Educator*, 2 (4): 50–1.

Thomas, G., Walker, D. and Webb. J. (1998) *The Making of the Inclusive School*. London: Routledge.

Trevarthen, C., Aitken, K., Papoudi, D. and Robarts, J. (1998) *Children with Autism: Diagnosis and Intervention to Meet their Needs*, 2nd edn. London: Jessica Kingsley.

UNESCO (1994) *Salamanca Statement on Principles, Policy and Practice in Special Needs Education*. Paris: UNESCO.

Van der Eyken, W. (1967) *The Pre-School Years*. Harmondsworth: Penguin.

Wall, K. (1996) 'Welfare and liaison', in K. David and T. Charlton (eds), *Pastoral Care Matters in Primary and Secondary Schools*. London: Routledge.

Webster, A. and McConnell, C. (1987) *Special Needs in Ordinary Schools: Children with Speech and Language Difficulties*. London: Cassell.

Welton, J. (1985) 'Schools and a multi-professional approach to welfare', in P. Ribbins (ed.), *Schooling and Welfare*. Lewes: Falmer Press.

Willis, M. (1953) 'Play areas on housing estates', in W. Van der Eyken (1967), *The Pre-School Years*. Harmondsworth: Penguin.

Witter, G. (1988) 'To see ourselves as others see us', *Support for Learning*, 3 (2): May: 93–8.

Wolfendale, S. (1989) *Parental Involvement: Developing Networks between Home, School and Community*. London: Cassell.

Wolfendale, S. (ed.) (1997) *Working with Parents of SEN Children after the Code of Practice*. London: David Fulton.

Woods, M. (1998) 'Early childhood studies – first principles', in: J. Taylor and M. Woods *Early Childhood Studies: An Holistic Introduction*. London: Arnold.

# Internet references

Internet 1   www.surestart.gov.uk
Internet 2   www.challengenet.com/~onemom
Internet 3   www.dfes.gov.uk
Internet 4   www.nas.org.uk
Internet 5   www.nasen.org.uk
Internet 6   www.network81.co.uk
Internet 7   www.nas.org.uk
Internet 8   www.portage.org.uk
Internet 9   www.nfer.ac.uk
Internet 10  www.unicef.org.uk
Internet 11  www.dfes.gov.uk
Internet 12  www.qca.org.uk
Internet 13  www.earlychildhood.com
Internet 14  www.ed.gov
Internet 15  www.inclusion.uwe.ac.uk
Internet 16  www.allfie.org.uk

# Index

ABC of behaviour 153, 154
Academic achievement 150, 174, 175, 177,
    187, 188
ACE 22, 118, 171
Access 14, 172, 188
ADHD 74, 170, 180
Affective needs 134–158, 167, 173, 175,
    177, 186
AIT 128
Alcohol abuse 69, 71, 78, 144, 183
Aspergers syndrome 123
Assessment 12, 13, 15, 17, 32, 50, 56, 66,
    71, 76, 77, 86–110, 111, 112, 114, 120,
    145, 152, 173, 184
Audiology 74
Autistic spectrum disorders 31, 35, 81, 87,
    111, 122–130, 170, 180, 181, 186

BAECE 22
Baseline assessment 89
Behaviour 24, 25, 92, 93, 96, 99, 100, 101,
    105, 107, 108, 120, 134, 138, 145, 146,
    150, 151–157, 174, 180, 186, 187
Behaviour support teams 72
Blind people 11
Bronfenbrenner 25, 65

Cancer and Leukaemia in Children (CLIC)
    37
Categories of disability 12, 13
Causal factors 13, 69, 107, 108, 109, 134,
    135, 143, 144–146, 152, 153, 154, 156,
    167, 180, 182, 187
Charitable organizations 10
Checklists 94, 102, 103
Child abuse 144, 174
Child psychiatrist 75
Childminders 10
Children Act 1989 7, 14, 32, 55, 66, 88, 106
Classroom management 92, 143, 145, 150
Clinical psychologist 74

Code of Practice:
    SEN 1994 15, 17, 31, 54, 66, 161
    SEN 2001 17, 18, 31, 32, 55, 61, 65, 67, 77,
        83, 86, 88, 90, 106, 112, 113, 115,
        116, 122, 136, 155, 159, 161, 181, 187
    Disability Discrimination 2001 18, 19
Consultant paediatrician 36, 73, 82
Consultant psychiatrist 75
Continuum of special needs 12
Counsellors 75
Court Report 1976 12, 66
Culture 92, 138, 140, 151, 166, 188

Day nurseries 10
Deaf children 11
Definitions 13, 14, 20, 64
Deprivation 5, 173–178
Derbyshire Language Scheme 120
Desirable Learning Outcomes 8
Diagnosis of autism 124
Diagnosis of special needs 28, 31, 33, 53, 86
Differentiation of curriculum 114
Disability Discrimination Act 1990 14
Disability Rights Commission 22
Disadvantage 173–178
Domestic violence 68
Down Syndrome 36, 170
Drug abuse 69, 71, 78, 144, 183

Early excellence centres 9, 67, 80
Early learning goals 8, 53, 88, 105, 108, 114,
    136, 137, 144, 182
Early Years Action 18, 55, 56, 77, 89, 90,
    108, 116, 136, 162
Early Years Action Plus 18, 55, 57, 77, 89,
    90, 108, 136, 162
Early Years Development & Childcare
    Partnerships 9, 67, 78, 80
Early Years Development Plans 31
Early years provision: Range of
    10–11, 181

196

Early Years SEN support teams 72
Education Acts:
  1908 2
  1909 11
  1918 4
  1944 5, 12, 160
  1970 12, 160
  1981 13, 15, 54, 66, 161, 162
  1988 14
  1993 15, 66, 162
Educational psychologist 37, 71, 78, 83
Effective schools 142
Emotional development 92, 141–143
Emotional difficulties 105, 107, 113, 134,
  135, 148, 149, 152, 156, 186
Ethical issues 94
European provision 2
Event/frequency sampling 96, 107

Families 23–26, 39, 40, 47, 48, 49
Families of children with special needs 15,
  23–42, 64, 65, 68, 69, 75, 76, 91, 181
Family centres 10, 47, 67, 83
Fathers 27, 29, 36–38, 39
Focused observations 98
Formal (statutory) assessment 13, 17, 18,
  37, 57, 78, 161
Forsters Education Act 1870 11
Foundation stage 56, 86, 89, 104, 108, 115,
  135, 136, 181, 188
Foundation stage profile 89
Froebel, Friedrich 3
Funding 18, 19, 68, 80, 81, 168, 169, 170,
  171, 172, 178, 184, 188, 189

Gender 92, 140, 145
General Practitioner (GP) 30, 36, 72
Grandparents 33, 34
Griffiths Developmental Scale 94

Handicapped Pupils & School Health
  Regulations 1945 12
Health Visitor (HV) 30, 36, 68, 71, 73, 76,
  82, 104, 118, 177
Hearing impairment 72
Higashi 128
Historical development:
  Nursery provision 1–10
  Special needs provision 11–19
Home-school liaison teachers 47
Home visits 32
Human Rights Act 1998 19

Identification 13, 15, 17, 50, 58, 77, 86, 87,
  89, 109
Inclusion 19, 21, 54, 81, 112, 116, 120, 122,
  137, 145, 159–179, 180, 181, 186, 187,

188, 189
Independent Panel for Special Educational
  Advice (IPSEA) 22
Index for Inclusion 165, 168, 187
Individual behaviour plans 154, 184
Individual education plans (IEPs) 32, 54, 55,
  57, 77, 106, 111, 116–118, 121, 131,
  144, 154, 185
Integration 13
Interagency working 64–85, 131, 168, 183,
  184
Intervention 40, 77, 86, 87, 90, 96, 97, 107,
  109, 111–133, 154, 156, 173, 177, 184,
  185, 187
Itard 11

Key Worker 69, 71, 78, 84

Labelling 152
Language impairment 72
Learning support workers 171, 188
Listening to children 88, 106
Local education authorities (LEAs) 12, 13,
  15, 16, 18, 55, 57, 60, 80, 160, 161, 162
Locus of control 148, 187
Lovaas 126–127
Lymphatic leukaemia 37

Maternal & Child Welfare Act 1918 4
Makaton 121
McMillan, Rachel & Margaret 3, 181
Medical needs 79
Mental health team 75
Models of disability 163
Mothers 30, 36–38, 39
Movement charts 102
Montessori, Maria 4
Multi-disciplinary (see also interagency) 9,
  10, 13, 18, 19, 40, 64, 65, 66

Nannies/au pairs 10
National Association for Special Educational
  Needs 17, 22, 49, 76
National Autistic Society 35, 76, 122, 128
National childcare strategy 9, 80
National Children's Bureau 22
National curriculum 14, 53
National Early Years Network 22
National Foundation for Educational
  Research 80
Negative reinforcement 107, 155
Network 15, 22, 54, 161
Nursery classes 10
Nursery Education & Grant Maintained
  Schools Act 1996 7, 17
Nursery schools 10
Nursery vouchers 7, 17

Observations 30, 32, 56, 86–110, 111, 112, 114, 120, 145, 152, 153, 154, 173, 177, 184, 185, 187
Occupational therapist 74
Ofsted 8, 56
Oncology 36–38
Opportunity centres 83
Opthalmologist 74
Out-of-school clubs 10
Owen, Robert 3, 181

Paediatrician 73, 76, 83
Parental partnerships 13, 15, 18, 32, 40, 43–63, 64, 66, 78, 91, 114, 131, 145, 156, 168, 171, 182, 183
PECS 128
Peer appraisal 145
Personal, social and emotional development 137
Physiotherapists 74
Pioneers 3–4
Planning and provision 17, 18, 40, 44, 45, 50, 53, 58, 68, 81, 90, 93, 145, 177, 184
Playgroups 6, 10, 16
Playladders 94, 104, 106
Play therapy 105
Plowden Report 1967 6
Policies 15, 40, 41, 44, 53, 57–59, 60, 68, 80, 81, 169, 184
Portage 36, 37, 76, 83, 94, 104
Positive reinforcement 92, 107, 117, 142, 144, 145, 150, 152, 155, 187
Poverty 144, 173–178, 188
Practitioners:
    Practices 25, 40, 41, 183
    Concerns 169
Pre-School Behaviour Checklist 94, 153
Pre-School Learning Alliance 6
Primary Schools 10
Profiling 108
Psychotherapist 75

Questionnaires 102, 144

Record-keeping 58
Resources 17, 80, 81, 184
Rights:
    Of children 7, 19, 53, 87, 88, 188
    Of parents 7, 19, 53, 54, 94

Salamanca Statement 162
School Action 90
School Action Plus 90

School health service 73
School Standards and Frameworks Act 1998 31
Second world war 5
Seguin 11
Self concept 92, 120, 146–151, 156, 177, 187
Self-esteem 69, 107, 134, 135, 144, 146, 148, 149
SENCO 15, 16, 18, 31, 77, 78, 79
SENDA 2001 18, 19, 67, 163, 171, 172, 181
Siblings 33, 34–36, 71
SMART targets 115, 118, 131, 145, 155, 173, 185
Social and emotional development 68
Social development 134–141
Social difficulties 105, 107, 113, 134, 135, 148, 149, 152, 156, 186
Social services department 14, 69, 75
Social worker 71, 75, 78
Sociograms 101
Son-Rise 128
SPELL 128
Speech and language difficulties 111, 118–122, 185, 186
Speech and language therapist 37, 73, 78, 104, 119, 186
Statements of SEN 17, 37, 90
Surestart 26, 48–49, 67, 174

Target child observations 98, 107
Targets 114, 115, 117
Task avoidance 92
TEACCH 127
Time sampling 96, 107
Toolkit 115, 116, 187
Tracking charts 102
Training 16, 17, 18, 19, 67, 68, 77, 81, 82, 145, 156, 161, 168, 170, 171, 184, 185, 186, 188, 189
Transdisciplinary (see interagency)
Triad of impairments 123, 128
Tribunals 15, 54, 171

UN Convention on the Rights of the Child 1989 19, 87, 136

Visual impairment 72
Voluntary agencies 69, 75, 76
Vygotsky 105

Warnock Report 1978 12, 53, 66, 160, 161
Within child factors 13